"Young love may well be the most overrated phenomenon since the disposable diaper. No matter how nice it seems looking back on it all, it was still an ugly business."

Tom Bodett

THE
BIG
GARAGE
ON
CLEAR SHOT

"Tom Bodett's sharp-eyed accounting of life's perpetual disorders is one of those all-too-few gems that really make you laugh out loud."

Bob Elliot of *Bob and Ray*

"An upbeat, warmly human collection of people and their stories . . . Will give much pleasure to the reader weary of tragedy, violence and sordid scandal."

South Bend Tribune

"Tom Bodett is too normal to be this funny and too smart to be this nice."

P.J. O'Rourke, author of *Parliament of Whores*

"The Garrison Keillor of oil-spill country . . . Pleasant . . . Off-the-wall . . . Full of good will and optimism"

Kirkus Reviews

"A truly great and unique talent"

Homer (Alaska) News

"I know in my heart that if I ever get to the End of the Road, some kind soul will have left the light on for me."

Lewis Grizzard

THE BIG GARAGE ON CLEAR SHOT

TOM BODETT

AVON BOOKS 🔺 NEW YORK

AVON BOOKS
A division of
The Hearst Corporation
1350 Avenue of the Americas
New York, New York 10019

Copyright © 1990 by Tom Bodett
Published by arrangement with William Morrow and Company, Inc.
Library of Congress Catalog Card Number: 90–37376
ISBN: 0–380–71642–9

The William Morrow and Company edition contains the following Library of Congress Cataloging in Publication Data:

Bodett, Tom.
   The big garage on Clear Shot: growing up, growing old, and going fishing at the End of the Road / Tom Bodett.
      p.   cm.
PS3552.0357B54 1990   90-37376
813′.54—dc2O   CIP

First Avon Books Printing: November 1992

To Pete and Florence:
my folks

Thanks

TO Johnny B. and Sharon Bushell and Gary Thomas, who nursed me along to many a deadline and added much to these pages. Once again, to Steve Hibbs and Sharon McKemie for being the left-brain of the operation. To Bob Lindner, Dave Anderson, Ed Carli, Cindy Biele, Pauline Renner, Jackie Aase, Tom Parse, Billy Pepper, and all the other countless kind souls who worked with us on "The End of the Road" radio show. And once again to Dick Brescia and Dave West for putting it out there for us.

Thanks to Rafe, Lisa, and Leigh at the Sagalyn Agency for continuing to keep this all in the proper context for me. And most especially, to the mysterious blue-haired lady, wherever you are.

Contents

Introduction

by
Ruby McClay

I remember when the Big Garage on Clear Shot still had trucks in it. That first orange city snowplow and the fire truck used to sit there side by side. Young Ed Flannigan would come in to wax and polish them. He'd listen to the stories going on around the coffeepot, rub on the trucks, and wait to grow old enough to run them.

Those seemed like simple times around here. Not that they're very darn complicated now, but there seemed to be less fussing. If you were one to have your coffee with a little conversation in the morning, you'd be down at the Big Garage like I was, sitting on oil cans or leaned up against doorways talking about the same things over and over: young Ed's eye for equipment; Argus Winslow and Bud Koenig's latest feud; what's going on with the new water line; who got rich fishing and who went broke trying.

There weren't so many kinds of people here then, but there were still plenty of stories to tell, and as new people came in the stories got better and the town got bigger, and we've all grown out of that coffeepot in the back of the Big Garage on Clear Shot.

When the mayor's sister opened up Clara's Coffee Cup, that was pretty much the end of the powwows down at the Garage. The city built itself a fancy new city hall some years back with a shop and fire hall, and all the trucks have long been moved over there. Most of us old-timers head down to Clara's in the mornings now, but that doesn't mean it's the only campfire in the woods anymore.

This town's grown up and there's lots of little corners in it now. Tamara Dupree and her gang over at the Natural Food Coop have carved themselves out a fine little niche to sit in. Pastor Frank's flock up at the First and Last Baptist Church hang together pretty well. The Organization of Fishermen's Wives seems to keep busy enough, and between all of this and all the new faces, it's a wonder we find a chance to get together at all.

I guess what I like best about this town is that we *do* find the time and reasons to get together. And no matter what camp you come from, whether you just fell off the truck or have been here all your life, everybody's equally welcome.

And I think the nicest part of it all (and the reason I brought the whole thing up) is that the only place in town big enough to hold us when we do decide to get together is still the Big Garage on Clear Shot. Whether it's two-stepping at a square dance or chewing somebody's ear off at a town meeting, the Big Garage is the one place in town where everybody feels at home.

It's different now than it was when there were trucks in it and it was just us few. Ed's a man now. The oil cans have become folding chairs, and the coffeepot now serves fifty. But there still seems to be plenty to talk about. There's other young ones to watch and old ones to consider. Each new person brings us a new story and there's times down there, when I'm leaned into a doorway listening to us yammer, that it sounds just like the old days.

It doesn't make me miss them, though. I like these stories as well as the ones we used to tell over and over and over.

R. M.
End of the Road

part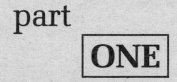

DOUG'S AMERICAN DREAM

DOUG McDoogan walked along the spit beach trying to keep his mind on what he was doing. It wasn't easy. Not only did Doug have very little mind to work with in the first place, but his life had sort of turned against him these last several months.

As he shuffled down the tide line late Monday evening looking for more material to work with, his fragile mental faculties were being overstressed and it was making him tired. It wasn't looking for driftwood that was doing it. It was everything else.

It all started back in November, when the mysterious blue-haired lady from Anchorage started paying him money to do driftwood carvings that he'd always done for nothing and left to lay. Things got better, then things got weird, and Doug wasn't sure which was who or when was where anymore.

At first, it was the best. The blue-haired lady gave him almost a thousand bucks right out of nowhere so she could put some of his whittling in her art gallery. He'd sunk that money into a winter's rent on a warm and dry sleaze-bag apartment and would've been pretty happy if it all quit there, but of course it didn't.

Soon enough the woman returned for more carvings, left more money, and Doug started to get *stuff lust*. That led to a murderous spree of garage sales that satisfied some inner desire to own things, filled his apartment to the brim with somebody else's old junk, and set Doug on the road to the American dream.

Last February the blue-haired lady featured him in a gala opening and reception at her gallery in Anchorage and nothing has been the same since.

The first thing that changed, that Doug noticed, was the blue-haired lady herself. When they'd first met outside Doug's

3

shack on the beach on that cold rainy day, she seemed genuinely warm. Doug thought she might have even *liked* him, which was not an experience he'd had a whole lot of in his thirty-odd years.

After that, whenever she came down for more carvings she was always glad to get whatever Doug had done, said nice things to him, left the cash, and got the heck out of the way. Even at her gallery in Anchorage when he'd fallen into the food table and dragged the president of the state council on the arts down with him, she'd passed it off as if Doug were the victim of the circumstance. Outside of Ruby McClay at the video store, Doug figured the lady from Anchorage as his best friend. Doug had few lines of reasoning to justify his figuring. Only that she was always so nice to him.

But lately it didn't feel so good when she came around. Ever since that messy business at her gallery, she'd been coming down more often.

"Five pieces?" She'd lean on her walking cane in Doug's kitchen shaking her head, not exactly aggravated, but obviously not pleased. "Doug, the demand for your work is phenomenal right now. They've tripled in value since the opening, and I'm still sold out constantly. You're going to have to do more."

Now when she left him, there was an air of urgency that remained behind. Doug knew that something felt different, but he gave it little thought even for him and continued to be fascinated by it all. The idea that this strange old woman would show up at his door one day, take a bunch of remodeled driftwood, and leave a pile of cash on his table—it still didn't make any sense.

A year ago he was living in a shack made of driftwood and Visqueen, carving on things that floated up with the tides and mostly letting them float out again with the next. Now he was getting paid close to two hundred dollars apiece for 'em. It felt pretty good, but he didn't have the faintest idea what was going on or what came next.

The thing Doug noticed mostly happening next was that the money was piling up, and that just wouldn't do. Doug had never had more than two cents to rub together and he wasn't about to change that now, no matter how much she paid him.

Every time his benefactor would grace him with one of her visitations, he'd stuff the wad in his pocket and head to town to spend it. A fool and his money are soon parted, and there are few as foolish as Doug. He'd buy anything, and FOR SALE signs were like beacons in the night to him.

He had a cord of firewood stacked in front of his apartment, which was heated with an oil-burning heater. It was only fifty dollars and the guy delivered it, so Doug figured it was a good deal. He bought a set of glass cookware to replace the garage-sale aluminum junk he thrived on and had to re-replace it with the old stuff after breaking every single piece of it in three days' time.

Everything was going that way. He bought a VCR from Ruby at the Video Roundup but has only gotten it to work a few times, by lucky pokes at the right buttons. It just sat on his table, its clock interminably blinking twelve o'clock high, like it was challenging Doug to do something, until he unplugged it for good.

The cherished clock radio with the lighted dial he'd bought at a garage sale months ago was replaced by an AM/FM home stereo system with a digital dial, automatic frequency control, programmable station selection, and local/distance loudness augmentation and Doug has never once successfully tuned in a radio station with it. He makes periodic stabs at pulling something in but invariably gives up and surrenders to the television.

Actually, it probably is the television that has affected him more than anything else lately. Doug has that quality of fixation often found in dim farm animals. From the moment he first turned it on, a glazing came over his already dulled gaze and his carving came nearly to a halt. The woman from Anchorage spotted the destructive potential of this sad development right off the bat and attempted to short-circuit it by talking Doug into getting a telephone installed.

Now Doug is not even left alone with his wispy thoughts. With uncanny ability, the blue-haired lady calls as soon as he's starting to slip into the abyss of a nineteen-inch-diagonal Tru-Color screen and coaxes him back to working on his carving.

Doug's life had always been somewhat of a challenging horse for him to ride, but now it was absolutely bucking. Nothing seemed to be working out as expected. Even the brand-new deluxe wood carver's tools Ruby'd helped him order turned on him.

After working all this time with an unremarkable five-inch jackknife, Doug's abilities weren't exactly honed to near as sharp an edge as the new tools held. When he wasn't digging in way past where he'd intended in a block of wood, he was going clear on by it and butchering himself in so many small and hideous ways that Ruby talked him into sending them back.

Ruby McClay represented the only real restraint in Doug's reality. Doug trusted Ruby with the secret of his semiliteracy, and she was slowly helping Doug improve his reading abilities. But as she coaxed Doug toward expansion in the cerebral areas, she was always preaching moderation in others.

When Doug wandered in one day with another fresh wad of cash and announced he wanted to buy a car, Ruby took him quietly aside, explained the responsibility of vehicle ownership, the licensing process and, for the good of the entire driving population, was able to talk him out of it. She had an equal amount of luck steering him away from an outboard motor he had no boat for, a lawn mower he had no grass for, and a horse, two pigs, a portable welder, and six hundred feet of used barbed wire.

Last Saturday Ruby finally had a long talk with Doug when he walked into her store to buy another television set.

"Doug, you live in a one-room apartment. What are you going to do with two TVs?"

"I dunno." He shrugged. "Maybe 'cause I like the other one so much?" It was then that Ruby realized Doug didn't have the faintest idea what he was doing.

"Doug, you know, just because you have some money doesn't mean you have to spend it."

Doug jutted his jaw forward as if he were making room in his head for this new thought. "What do you do with it if you don't spend it?" He looked down at the pile of bills in his hand, and Ruby realized that this was the first time in his life that Doug had more money than he absolutely needed to buy food and other essentials.

She poured her young pupil a cup of coffee and patiently interpreted the concept of savings. She pointed out that this roll he was on right now couldn't last forever and that he should be stuffing some aside for that day to come when things weren't so good. She also advised against keeping cash in his apartment and explained how to go to a bank and open a savings account.

"I'd never wish a checking account on you, Doug, but a savings account will save your hide someday. You gotta take care of yourself. You don't want to end up back in that beach shack, do you?"

Doug didn't know what he wanted, but he knew enough to listen to his friend and that was to his credit. On Monday he sat through a long and painful hour at the Fair Deal Bank and Trust with the new-accounts person. The woman had no idea the caliber of individual she was dealing with and her explanations of regulations, identification, floating interest, and overall bank policy went completely over his head. A head that also had a splitting migraine throbbing over his disillusionment with the whole experience. He walked out of there with a little blue plastic book and a free Frisbee, and it had cost him over five hundred dollars. He'd have to go back to Ruby's someday soon and have her explain this process to him again.

It had been an exhausting afternoon for Doug, and back at his apartment he'd settled in for a long evening of TV. But no sooner had his brain begun to crystallize in formation with the tube when the phone rang.

It was, of course, the blue-haired lady calling to find out how Doug's latest batch of work was turning out.

"Oh, great," he lied. She'd been after him for two weeks this time. "I'll have 'em all done by the time you come down again."

"I'm coming down Thursday," she said in her most current cool manner. "And I don't want to be disappointed."

And it was this phone call that found our hero walking down the tide line in the late gray light of Alaska spring looking for material. He hadn't even started on this batch, and it didn't look like it was going to be easy. Normally these beach walks quickly produced some subjects. He'd always spot dozens of washed-up pieces of wood that reminded him of bears or otters, seals or whales. They would sometimes leap from the wood so sharply at him that at first glance he'd think he'd already carved it.

It all, of course, was a fortunate and God-given hallucination Doug had that allowed him to see form where there was none and turn nature's own litter into beauty again. But tonight it wasn't happening. He was just too tired.

As Doug walked down the row of smelly kelp, twisted limbs, and occasional fish carcasses, he could see nothing. Up ahead there were the rattled remains of his old beach shack, and he walked over to look at it. The Visqueen was blown off, and the walls were a little knocked down, so he planted his butt in the sand and let himself recline on one bent-over old plank.

He closed his eyes to the stuff on the beach. It all looked just like debris. Nothing begged to be picked up. And in his weariness Doug let his mind roll over in his head and pictures of blinking digits, trailing seaweed, televisions, sun-bleached branches, and little blue books with numbers—seals, birds, and dollar bills all mixed together in his head like a washed-up shipwreck.

And it all made Doug so tired to see that his old beach shack could only creak and give just a little when he fell fast asleep against it, the pictures still rolling like a dream come unglued.

EGG HUNT

THE Rod and Gun League's annual Easter Egg Hunt was a medium-size affair by End of the Road standards. As always, it was held in the Big Garage on Clear Shot and the lot out back. It wasn't the most well thought of family activity, because even though there was a traditional egg hunt for the kids, some of the adult games were of questionable taste.

The Rod and Gun League had over the years developed contests of skill around this event to determine who would belong to its elite board, the Predator Club. These contests included the Egg Shot Skeet Shoot, the Shell Tap Fly-Rod Competition, and the City-Wide Egg Stalk.

The egg stalk was probably the least entertaining of the three but drew the biggest participation, because of the prize. The way it worked was that one single plastic egg was camouflaged and hidden somewhere on the main drag. Anybody qualified to win, and whoever found it got the grand prize and also became an honorary member of the Predator Club. This year's prize was a free ten-day trip to the Western States' Rod and Gun League Annual Convention at the Big Kahuna Hotel in Honolulu and promised to really bring some spring stalkers out of the woodwork.

You see, this is an uncomfortable time around the End of the Road and everybody is looking for distraction, particularly distractions of the tropical persuasion. It's bothersome right now because the calendar says it's supposed to be spring, but it's still winter in every other way, with a month or so yet to go.

The Easter bonnets and spring grasses of our southern youths are lost in a sea of bad attitudes. So it was a bit of a somber crowd that gathered at the Big Garage on Clear Shot.

Sissy Tuttle and her gang from the Organization of Fishermen's Wives had been out in the lot since dawn hiding colored eggs around in the snowbanks, perching them on truck bumpers, old wire-spools, and wooden pallets. The kids were being assembled inside and outfitted with gathering baskets, while the governing members of the Predator Club set up the games of skill. It was a miserable snowy morning and had all the Easter charm of fresh frozen peas.

Other members of the Rod and Gun League were setting out food on folding tables. Stormy Storbock unpacked about thirty pounds of barbecued bear ribs. Frank Tuttle was arranging a mound of alder smoked red salmon. There was Fritz Ferguson's venison stroganoff from an old family recipe and Argus Winslow's inevitable and annual rabbit stew, the indelicacy of which had never been fully explained to Argus. Not that it would have made any difference.

The Egg Shot Skeet Shoot was held out on the bluff and was being assembled by Bud Koenig and Ed Flannigan, two of the best trapshooters in town and lifetime members of the Predator Club. The history of the Egg Shot Skeet Shoot is not a pretty one and it hasn't improved with age.

Years ago, after the very first egg hunt, the gentlemen of the Rod and Gun League discovered that the kids didn't give a hoot for all the eggs they found. They were traded in for prizes and left to the members to dispose of. Everybody likes a boiled egg every once in a while, but nobody was going to volunteer to take ten dozen of them home for lunches.

"Make for good target practice," someone must have said in the offhand way that men will say such things, and it caught.

Bud Koenig had devised a hand sling that could send an Easter egg well into sporting range, and ever since then, the Rod and Gun League's annual Easter Egg Hunt had been shot-gunned into seagull feed.

As Bud and Ed were putting the trapshoot together, Mayor Richard Weekly was behind the garage distancing the targets for the Shell Tap Fly-Rod Competition. Mayor Weekly was a fly fishing fanatic and it was he who devised this highly skilled event.

What it consisted of was five golf tees stuck in the snow with five raw eggs on top of them. The contestants were to stand twenty paces back with the rod and dry fly of their choice and tip the eggs off the tees in the shortest time possible. It took a good eye, a steady hand, and a calm day, most of which Mayor Richard Weekly had at his disposal. He was whistling a merry tune as he set up his marks and watched all the little children pouring out of the Big Garage to find the colored eggs scattered around that morning.

One of our more earnest citizens was not present for this orgy of wild game dishes, gun lust, and plunderous outdoor talents. Not surprisingly, Tamara Dupree had stayed home that day, and she was disgusted. What she was disgusted about was a number of things.

Number one, of course, were the activities going on in town. They were a hideous public violation of everything Tamara stood for: environmentalism, vegetarianism, and good taste. It disgusted her more that it was being done in front of and in cooperation with children, and even more that they were doing it all on such a crummy day.

This is getting to the real root of Tamara's revulsion. You see, it wasn't so much that she was overly offended by the Rod and Gun League, because that's no surprise to anybody who knows her. It's that she could not for the life of her muster the energy to do anything about it. This is what disgusted her.

Protest and intimidation were Tamara's lifeblood. She wore fanaticism like a diamond tiara. On any other day she'd be down there with her card table and signs denouncing the taking of wild animals for any reason and for assigning such words as *hunt* to a playful children's game of finding eggs, which by the way are murdered chicken fetuses. And she would have successfully irritated everybody, confused the kids, and gone home with a real sense of accomplishment.

But today Tamara could hardly get out of bed. It had been this way for a couple weeks now. Ever since she'd returned from Anchorage and the disastrous reunion with her old friend Tony, who had, of all things, become an army surgeon. She couldn't be sure if it was all that, or just what it was for certain, but she suspected it had plenty to do with the weather. It has been a long, gray March. It would snow for two days, rain for three, blow for two more, then turn around and freeze solid again. The roadsides were monuments of dirty slush hard as granite, and even the longer daylight hours seemed to offer no relief. The sun never really rose or set. It just oozed a languid gray light into the morning and waned again at night. Not in any grand fashion of colors or magnificence, but a dull lingering death, the way a flashlight wears down.

Although she would never admit it, because it seemed so pedestrian and unholy, Tamara Dupree had cabin fever.

What cabin fever is exactly or what brings it on is hard to say. Running out of dry firewood, like Tamara did, can trigger it. Getting a person's van stuck in the vanilla-fudge twirl of snow and mud that passes for a person's driveway this time of year, like Tamara had, could spark a fit of cabin fever. Holding up one's shirt in front of one's mirror to see how absolutely corpse-like one's white belly skin has become, like Tamara has been doing, can also bring on a bout of the fever.

Cabin fever can manifest itself in any number of odd and ugly ways. You know you've got it if, say, like Tamara, you've been having homicidal fantasies about your dog at night because you can hear it breathing. You know you've got it if, like Tamara, during your Yoga Nutritional Visualization class, all you can feature between your ears is a hot white sand beach, palm trees wafting in the tropic breeze, and innocent young Samoan beach boys dancing Frisbees about your medulla. And you also know you've got it if you can scarcely muster the strength to boil water for tea on a day when the Northern barbarians are celebrating their primordial prowess unchecked just three miles away.

A disgusted Tamara Dupree stood in front of her little mirror and raised her shirt to finger at her cadaver of a belly.

"You're a mess, girl," she said to her pale reflection, and decided to take a walk. Maybe a shot of wheat-grass juice from the Natural Food Coop would pick up her spirits.

While Tamara was fighting off the fever, Ed Flannigan was having a good day at the Egg Shot Skeet Shoot. He'd finally beat Bud Koenig in a tiebreaker after eliminating Stormy, Argus, and Frank Tuttle in the first round.

Mayor Weekly had neatly sewn up the fly-rod competition as he did most every year. And the only real entertainment to the whole bleak function was when Doug McDoogan caught Argus Winslow behind the ear with a dry fly on his back swing and tugged on it six or eight times before the mayor took the rod away from him. The string of curses that followed sent most of the wives and children home for the day. Which was just as well, because it was about time to start the City-Wide Egg Stalk anyway.

Police Chief Peter Bindel was the designated concealer this year. He verified to the gathered group of hopefuls that he had indeed placed a camouflaged plastic egg somewhere in plain sight, somewhere in town. The person to find it wins a ten-day trip to Waikiki and an honorary membership to the Predator Club. And with that, a dozen or so stalkers began a cautious wide-eyed march down Clear Shot to town.

The egg stalk could go either way. Sometimes it lasted less than an hour, other times it took days. If it lasted too long, people started seeing eggs in their sleep, but sooner or later somebody would pick it out of the scenery and everybody wanted to be that somebody. Especially since this year that egg held Polynesian promises.

Tamara could see the gang of Rod and Gun Leaguers wandering up the street as she rounded the bend into town. Her walk was having the reverse effect on her than what she'd intended. As she came slogging down from Far Road along the shoulder, she could hear the shots coming from the trapshoot and had let the whole idea of the thing gnaw at her already chafed composure. Then when she saw these goof-eyed would-be stalkers pacing up the main drag like some kind of play army, she wanted to grab them all and slap them silly.

"Isn't there one civilized person in this town?" she said out loud to herself as she crossed the street toward the Natural Food Coop.

When Ed Flannigan spotted Tamara coming, he got a little self-conscious. He straightened up his gait and tried to stop his head and eyeballs from sweeping side to side. Neither Ed nor Tamara had fully recovered from their encounters of last fall. It had started and stayed innocent enough but had ended so badly that there was implied guilt left all over the place. Guilt that threw even our iron maiden off her balance a little as the two unavoidably drew up to one another.

"Hello, Ed. Looking for your little egg?" Tamara could be so cruel so easily it scared her sometimes.

"Yeah, sorta." Ed shuffled to a halt facing Tamara and squirmed.

Taking note, Tamara went for more. "What's the big prize? Another automatic assault rifle, or have you come up with some fresh new killing toy this year?" Tamara tried to look Ed in the eyes as she ridiculed, but she couldn't meet them and let her gaze wander as she finished. "I hope I find that egg. I'll take your prize and throw it away where nobody could use it."

Ed took in a breath of resignation. "You'd throw away a ten-day trip to Hawaii?" And it was just at that moment

Tamara's wandering eyes chanced upon a dull green plastic egg taped to the downspout on the Natural Food Coop.

"Did you say a trip to Hawaii?" Tamara's eyes widened, and naturally, instinctively, she started to circle away, turning Ed's attention far from her prey.

"Yeah, that's right. An all-expense-paid trip to Hawaii for the Rod and Gun Show, and an honorary membership in the Predator Club." Ed, seeing a change come over Tamara, added importantly, "A lot of people would kill for that, you know."

A lot of people *would* kill for that. Tamara was sure of it. Her eyes darted nervously from Ed to egg, to the ragtag band of stalkers wandering about the street. At any moment, any one of them could glance over and claim her prize. The thought of it made Tamara's nostrils flare and her fingers curl. Steadily and deliberately, Tamara brushed by a confused Ed Flannigan, took six long strides, and seized her quarry with both hands.

Tamara turned around with her spoil and held it jealously in front of her. With a greedy grin that handsomely displayed her upper incisors, Tamara gushed, "I got it. I win."

Ed, not knowing what else to say, scratched around and said the first appropriate thing that came to mind. "Congratulations, Tamara, and welcome to the Predator Club."

Tamara closed her hands around her egg, closed her mind around a white sand beach with palm trees wafting in a tropical breeze, with beach boys teasing Frisbees about her medulla, and she went inside for a shot of wheat grass.

NORMAN'S ENEMY

THERE are many firsts in a thirteen-year-old boy's life, and Norman Tuttle, as you know, has had his share. Long after the novelty of growing up leaves him, Norman as a jaded adult will still recall these firsts of his with clear and fond regard. They'll be the subject of pleasant evening conversations with some future front-porch friends. Even the firsts that are not so fond to recall. Like Norman's first enemy.

It started innocently enough, playing volleyball in phys ed class. Norman was tall for his age and was playing the net. He wasn't terribly coordinated, but he did try hard and he played fair and he had fun. But all the fun came to a halt when he jumped up to block a spike and accidentally hammered the ball back into the face of Leonard Kopinski. Leonard wasn't paying attention and it hit him square in the nose. The kind of hit that brings instant tears and wide-eyed nosebleeds.

The blow sat Leonard right down on his butt, and he held his nose while the rest of the boys, in a fine display of eighth-grade sportsmanship, laughed at him and clapped Norman on the back.

"Hey, hey. Way to go, Tuttle!"

"Yeah! Nailed it!"

Norman started to cross under the net to help, but Coach Crawley beat him to it. Leonard wouldn't accept any assistance. He pushed the coach away and stood facing Norman. Then Leonard pointed a bloody hand and, in a voice that sent dread reeling through Norman's skinny body, hissed, "You're dead, Tuttle."

Tuttle, he spit the word like it was the worst insult he could deliver. And it had that effect on Norman. More effect than the threat did.

"It was an accident." Norman hadn't intended to plead, but

it came out that way. This wasn't wasted on Leonard, who strutted out of the gym letting his nose bleed freely. In this unwelcome bout with his earliest enemy, Norman had lost the first round.

Norman didn't know very much about Leonard Kopinski, but what he did know unsettled him. He back-talked teachers and smoked cigarettes. He'd been caught stealing. Norman couldn't understand this. His own parents would have had him executed for any one of those things.

Leonard had also been held back a grade somewhere and that made him a year older. One year is a millennium of mutation in adolescence, and Leonard's advanced physical maturity was evident. Painfully evident to Norman, who, though taller than most boys including Leonard, was slow on the hormonal draw.

Norman had boyishly bald and largely untrained long legs and arms while Leonard looked to be on the eve of shaving. In the wide and weary scope of things, it was never likely that Norman and Leonard would become good friends. But at the same time it was never in Norman's plans to have an enemy, and he wasn't quite sure what to do with the experience.

One thing Norman soon found out was that you don't have to do very much at all with enemies. They pretty well take care of themselves. On his way to algebra class from the gym, Norman ran into Leonard's two perennial sidekicks, fat Eddie Talbot and Glenn Ferguson. They were rough-looking boys like Leonard and were leaned against their lockers sneering and watching Norman coming for a long way. Norman could see them and it made him self-conscious. His feet didn't want to work properly and he stumbled at least twice on a smooth floor, to the boys' immeasurable delight.

"You're dead, Tuttle," they mocked, and fell in beside him just enough to jostle Norman loose of his notebook.

While he was stooped to pick up his papers his best friend, Stanley, even came in on the action. "What did you hit Leonard Kopinski in the face for?" he said as Norman stood up. "He told the whole school he's going to kill you."

"It was an accident," Norman said, not meaning to plead, but it came out that way.

Norman was a miserable student of algebra that day. Not even Laura Magruder's bra strap showing through the back of her blouse could offer him any comfort or distraction. All he could think about was Leonard Kopinski. The menace in his voice. The power in his gait. And those tears of rage in his eyes. Rage and something else. Something that chewed at Norman and soured his stomach. Something he couldn't identify.

As miserable as algebra class was that day, it was still far too short for Norman's taste. Soon he was out of the protective custody of the school building and standing with Stanley Bindel waiting for the bus. The rest of the kids were carrying on in their typical after-school manner, tearing around, raising Cain, and generally being jubilant, which irritated Norman to no end this particular day.

Norman was deadly serious as he scanned the gangs of kids for one specific face. A face he knew was out there. But he didn't see it. Then from nowhere Norman heard a POP in his head like a knock on a wooden door and an instant later he felt the sting and wet of an iceball, which had found him right at the temple.

He grabbed the side of his head in agony and spun to see the face. The taunting face of Leonard Kopinski. His arms were at his hips and his feet were set apart in challenge. Eddie and Glenn stood on each side like lieutenants to the general, and all three wore the obnoxious smirks of bad boys on the high ground.

Norman, caught entirely off guard by all of this, could do nothing. It was the kind of a hit that brought tears and rage and menacing thoughts and something else that chewed at his will and soured his stomach. Something Norman could now identify as humiliation. To the dismay of three bad boys and one disappointed best friend, Norman Tuttle climbed on to the bus and pretended to be looking for something in his book bag.

By the time the bus pulled away, Leonard and his friends and at least a dozen neutral bystanders had a taunting chorus going that boiled Norman's dignity and burned hot into the tender spot on the side of his head. "Tuttle is a chicken baak-baak-baak . . . Tuttle is a chicken baak-baak-baak . . ."

Stanley didn't talk to Norman about it on the way home. Norman was making it pretty clear with his manner that it was not an open topic of discussion. But Norman knew that it was not a closed topic, either. He sensed that the Leonard thing was not concluded with his defeat. Leonard had only tasted blood. Now he would want the kill.

Norman's father inquired over dinner about the red mark on his face, and he passed it off with, "Just a snowball fight at school." But he was too quiet about it. Norman was too quiet about everything that night to suit his dad and he soon found an opportunity to corner him.

"How's it goin' at school, bub?"

Norman knew this kind of question from his father. What it meant was *I know something's wrong at school and you better tell me straight*. So Norman did tell it straight, in Norman's way, with a question, "Have you ever been in a fight, Dad?"

Frank Tuttle looked at his son and understood immediately. His boy was mixing it up with somebody at school. A rage started to build in his chest, his teeth locked, and his face went red. It was unclear what was making him madder—the fact that somebody had hit his boy or that his boy might be hitting somebody else. There was nothing that the Tuttle family despised more than violence, and it took Frank several beats to compose himself before answering.

"Normy, I don't want to know what's been going on here, but I want to tell you one thing. No, I have never been in a fight. Not in my life. I've had opportunities, and some might say I've had reasons,"—Norman's dad held his meaty fisherman's hands out in front of him—"but these hands have never hit another human being, and they never will. There's no good reason why a civilized person should ever use his fists. I'm very proud that I haven't. As proud as I am of anything, and you will be too when you're my age. It takes a big man to win a fight, Norman. It takes a bigger man to walk away from one. So just leave it alone. You'll be glad you did as long as you live."

And that was it. No questions from the gallery. No explanations or "but, what if's" *Just leave it alone*. Norman knew his dad, and he knew when the law had been laid down.

Norman's dad left the room, and left his son to puzzle on this new information. It sounded grand, even noble. But as hard as he thought about it, and he would think about it all night long, he still couldn't figure out what he was supposed to do about Leonard Kopinski.

Norman was still puzzling over what to do with Leonard Kopinski when his bus pulled up in front of the school the next

morning. When the doors swung open and Norman stepped
out, he couldn't believe his ears.

"Tuttle is a chicken . . . baak-baak-baak . . . Tuttle is a
chicken . . . baak-baak-baak." Like they'd been standing there
all night long, Leonard and his cronies were posed in their
tough-guy stances and chanting at him.

Norman was too surprised to do anything meaningful or
even honorable, so he just tucked his head and tried to walk
around them. Leonard stepped into his path, and Norman had
to either stop or run into him. He stopped.

As the bus pulled away, the other kids gathered around and
more arriving students saw the action and moved in. Leonard
Kopinski glanced at the assembling mob and seemed to collect energy and confidence from the invisible blood lust that
school-children seem to emanate in these situations. "Why'd
you run away yesterday, chicken butt?" Leonard stepped closer
and had to look up slightly to Norman.

"I didn't run away. I got on the bus." Norman tried to sound
calm and reasonable even as his heart raced in his ears and his
knees shook.

" 'I didn't run away, I got on the bus,' " Leonard mocked,
employing the universal tact and wit of cretins young and old.
Then he reached out and knocked Norman's book bag out of
his hands. A notebook fell and some papers scattered as a quiet
gasp went up from the spectators.

Norman bent down to pick them up, and Leonard took the
opportunity to push him with his foot. Norman stumbled, but
he kept his feet and he turned again to face his attacker,
petrified. His breaths were short and worried and his eyes
darted around the faces, looking for support, an answer, a
rescue . . . anything. All he saw was his best friend, Stanley
Bindel, looking at him, embarrassed.

Leonard continued his assault, circling around Norman,
pushing at his chest and taunting, "C'mon. C'mon, chick-
en butt."

Norman's head was swimming. *Walk away. How do you
get away? Big men win. Proud men walk. Leave it alone. It
was an accident.*

Norman didn't want to fight. Not at all. But what he didn't
realize was that he was fighting. In the world of eighth-grade
warfare, pushing a person around until he cries is a righteous
fight. Two people pushing each other around is a real barn
burner. Leonard knew this, but Norman didn't. He couldn't.

He'd never been in a fight before. He'd only seen it on TV and it scared him to death.

"C'mon. C'mon, chicken butt." Norman could smell Leonard's breath as he kept taunting and kept hammering his fingers into his breastbone. Norman wasn't getting mad. He was getting panicked. All thoughts were leaving him and instinctive reflex was taking over.

His instinct told him that any moment he was going to be hit and injured, and his reflex took it from there. Without conscious direction or strategic forethought, Norman's long thin arm cocked in a tight little bony fist behind his back and came forward in the worst possible roundhouse swing ever devised. A swing that just happened to land smack-dab and start the count right on the end of Leonard Kopinski's nose.

It was a solid hit. One of the kind that brings instant tears to the eyes and wide-eyed nosebleeds. A moment of silence that lasted a long harsh month hung in the air. Leonard went to his knees holding his nose, and Norman held on to his own right hand. He was stunned. Stunned at what he'd done, and surprised to find out that hitting somebody in the face hurt so bad.

But the most staggering things of all during that long harsh moment were coming up from deep inside him as he looked at Leonard Kopinski's eyes. There was no rage, no menace, no threat. Not even humiliation endured. The tears on his enemy's face were tears of pain, and Norman realized suddenly, and sickeningly, that he'd hurt him.

"Hey, hey! Way to go, Tuttle."

"Nailed 'im."

Norman's friends closed around him, and Norman watched as Leonard walked quickly away. Still bleeding. Still crying. Not even his lieutenants thought to go with him.

They were dazed. Norman was dazed. He couldn't even hear what was going on around him. That Coach Crawley had him by the elbow pulling him into the school with threats of suspension. That his father would have to come down. None of it got through to Norman.

All he could hold in his mind was that forever, as long as he lived, Leonard Kopinski would be the first and only person he had ever hit. And there was nothing in the world that could be done about it now.

TAMARA GETS
SOME SUN

EVEN the prospect of going to Hawaii and raising hell with the entire convention of Western States' Rod and Gun Leaguers gave Tamara no joy.

Ever since she discovered that her first and only true love had become a military heart surgeon, she was inconsolable. Anthony Tobias: The man who put the "pro" in protest—who'd made activism an art form for Tamara, the Sheik of radical, her Tony—had shown up after eight years a major in the army.

She hadn't let him explain himself when she found his uniform in that Anchorage hotel room. And she wasn't letting him explain still as she read through yet another of his letters of rationalization, which had been arriving regularly from Seattle ever since.

This one was more of the same. How he'd originally joined the army as his only means to get through medical school. He told her not to think that everybody in the armed forces voted Republican or belonged to the NRA. He'd been in the service over eight years and had never even held a weapon in his hands. He was a doctor. A healer. The uniform was incidental. It was like a credential, a résumé worn on the outside. He was respected, and most importantly, he was able to introduce some of his idea of holistic medicine to the military medical establishment. The uniform was his way in.

All this bounced off the iron doors of a tightly closed mind. Even as her heart begged for understanding and her eyes couldn't leave the seductive flowing gait of Anthony's handwriting, Tamara could accept no explanation. Could Sirhan Sirhan warrant what he did to RFK? No. Could Union Carbide excuse Bhopal? No. Could Tony Tobias exonerate himself to Tamara of wearing the uniform of the very military-industrial

21

complex that she held responsible for every ill and bad vibe on the planet? Stupid question.

Tamara had set her heels to be miserable and there was going to be no talking her out of it. She returned the letter to her backpack and looked over the crowd milling around the Anchorage airport. The plane to Honolulu was ready to board and a colorful collection of Alaskans were queuing up in front of Tamara. Hardly the sort of people to take her mind off her heartache. They were revolting to her. Painfully white people with stooped backs, bad feet, and lives that smelled of Laundromats.

Some wore furs. Some wore shorts. And they all wore the foolish smiles of people expecting a big wonderful surprise. Tamara knew they would drink too much on the plane, and all their noses would be in intensive care by sundown tomorrow. She joined the group at a bit of a pompous distance.

Tamara was giving no consideration to herself and how she might look, but that is her nature. She'd already forgotten how she'd craved this very trip two weeks ago. How after winning this vacation with the City-Wide Egg Stalk, she'd fairly danced back to her cabin.

She'd been absolutely delighted by the prospect of getting some bona fide ultraviolet light back into her own lifeless skin. Letting some warm fresh sea air pass between the appendages of her body before they grew permanent webs. It was the cure for all her ills. This long, dark, heartbreaking winter was going to get a welcome interruption.

But somehow since then this big wonderful surprise interruption had turned into another of Tamara's crusades against tyranny, torture, and the world of sports in general. It happened when the gentlemen at the Rod and Gun League suggested she stay away from their convention while she was in Hawaii.

Little did the men know that Tamara had absolutely no intention at all of attending that hideous affair. In fact, she laughed herself to tears over the idea that she was going as the End of the Road delegate. She fully intended to cash in her room at the hotel and go beach camping around the islands for two weeks. Eating mangoes, meditating, and making up to sun-tanned natives. And she would have done that had not the men of the Predator Club of the Rod and Gun League suggested that she do that very thing and forget about the convention.

"Why?" she'd said immediately. "I have the right to go, don't I? And don't I get an honorary membership in your

Predator Club as part of this prize too?" Around the big table in the back of Clara's, Tamara stood over the governing board of the Predator Club, arms crossed and eyes blazing.

The men shuffled, grunted, and allowed as how she did have the right and the membership but didn't figure she'd be interested. Tamara, in another of her knee-jerk vaults into pure contrariness, had insisted that not only would she be wanting to go to the convention, but that certainly she would want to wear the colors of her home organization.

She demanded that they present her with the jacket, hat, and lapel pin of the Predator Club. Their proud insignia on each was an eagle claw holding a wriggling fish over two crossed gun barrels. The jacket had a sewn-in game pouch, and the hat could hold up to ten rounds of ammunition in the elastic brim. She also got the No Spill'em Insulated Beer-Can Truck Caddie and the "Li'l Bugger Pocket Dry-Fly Kit."

"Lovely," she said, and left a very paranoid Predator Club to their afternoon coffee.

In the two weeks since, Tamara has crafted probably one of her more astute and subtle political moves to date. Instead of her usual tact of bowling headlong into the opposition, she would go among them as one of their own. She would make herself respected, appreciated, and approved. Then she would go to work on them.

She'd collected at least twenty pounds of consciousness-raising paraphernalia as regards everything from the leg-hold steel trap to the humanlike mating customs of migratory birds. She had pamphlets on endangered plankton in Indonesian tide pools. Studies on the pain that fish feel. Rain-forest devastation in the Amazon basin. Everything. Every single thing that could possibly go wrong with an environment was graphically and righteously represented in Tamara's backpack.

She thought about it all as she rode not so merrily along at thirty-two thousand feet, heading due south for paradise. It's all she could do to take her mind off herself and one particular officer in the army thousands of miles away, who had finally gotten hold of somebody to find out where she was.

Tamara was uncomfortably warm in her Predator Club jacket, but she decided she'd better wear it while she checked into the hotel. The Big Kahuna Hotel and Convention Center was swimming with the opposition. Middle-aged potbellies adorned with Polynesian prints were streaming up escalators, pouring from elevators, and four deep at the bar. Half of them had decorated wives in tow, the other half were fine-tuning their leers toward every female form that made a move, including Tamara.

"Ms. Dupree, there was a call for you from a Mr. Tobias." The desk clerk handed her a pink message slip. Tamara's blood surged for a moment, then her eyes narrowed as she crumpled it.

"Thank you. Please put a *do not disturb* on my phone."

"Very well, miss, and here is your conventioneer packet."

Tamara went through her packet and chuckled viciously in the elevator up to her room. There was a name tag. TAMARA DUPREE, ROD AND GUN LEAGUE, HONORARY PREDATOR, ALASKA DELEGATION, along with a conglomeration of banquet passes, sunset cruise discounts, and announcements for a myriad of sporting demonstrations from skeet shooting to salmon skinning.

Tamara stepped out onto the balcony of her room and looked over the busy white sand of Waikiki Beach. The huge red orb of sun was compressing itself into the tropical waters and a south-Pacific breeze as warm as breath teased Tamara's blouse and arranged her hair.

It almost did it. The great iron doors of Tamara Dupree opened a crack, letting in just the tiniest ray of glorious light before she wrestled them shut again. She had a big day tomorrow. She closed her drapes, turned on her lights, and read until she fell asleep, exhausted, into a sea of consciousness-raising bulletins.

Tamara dressed carefully the following morning and went down to the get-acquainted brunch sponsored by the convention. She dressed as she expected a sporting woman from Alaska might—Western-cut flannel blouse, dungarees, and of course, her nylon Predator Club jacket. Her one concession to climate and sanity was sandals. She looked less than her svelte self with the bulk of pamphlets stuffed into the game pouch of her jacket.

Down at the brunch, after grabbing hold of a fruit plate, Tamara easily attached herself to a handsome foursome off to the side. There were Hank and Mitsy from Boise, who had just met Bill and Veronica from Spokane. They were very excited to be there and had loads of questions for Tamara, her Alaska home and Predator Club status making her a bit of an instant celebrity.

"What do you do in Alaska?"

"Oh, you know. Usual stuff. Shoot moose. Trap beaver."

Hank and Bill laughed nervously while Mitsy and Veronica could only gape and change the subject. "Is your husband here with you?"

Tamara could see she was making everybody edgy and figured maybe she'd back off a bit. "No, Butch couldn't make it. He's, uh, tyin' flies and gettin' his, uh, *gear* ready for fishin' season."

"Oh, a fly fisherman." Hank from Boise seemed to relax. "That's us, too. I'm a fishin' fool. I wouldn't know about hunting moose or trapping. Jes' give me a dry fly and a wet trout any ol' day."

That seemed to break the ice between everybody, and soon Tamara was invited along with their group to wander the displays in the convention center. Tamara stayed pretty quiet, getting by mostly with a lot of "uh-huh's" and "I'll be's."

Hank and Bill stopped at every booth that had any sort of fishing gear displayed, while the women stood off to the side talking sunscreen and shopping trips. Tamara could sense that she'd picked a fairly benign representation of the opposition and decided to troll for more malignant game. "I'm gonna go see about a new gun" was all she could think to say to Mitsy and Veronica as she waved goodbye to their puzzled smiles.

Tamara roamed around awhile, discreetly placing pamphlets on counters here and there, and finally settled on an exhibition of custom shotguns. There were several half-naked women demonstrating the action and assembly of a variety of guns as the melodious-voiced salesman with a microphone pointed out the finer features of each. Several other assistants worked the counter around the display, and as Tamara walked up, one of them pushed a shotgun into her breasts, forcing her to take hold of it. Tamara's first impulse was to throw it back at the woman like a live snake, but she fought the urge, knowing this could bring her miles inside enemy territory.

The woman launched into her pitch, describing the solid-cherry buttstock, stainless-steel receiver, ventilated rib site ad nauseam, and actually had Tamara sighting on an artificial duck hanging from the ceiling when a familiar voice came through the din.

"I never thought I'd see the day."

Tamara whirled around and ended up pointing the gun right in his face. "Tony!"

Major Anthony Tobias, dressed in cutoffs and a Grateful Dead T-shirt, pushed the barrel away and the woman behind the counter quickly recovered it. Tamara was too shocked to think and could only blurt out the obvious: "How did you find me here?"

"I finally got hold of that friend you mentioned, Ed Flannigan. He told me you were here. And he told me you were probably looking for trouble. I see that you are."

Tamara took this moment to gather herself together. "I have nothing to explain to you—*Major*." With a toss of her hair, she strutted away with Tony hot on her heels.

"Oh yes you do, Tamara Dupree." She didn't stop, but she was listening as they paraded toward the exit. "You explain to me what's made you such a mean, unhappy person. Look at you!"

Tony grabbed an arm of her Predator Club jacket and spun her around. Some pamphlets fell out on the floor. He picked a couple up, glanced at them, and wagged them in her face. "What are you trying to do, just make these people feel bad? You think they're stupid? Where's your heart gone, and where's your sense? It's eighty degrees in here, and you look ridiculous. The Predator Club—it's insulting!"

Whether it was the surprise, what he was saying, or just if it was time, Tamara could feel herself start to fold. "I wasn't trying to say anything with it. I just wanted to get inside. Just a way to get something done that I had to do."

"Where have I heard *that* before?" Tony loosened his grip on her jacket, and she allowed him to slip it down her arms.

He let it drop to the floor, and when he looked back up, Tamara's eyes were on him. Something grand was happening behind those walls of pure blue calm. Huge iron doors were folding back and a majestic light was seeping in. A light like realization makes.

Tony put his arm around her waist, and as if they had thought of it together, they continued toward the doors.

"Let's go outside," Tamara said. "I think I could use some sun."

EMMITT MEETS HIMSELF

YOUR first thought in the morning is the last honest thought of the day. It's a thought without pretense. None of the little beliefs and assumptions we superimpose on our world are in play yet. We're just ourselves. It's a raw and undisciplined viewpoint that tells the truth.

Emmitt Frank's first thought on Monday morning was a frightening one. Not a clear one, mind you, but frightening all the same. It caused him to draw his knees up to his chest and close his eyes tighter against the morning light.

All he'd thought about was where he was. But that was enough. It had been happening almost every morning since he arrived at the End of the Road three weeks ago. He'd wake up, remember where he was, and a moment of alarm would grip him. But it would pass as quickly as it came.

Soon Emmitt's ego would wake up, start unpacking his self-assurance, ambition, willpower, image, and various and sundry other allies we all surround ourselves with every morning in order to get out of bed. And everything would be all right again.

Emmitt's first few weeks of employment at the End of the Road were going well. Within a few days he had discovered the problem with the new sewer system and devised a remedy. Although his employers, the city council, didn't seem to appreciate his fastidious presentation.

After thoroughly investigating the construction contracts, project specifications, permits, payment vouchers, as-builts, and gradient inspections, Emmitt had compiled an elaborate exposition on his findings. Armed with chalkboard visuals, over-head projector, handouts, graphs, and municipal-code books, he had assembled the council at the city offices and proceeded on a two-and-a-half-hour faultfinding fest.

He had sixteen pages listing misfiled forms by the previous administration. He produced Xerox copies of dozens of unsigned payment vouchers, unstamped engineering specs, and untouched Federal Environmental Cautionary notices. He droned on interminably about the seriousness of the situation, the legal exposure of the municipality, and the unprofessional execution of duties of apparently every manager they've had since the city's inception.

Finally, Mayor Weekly couldn't keep his eyes open any longer and interrupted Emmitt. "Frank, did you figure out why the sewer's backed up?"

Emmitt, impatient with the delay in his report, straightened his tie. "Of course I did, but that's not the point . . ."

"What was the problem?" the mayor continued.

Emmitt sighed peevishly. "Very well. If you'll all refer to the blue handout, section six, part three of the as-built documentation, you'll notice a discrepancy in the gradient-survey figures as regards the primary line on Clear Shot Avenue and the branch lines off Main Street. Comparing these to the contract specifications in your pink handout, section two, you'll see . . ."

"Excuse me, Emmitt." It was the calm voice of Bud Koenig. "Tell us why the toilets don't flush."

Emmitt, as if talking to children, said, "It's obvious. The main line wasn't buried deep enough and you're trying to make sewage flow uphill."

"Can it be fixed?"

"Of course. With a relatively inexpensive pump station that is on order and is due to arrive next month." Emmitt threw this off as an annoying detail and was trying to find his place back in his presentation when Mayor Weekly adjourned the meeting.

Emmitt was dumbstruck as the council filed out. He was only halfway through his report. He was about to call after them when Bud Koenig walked into his line of sight.

"Good work, Emmitt." Bud took Emmitt's hand and shook it.

"Where is everyone going? There's a lot more to cover." Emmitt held up a four-inch-thick portfolio of papers with the same reverence one would display Moses' tablets of stone.

"You gotta know when to quit, Emmitt." Bud put his hand on top of the portfolio and lowered it to the table. "You fixed the sewer. That's all we cared about. You deal with the paperwork."

Emmitt didn't understand. The sewer was the technicality. It was going to work fine, but the project files were a disaster. He could only speak his mind. "I don't understand."

Bud put a fatherly arm on Emmitt's shoulder. "You will once you get to know us. You did a good job. Leave it alone. And try to lose that necktie would you? Just be yourself."

Bud left the office, and only momentarily did Emmitt turn to his reflection in the window to consider himself. He looked like Emmitt Frank to him. Dark suit, white shirt, plain tie. *Be yourself. What a curious thing to say*, he thought. Who else would he be?

The man who would be Emmitt Frank dressed himself Monday morning and mentally braced for the day ahead. He had some disturbing news to present to the council at their lunch meeting. He'd found discrepancies in the city files that threatened to rock the town to its foundations. Irregularities so glaring and involving such key people that they could not be ignored or tolerated.

It was a solemn city manager who stood blue-suited, white-shirted, and plain-tied in front of his employers around the big table at Clara's Coffee Cup. Mayor Weekly, Bud Koenig, Lars Luger, Ruby McClay, and Pastor Frank were all eating the meat loaf special while council secretary Clara Weekly worked a crossword puzzle on the lunch counter.

"Mr. Mayor and members of the council." Emmitt fingered his tie. "I have some distressing information in my report today." Emmitt paused while the council, taking note of the seriousness in his voice, laid their forks down and focused their attention on the new manager.

Emmitt continued: "While conducting a routine audit of the city zoning chart, I discovered that there is a licensed retail outlet operating in a residentially zoned neighborhood."

The council members looked at each other, still waiting for the bad news. Emmitt assumed a Judgment Day manner and proceeded: "That business establishment is Ruby's Video Roundup, registered to councilperson Ruby McClay."

Emmitt was met with silence from the big table, and unable to look into their undoubtedly stunned faces, he went on: "Ahem—also in my audit it was uncovered that the city did not gain clear title to the lot that was donated by city benefactor

Argus Winslow for parkland in December of 1988. Because of this, the property cannot be covered under our public-liability insurance policy as it is currently written. I request direction from the council on both of these urgent matters." Emmitt laid down his notes and looked up to his bosses, who had resumed eating their meat loaf.

Mayor Weekly finally wiped his mouth. "Frank, did that sewer pump show up yet?"

Emmitt was mystified. Hadn't they understood what he'd said? Didn't official impropriety or exposure to civil suit concern these people? "No," Emmitt said, exasperated. "The pump isn't due until next month."

"Let us know when it's here. I'll call Argus and see if he can clear that title up sometime. Thank you, Frank." Mayor Weekly turned his attention back to his lunch, and Emmitt took this as his dismissal.

As he was walking across the street to his office, Bud Koenig caught up to him.

"You gotta lighten up on that stuff, Emmitt. You dig around in there too much and you're gonna start hurtin' people's feelings."

Emmitt had no idea what he was talking about. "We have a blatant zoning violation and an uninsured public park. Doesn't anybody care about that?"

"No, not really, Emmitt."

Emmitt turned and faced Bud. He was lost. The limits of his comprehension had been breached. "What *do* you people care about?"

Bud raised the fatherly arm once more to Emmitt's shoulder. "We care about living here well and doing the best we can. Emmitt, why don't you lose that necktie and come out to my cabin tonight. You need to get away from this office for a while and just be yourself."

Emmitt stared dumbly into Bud's kind eyes. *There it is again. Just be yourself. What is he talking about?*

Emmitt accepted the invitation as one would any ovation from one's employer. Bud gave him the simple directions, said dinner was at eight sharp, and warned him to watch for moose along the way.

On the way out to Bud's cabin, Emmitt's mind worked his bewilderment over like a dog chews a bone. *How can these people be so reckless? What is it about this country that allows it?* It was going to take Emmitt a lot longer than he'd estimated to straighten this place up. *Just be yourself. Isn't that what they're paying me for?*

In the gray light of dusk, he barely saw the big one in his high beams and he never saw the little one that landed on his hood. Everything happened at once as Emmitt's breath seized with the sound of the sickening bump, the screech of his tires, and the sight of a young moose catapulting back onto the pavement. The larger moose disappeared into the brush beside the road while the young one lay in the wash of Emmitt's remaining headlight.

Emmitt started breathing again and stared into the unreal scene. The young calf's hindquarters were twisted at an impossible angle. He could see a dark stain creeping from underneath it. The animal's raised head slowly lowered to the pavement, with quick breaths snorting steam out its nose.

Emmitt didn't know what to do. His first thought was that it was a collision apparently involving more than two hundred dollars in damage and that he should not leave the scene of the accident. And then he looked at his watch to see that he was going to be late for dinner if he stayed. He supposed that another car would come along eventually. Or should he go look for assistance? What was the procedure?

The young moose lay still, and Emmitt got cautiously out of the stalled car. He walked around to look at it, but no action to take came to mind. It was a big wild animal and Emmitt had no precedent to follow here. He didn't remember ever hitting an animal on the road before. Particularly never one the size of his desk. He moved a step closer to look, and the calf's head raised up again.

Emmitt screamed out loud and jumped back through his open door. He'd thought it was attacking him, and all his blood was pumping in his neck as he gripped the steering wheel, again looking out. A bizarre and tragic drama was unfolding before him.

The larger moose reappeared alongside the road and stepped into the headlight. The calf swung its head toward its mother and there was a quick nuzzle of noses. Then the large cow raised its head to Emmitt. Her nostrils flared, her eyes glared, and there was a rumble of wild muscle, a convulsion of sorts, that barely moved her but sent sharp spears of pure fright coursing through Emmitt's rigid form.

The cow relaxed and turned her attention back to her dying calf. The calf's head lowered slowly, swinging barely from side to side like a lone leaf falling from a tree. The steamy breaths came shorter and shorter, and finally as the homely head reached the road, one last long rush of mist escaped into the night and left with a shiver of legs. The mother dipped her head once more, whipped it back in rash resignation, and trotted off.

Emmitt's body relaxed back into the seat. He felt the tautness bleed out his feet and let his forehead down to the steering wheel. There was no sound but his own breathing and the hum of an empty place. And to his incredible surprise Emmitt Frank, just being himself, began to cry.

KIRSTEN AND
STORMY START OVER

KIRSTEN Storbock had been dreading the weekend for a long time. Ever since their house burned to the ground last November, she knew that one day they were going to have to finally go out and clear away the remains. Stormy had rented a D-6 Cat to bulldoze the debris into the ground and Kirsten was driving the pilot car behind. The big truck and lowboy carrying the Cat puffed dark smoke and slowed to a crawl on the way up the windy road to Flat Back Ridge.

It wasn't that she was dreading the job so much as the idea of it. Even though all that endured of their dream house was a scorched basement full of twisted, charcoaled lumber and black puffballs that used to be sofas, beds, and chairs, it was still their dream house and it always would be.

She and Stormy had invested ten years into the place. Every shovel load of dirt. Every concrete block, joist, plate, stud, rafter, and nail seemed like only yesterday's chore. Done with their own four hands, the hands of friends, and done as they could afford it. And they'd barely gotten to live in it. Just a few months. It was hardly even broken in when a freak kitchen-grease fire turned their dream to soot. She hadn't even taken the plastic wrappings off all the lamp shades yet.

Before the fire, Kirsten was prone to sitting in different places around the house and unashamedly admiring it. She'd sit in the living room at last light, cherishing the shadows on those perfectly textured Sheetrock walls. She'd follow the lines down into the plush, unruffled sculpted carpeting and across to the glass-topped wrought-iron coffee table that served no purpose but to look good and collect fingerprints.

She couldn't even enter her bedroom without turning around to look back down the hall: the way the kitchen opened off of it; the dining area and its warm wainscotting; the sheer distance

of it, and that it was all their beautiful house. And here she was
following a piece of huge machinery at a funeral's pace up to
her dream house to bury it.

Stormy dropped another gear in the truck and tried to think
through the roar of a redlined Detroit diesel. He'd been looking
forward to this weekend for a long time. The idea of that
old burned-up house sitting out here like that had bothered
him all winter. He and Kirsten had come up a few times to
look it over and it had always depressed him. Seeing all that
work and money burned to a crisp and piled up in a ruined
basement. Even the concrete had crumbled under the heat.
The only salvageable items from ten years of blood, sweat,
and tears were the well and the septic tank. At least it would
be a start on the new place, he thought.

The house had burned uninsured, but Stormy and Kirsten
were able to get financing to rebuild through the Fair Deal
Bank and Trust. It wouldn't be the same this time; working
with somebody else's money, and working with a deadline.
And when it was all done, they'd owe on the new place for
thirty years. But they had to do it. And they would do it. And
today was a great big starting place.

Stormy had been waiting weeks for the ground frost to go
so he'd be able to scrape the top off it. He'd pulverize the
basement with the D-6, then fill it in with what was dug out
of there to begin with.

They'd dug that basement mostly by hand. It took one long
summer of weekends, friends, wheelbarrows, and beer, but
they'd done it. God, it seemed like ages ago. Stormy checked
his machine in the side mirror and thought, *This time we'll do
it right*.

Stormy could feel the raw mechanical power all the way
through him when he lowered the Cat off the lowboy trailer.
The snap and pop of the steel tracks could be heard over the
blaring engine as Stormy did a three-sixty in each direction
to dry the clutches and test the brakes. He looked up once to
Kirsten, who was heading toward her garden plot with a rake
and a shovel. She never even saw his first stab at the crumbly
old foundation.

The wall went down easily, raising a gray cloud of ash and
dust. Stormy backed up and pushed about a foot of topsoil
into the basement. Then he backed up again farther and did

the same thing. Then again and again until he had dug himself a ramp down into the old basement.

Kirsten watched from the garden as Stormy disappeared into the hole on the huge yellow machine. She could hear the squeaky groan of burned timbers being ground beneath the tracks. Just the top of the Cat was showing and Kirsten could see it moving back and forth, back and forth. Grinding and compacting the debris into a solid mass. A mass that could be built on.

She raked absently at her muddy garden site and blocked the noise of her dream house being granulated by the fantastic sounds of nails being driven and boards being sawed.

She imagined the new construction project as a sort of resurrection. She saw them all—friends, neighbors, relatives, and good samaritans—sweating and laughing behind shovels of dirt. She saw glowing faces etched by the harsh shadow of a newly framed wall and the sweet, accomplished smell of fresh white lumber standing in the breeze.

She saw her man, Stormy, and Ed Flannigan, slaphappy and silly, laying asphalt shingles in the warm summer sun with cold beers shining like agates in a tub of ice for quitting time. And through it all, her dream house would be ascending from the ashes a stick at a time until it was a perfect thing again.

Stormy was rather enjoying himself down in the basement. Every time he'd ram the big Cat into the end of the hole, another big chunk of concrete wall and backfill would tumble in. He kept layering the sandy backfill over the ashes and debris and continued to compact it all together. He rammed hard on the gear shift and clutches. He was in a hurry. If he didn't get this done today, he'd have to keep the Cat another whole day and pay for it. There just wasn't the time or the money.

Stormy knew this house was going to be a whole different story. He'd have to start working six days a week at the boat yard to keep up with the interim financing, and Kirsten would have to take in more bookkeeping work so they could meet the mortgage payments when they started. He'd have to hire a couple of carpenters, he guessed. With the amount of interest they were paying on the construction loan, the sooner they got it put together the better.

Ed Flannigan already said he wouldn't be able to help much

this time around. He was going to take a second job with the road crew this summer so he and Emily could get a little extra laid aside.

Stormy ran the blade all the way down one side of the basement and it fell in behind him. What they'd taken ten years to do the first time they'd have to get done in four months. It was going to be a hectic summer.

Kirsten leaned on her rake and watched, not really focusing, as the D-6 Cat moved back and forth, inching continually higher out of the hole.

Country Morning, she thought. That's right. That was the name of the wallpaper in the kitchen. And the counters were all done in Plum Delight. The cabinets were the light honey oak with raised panels, and they had the slate-gray no-wax Mannington vinyl floor covering with the diamond pattern.

What was the name of that carpeting in the master bedroom? Sonoma Sunrise? Valley Wine? Something like wine, she was sure of it. She'd know it when she saw it again. It wasn't going to be that much trouble to replace the interior. It hadn't been that long, and they must still carry all the selections. Thank goodness she didn't have to make all those decisions again.

The rooms themselves would be easy to reproduce. She and Stormy had kept meticulous plans of everything as they'd built. The design changed several times over the ten years, mostly to accommodate the two kids who were born in the meantime, but they'd done it all on paper, and Ed and Emily had kept the copies that Ed had used to figure the Sheetrock with.

It's a darn good thing too, Kirsten thought. Oh, those late-night arguments in the kitchen. Stormy in his T-shirt, with a ruler and graph paper, trying to draw a bedroom addition. Kirsten looking over his shoulder, nitting and picking the whole while.

"No, make it longer and not so wide. Put the window on the end. Yeah, no. Bigger. There, whoops, where will the laundry chute be now?"

And on they bickered, trying to get everything just right. Just the way they wanted it. She certainly looked forward to not having to go through that anymore. This time they knew just what they were going to do and exactly what it was going to look like before they even started.

Kirsten snapped out of her reverie and centered her attention on Stormy, who continued to rise out of the hole. The machine was nearly all the way exposed to her now and she saw Stormy's hands working deftly and handily on the controls, his tongue out and his shoulders hunched like a busy man.

Stormy had the rhythm of it now. Two passes all the way across to pack, one back blade from the far edge, a fresh cut from the front, and pack some more. Another half hour and you'd never know there was ever anything there at all.

As busy as it was going to be, Stormy looked forward to getting a second chance at this place. They'd changed their minds a lot in ten years and left a lot of mistakes they wouldn't have to make over again. For one thing, they'd turn the whole works further toward the south. They'd missed by a mile the first time. The view was just as good to the south, and they'd get so much more light in the winter. And the windows. They'd been cheap on the windows. They'll put in some great big ol' triple panes. Change that whole room around.

They'd move their bedroom to the south of the house, too. Was like sleeping in a tomb back there on the north side. And that purple carpet, whoa. Never do that again. Looked like a Belgian cathouse in there.

Not as bad as the kitchen, though. That wallpaper. Jeez Louise. Little butter churns and windmills on the walls. Stormy hated pictures on the walls. Especially those butter churns and the fat little babies with bows and arrows in the master bath. This time no pictures, just Sheetrock.

Stormy'd seen a picture of a house in Kirsten's *Better Homes and Gardens* that gave him ideas. The place was just white and wood. Tall ceilings, lotsa light and open places. They didn't need to do any of that cutesy stuff again. Kirsten got her way once, but that was her first house. They both knew better by now, he thought. Stormy wasn't sure just exactly what he wanted to build, but he knew it wasn't going to be anything like the other place.

After Stormy walked the Cat back onto the trailer and shut it off, the silence that was left was like a vacuum sucking. Kirsten leaned on her car and looked out over the perfectly groomed lot. The only two things visible above grade were the stakes Stormy had marked the water and sewer lines with. Everything else was flattened. Flattened and textured, like you could rake it, plant it, and never know they'd been there at all.

Stormy climbed down from the lowboy and leaned up against Kirsten and her car.

"Well, there she be, Kirsty. A virgin lot."

"She's a virgin, but she knows what she's doing." Kirsten leaned back into Stormy's greasy overall. "It's almost fun starting over, isn't it?"

"Yeah, maybe it is. I can't make up my mind."

"What's to make up your mind about? It's already been figured out."

But Stormy wasn't listening. He was sitting in a bright room of white and wood admiring the light a little farther to the south.

And Kirsten didn't wait for a response as she'd finally remembered the name of that carpet, Belgian Boudoir. Yeah, that was it.

"Oh, Stormy," she said. "Isn't it so nice we've been through this once? What could we possibly find to bicker about a second time around?"

ARGUS AND RUBY

YOUNG love might be the most overrated phenomenon since the disposable diaper. No matter how good it seems looking back on it, it was still an ugly business.

Young love is an all-consuming thing that lends full frontal lobotomies to young men and women who should have been celebrating their lingering childhood.

There is another side of love, though. A side that makes up for what it does to us in our faded youth. A side that you have to live a long time for.

Argus Winslow had lived a long time, and as he stood beside his Argus Salvage and Sales tow truck in front of Ruby's Video Roundup trying to muster the courage to go in, he couldn't remember ever feeling so fidgety. Of course, he wasn't remembering a lot of things these days, he had to admit.

Ever since he banged heads with Bud Koenig during that New Years's Day fiasco, he'd been having memory lapses. The doctors told him honestly that it might probably, with no real certainty, clear itself up to a point someday, but then it might not. In the meantime Argus was making the best of them—laughing them off as he went, covering up for them where he could, and troubling over them always.

But it wasn't his memory troubling him right now. It was his heart. A sixty-seven-year-old heart that was beating like a teenager's as he finally pushed through the door into Ruby McClay's video store.

Ruby heard the jangle of the bells on the door, glanced up from her catalog, and did a double take.

"Well, if it isn't the old junkyard dog himself, Argus Winslow. In here to rent *Ole' Yeller* again for your dog?"

"No." Argus showed his uneasiness by pulling off his greasy cap and fingering it in front of him.

Ruby registered his seriousness and was frightened for a moment. "Barney's okay, isn't he?"

"Oh sure, that dog'll outlive us both, Ruby." Argus walked up to the counter, set his hat down, and got to business. What Argus Winslow might lack in courage, execution, or style he made up for in plain straight-ahead forwardness. "Miss McClay, they're having that big fish fry over at the lodge Friday night and I was wanting you to go eat with me."

Ruby McClay looked at her old friend with his rugged red face and smiled an old-friend smile with just a little more. "Mr. Winslow," she said, imitating his manner. "I'd be honored to go eat with you."

Argus was warmed and calmed by her answer and demonstrated this by putting his hat back on and leaving. He paused on the way through the door and over the jingling bells called over his shoulder, "I'll be here with the tow truck at six."

Ruby smiled after him over what a little boy Argus seemed, then she took stock of herself and smiled even deeper at what a little girl she felt.

You see, Argus Winslow and Ruby McClay have been circling each other for years. When Ruby came to town a quarter century ago, Argus had already been here twenty years. Ruby was one of the few single women to ever venture out to the End of the Road, and being a trim, thirty-five-year-old redheaded fireball didn't hurt her popularity any. She'd have five to six suitors tethered around her at any one time, but she never seemed to show any enduring interest in any particular one of them.

By the same token, Argus couldn't seem to give a whit for Ruby. He was nice enough to her when he was around, but he never got goofy-eyed like the other men. Those first few years, whenever Ruby would walk into a room full of men, voices would rise, postures would improve, pocket combs would be drawn and fired, and she'd have as many drinks in front of her as there were guys in the place. Every guy but Argus, that is. Argus would look up, maybe tip his hat, then return to whatever argument he happened to be having at the moment.

Argus was a real dilemma for Ruby. She'd known men she couldn't hook before, but she'd never known one who wouldn't at least sniff the bait. Ruby knew it couldn't be her, and her woman's instincts told her it must be somebody else. Argus was no celibate. She could sense that for sure. He must have a companion. Someone, somewhere he was being true to.

Ruby's instincts were good ones, and although she couldn't be certain about Argus's girlfriend in Anchorage, she could see the before and after difference in the man around his monthly scrap-selling trips. He'd leave town short-tempered and struggling along with a fifth-wheel trailer loaded to the gills with scrap iron, then come back with an empty truck, a crooked grin, and a walk that came right off the balls of his feet.

Ruby rested her graying head on her open hand at the video store and wondered what had changed for the man that he'd start coming around after all these years.

Argus Winslow poked around a pile of rusty water-heater tanks out at the junkyard and pondered the same thing. In the less-than-romantic din of metal tanks having the pressure valves beaten off them with a crowbar, Argus thought about the circumstances at hand. How after twenty-five years of avoiding the subject he was making a move on his favorite lady. Of course, he'd never let her know she was a favorite, but he was busy enough with Dolly most of that time.

You have to understand that Argus Winslow lives his life by a few hard and simple rules and two of them concern women. The first one is always tell the truth to women because they can smell a lie. The second rule is never to get mixed up with more than one woman at a time because of the first rule.

Argus's friend Dolly was the perennial bartender at his favorite Anchorage watering hole and for thirty years he'd been warming a stool at her bar and a seat at her breakfast table whenever he got to town. It was a relationship built on laughter, nonsense, and naughtiness and gave Argus and Dolly each what they needed for the last half of their life so far.

Dolly took sick and left the state sometime around Halloween, and Argus's eye started to wander about the same time his memory did. *Better go talk to Ruby before I forget what to do with her*, Argus thought. And that's exactly what he'd done.

Argus finished knocking the last of the valves off the water tanks and stood up to survey his work. "Barney?" The black dog at his side leaned against his leg. "I can't for the life of me remember why I did that."

Argus dressed carefully in his trailer Friday night. He'd spent the afternoon trying to make the front seat of his tow truck respectable, but it was fruitless. Too many years of rusty car parts, empty oil cans, and a Labrador retriever. Argus could only hope that Ruby had the sense to wear dark clothes.

As far as his own clothes went, he was pulling out all the stops. He had a fresh red-checked flannel shirt that barely buttoned over his belly and a brand new pair of canvas bib overalls in case the buttons failed. Argus was feeling so infected with the spirit of the evening ahead, as he slicked his remaining hair back in the mirror, he decided he'd leave his hat at home. "Barney, they're never going to recognize your old man tonight."

Ruby, for her part, had spent the entire day in curlers and even closed the store early to get ready for her date. She did have the sense to wear dark clothes and was still grooming the pleats in her denim skirt when she heard the tow truck pull around behind the store.

Ruby's apartment in back of the store was small, and Argus seemed to take up the whole kitchen just by standing in the doorway. But he took it up in a nice way.

"You are still quite a handsome woman, Ruby McClay."

"Pretty well preserved yourself, Argus Winslow."

Argus held back the door for Ruby to pass, and a shiver went through his body when he smelled her perfume. *Why didn't I think of this twenty years ago*, he thought, then said out loud, "Let's go give this town something to jabber about."

Argus and Ruby were among the first to arrive at the Organization of Fishermen's Wives annual Fish-o-Rama Banquet Benefit and Fishermen's Ball at the Bluff Lodge. They worked their way down the huge buffet not saying much, and since the place was just beginning to fill up, they took a small table for two back in a corner.

The late-spring sun hung in the sky outside the big plate-glass windows of the lodge. Sissy Tuttle went down the wall lowering the blinds but got called away to an emergency with the beer batter before she got the last one. This happened to be the one shining right on the small table of Ruby and Argus. And as if they hadn't already captured the attention of everyone, they certainly were now firmly in the spotlight.

The glaring sun had just the reverse effect for Argus and Ruby, who couldn't look out into the room without blinding themselves. They hardly took notice, though. It all sounded like the typical banquet going on whether they could see it or not. A constant dinging of silverware, children complaining, glasses breaking, renegade laughter, and that low-pitched rumble of small-town talk.

"I knew those two would get together."

"Never thought I'd see the day Winslow took his hat off."

"Don't believe I've seen Ruby in a skirt since Fritz's wife's funeral."

"Mommy, are they going to get married?"

And as the talk droned on Ruby and Argus ate quietly, waiting for the other to start. Ruby, in her own direct manner, did. "Argus, how come after twenty-five years you finally asked me out?"

Argus, employing his first rule of women, told the bare fact of it: "My girlfriend left the state and died."

Ruby, not knowing Argus's first rule of women, could only think he was being cute and absurd, and she laughed. Argus looked up and chuckled a little just to be in on it, and their feet shifted under the table.

Argus's foot lit on what he was sure was a piece of the table, and just to the north of there Ruby's foot decided the same thing. Simultaneously, each felt the other's foot resting on their own, but neither one knew they were giving it back. They were both a little rattled and this caused them to squirm their feet back and forth. This only added to the exhilaration of the whole thing, and Argus felt blood rushing into his cheeks for the first time since he forgot what he did for a living and called the cops to find out who put all the junk in his front yard.

So as Argus and Ruby ate in a stunned silence, deliciously shocked that the other was being so bold, the rest of our happy diners certainly were "getting something to jabber about."

"Holy smokes, look at that old goat move in."

"Ruby hasn't lost her touch a bit, has she?"

"Too bad Winslow's too old for children. Probably make good sled dogs."

And as the audience had their fun, our players had *their* fun until Argus finally wiped his mouth. "I eat one more bite and I'm gonna pop like a road kill."

"You say the sweetest things," Ruby said, wiping her own mouth, and they chuckled a little while their feet returned to neutral territory under the table.

"Let's get outa here before people start talking."

The ride back to Ruby's in the tow truck with Barney in between them was a quiet one. Neither one of them really knew how to follow up on the dinner entertainment. And they both felt shy and guilty that they hadn't reciprocated the overtures. *I shoulda sweeted her up a little*, Argus was thinking. *I hope he doesn't think I'm prudish*, thought Ruby.

And since neither knew what had really happened, or what might come next, it was a quiet parting at Ruby's back door. She searched for any viable reason in the world for having Argus in while Argus reached deep down in his crusty old bag of tricks for a reason to keep her out.

"Well good night, Argus."

"Good night, Ruby."

Argus was pulling into his driveway before he even realized he'd driven there. His head and body had been sent swimming and the whole drive home went unnoticed. All he had on his mind was a gray-haired sweetheart of a human being. He was thinking of every word she'd said, every move she'd made, and every time she looked at him.

Ruby lay back in her La-Z-Boy with two of her cats and was paying about as much attention as they were to the video on TV. It was *Charade*, with Cary Grant. Usually she couldn't keep her eyes off Cary Grant, but tonight she couldn't even look at him. She had another man on her mind. A sweet, reckless old goat who'd left her tongue-tied as a schoolgirl all over again.

Argus stood in his trailer dazed and undressing. As he took off his shirt, he felt something in the pocket. He pulled out two paper tickets and read them, THE FISHERMEN'S BALL.

"Oh no," he said out loud. "I forgot to take her to the dance." Argus sat back in the kitchen chair and wanted to cry. He'd taken her home after a one-hour date only because he couldn't remember what he had meant to do. His cheeks flushed for the second time that evening, and this time from pure embarrassment. "First I won't play footsies with 'er. Then I take 'er home before the band starts. She must think

I've gone over the hill." Argus reached for the phone without thinking. When he heard her sleepy voice come on the line, his embarrassment vanished and his hot face was replaced by a warm, and active, heart.

"Ruby, it's Argus. I forgot to take you to the dance tonight."

There was a silence on the line for a moment. The silence a person leaves when she wants to say the right thing.

"Argus, I forgot to take you to the dance tonight too."

There was another silence on the line like a person leaves when he's heard the right thing. And then there was nothing. And late into that night, long after the band had stopped playing, two old players lay awake and wondered how something as overrated as young love could live so darn long.

MATTY AND EMMITT

IT was the way he said her name that first turned Matty's head. And Matty Pierce was not one to have her head turned easily. Especially not by her boss. And most especially not by a boss like Emmitt Frank. She didn't really know Emmitt all that well, but his appearance and mannerisms alone should have disengaged any interest at all. If it wasn't for the way he talked to her. Actually, it was only the way he said her name.

"Matty." Even if he was just calling her into his office for something, he said it so easily and comfortably, it made it sound like something special. Like it belonged there. Never a question mark on the end like one might use a stranger's name. Nothing sounds sweeter to a person than her own name, and if it's done just so, well, it does things.

It lent an instant familiarity to Emmitt. It seemed almost affable, which was so unlike everything else about the man that it was curious. Curious enough that Matty found herself studying Emmitt.

Matty had worked as the city clerk and assistant to city managers at the End of the Road for nearly ten years. In that time there had been nineteen different city managers. The longest one lasted nine months, the shortest, two weeks. She had looked forward to Emmitt Frank's arrival six weeks ago like some people crave cold oatmeal. Hardly at all.

These managers were such an inconvenience. They'd always come in full of important ideas, change everything around in the office, then get themselves fired by the city council, leaving Matty to pick up the pieces. They were all just tourists to her.

But Emmitt seemed to be a little different. For one thing, the city council liked him so far. Emmitt was either extremely competent or very lucky. He'd come in and fixed the new

46

sewer system in a matter of weeks, something that had cost the job of the last two managers. He was sharp, Matty couldn't deny that, but he was about as entertaining as the aforementioned cold oatmeal.

Matty remembered his first day on the job.

Oh my God, she thought when she walked in that morning. She was pulling off her rubber boots and getting into her work sneakers when she spotted Emmitt in his office. He had on a three-piece suit that was impeccably pressed and he sat square-shouldered in his chair with his hands folded on the desk in front of him. That's how Emmitt relaxes, she knows now, but it struck her as being a mite formal that first day.

"You would be Margaret Pierce, I presume? I'm Emmitt Frank and I believe we'll be working together." Emmitt stood behind his desk and extended a hand across.

Is this guy for real? Matty took the hand. "Yes sir, I'm your gal, and everybody calls me Matty."

"Matty," he said. That was the first time she heard it in his voice. Some sort of remark on the name. "Matty." He said it again and a barely visible shift went through his rigid frame. "We have a lot of work to do."

And then he'd launched into the most boring one hour of Matty Pierce's life—outlining procedural changes he hoped to implement, programs he intended to introduce, and filing instructions that would have made little or no sense to Matty even if she had been listening. *This one isn't going to last a week*, she'd thought.

Being a good-looking forty-year-old single mother at the End of the Road left Matty with no dearth of men friends, and she has been known to indulge, however difficult she's made it on the guys involved. Her husband was a bush pilot and had died in a crash five years ago, leaving Matty and her ten-year-old son, Willy, to carry on. She'd been deeply in love with her husband. Even after five years, she found other men didn't compare favorably to her man, and few held her interest.

A person would think that no man could hold her interest less than Emmitt Frank, but that wasn't the case. She watched him very closely and found out as much as she could about him. Which wasn't very much.

She knew he came from Chicago. He was forty-three and had worked only one job his whole life, with the city of

Chicago. He'd left after twenty years, to take this job at the End of the Road. That was all on the résumé in his file. She also knew he had been married and was getting divorced. That wasn't on his résumé, but he'd gotten a couple of letters from a law firm in Chicago and she'd held one up to the light.

The idea that Emmitt had been married made him even more interesting to Matty. She could hardly picture him with a woman. It wasn't that he was ugly. No, but he wasn't particularly handsome either. He was just sort of *there*. He had the look of someone who was perpetually overlooked at service counters. So much so that he'd developed the habit of turning his head around quickly when spoken to, to make sure you weren't talking to somebody behind him.

He might have had a pleasant smile if he ever tried one. His face was always the same—that professional pleasantness that lingered somewhere between a smile and a wince, which has been mastered throughout the business world by bankers, brokers, and insurance salesmen. The ability to look a person in the eye, nod appreciably, and say, "Terrific," and not be listening to a word they're saying.

If he had a sense of humor, he'd left it in Chicago. In a giddy mood one morning, Matty had tried to make a joke about her boss's business attire.

"You oughta do something about that necktie," she said. Emmitt looked at her, puzzled. He looked down to his tie as if there might be food stains on it or something, but he seemed to know there wasn't. He just looked back up to her and asked her to bring him the as-built survey for the sewage outfall.

Matty would lose interest in Emmitt for days at a time and then something would happen to rekindle the fascination. One day she read a memo he'd left on her desk and noticed how he'd written her name, Matty. He'd brought the tail of the *y* around and crossed the *t*'s with it. She did that herself with her signature. Was he trying to tell her something? Was he trying to impress her in his awkward way, or was he maybe mocking her? What an interesting man.

She asked him to lunch one day and was nearly bowled over when he accepted. She'd asked him to lunch no less than twenty times since he arrived and he'd always waved it off with a pleasant, "Thank you, you go ahead. I'll eat later."

She expected the same thing that day, but when she asked, he was sitting at his desk with his hands folded in front of him and not paying attention. He may have agreed to go to lunch with her before he realized what he was doing, but by then it was too late.

Emmitt was in a particularly thoughtful mood that day. He was never a chatterbox even on his best days, but he at least seemed to be busy all the time. That morning he just seemed to sit and muse.

On the way across the street to Clara's Coffee Cup, Matty noticed the front of Emmitt's station wagon was smashed in. "What in the world happened to you?" she said.

Emmitt kept on walking. "I hit a moose on the road last night." Then he stopped and turned to her. "It died, Matty."

There it was again, "Matty." And a flicker of emotion came with it. Not just "It died," but "It died, *Matty*." What was this man trying to say to her?

They kept walking into Clara's and both ordered the turkey-sandwich special.

Emmitt spent most of the meal discussing various computer programs he was considering implementing at the office. "There is a program I read about in *Manager's Monthly* that will cross-file utility billings by usage, property value, name, date, or payment history. It could be extremely useful when it comes time for service upgrades."

He droned on interminably, and Matty began to realize that these things were incredibly interesting to Emmitt. It's what he liked to think about. Or was it? Did he only think about these things to force more unpleasant things from his mind? Like ex-wives, or dead moose? She watched him eat his lunch.

He had his napkin folded lightly and perfectly in his lap. He'd removed his jacket and hung it on a hanger by the front door. The only hanger in the place, and one he must have put there himself for just this reason. His back was ramrod straight on the counter stool and he talked mostly to his hands, eating meticulously. He'd cut the slightest signs of fat or gristle out of the turkey with his knife, switch hands, and delicately move a bite to his mouth. He'd chew pensively, as if he were counting, which in fact he was, but Matty had no way of knowing that.

She had no way of knowing much of anything about this man. Never in her life had she run into a person who revealed less about himself than Emmitt Frank.

But he had revealed something by saying her name. Was this newly divorced, anal-retentive bureaucrat making some inept play for her? The thought, however distasteful, was somehow flattering, as it is to anyone who suspects an admirer.

Or maybe, she thought, *it's deeper than that. Maybe it's just his soul reaching out to me.* Matty had been reading a lot of stuff on spirits and kindred souls since her husband died. There was definitely the possibility that Emmitt and she were connected in some spiritual way they hadn't discovered yet. It certainly would explain a lot of things.

"Thanks for lunch, Emmitt," Matty said on the way back across the street.

"It was my pleasure, Matty."

Matty. How did he *do* that? There was something going on here. Matty expected something more as they walked by Emmitt's smashed car, but nothing came. They reached city hall, Emmitt took a left at his office, and Matty resumed her roost around the corner.

It was an uneventful afternoon. A couple of complaints about water pressure. Another light got shot out at the harbor. Emmitt was working in his office on some zoning ordinances he was going to recommend to the council on Monday. The copy machine broke down again. Then there was one long-distance call that changed not only the afternoon but pretty much everything.

It was a woman's voice, and she just asked to speak to Emmitt Frank. Emmitt got so few calls that it never even occurred to Matty to ask her name. "Emmitt, long distance, line one."

Matty could barely hear Emmitt's end of the conversation, and she wouldn't have been listening at all, but she heard her name. It drew her attention, then she heard it again. She thought maybe he was calling for her, and she was already on her feet and on her way when she started hearing the whole of it.

"Yes, Matty, that would be fine. Certainly. I think your lawyer is correct in demanding you keep the house and second car. The papers will be signed and returned within the week. Good-bye, Matty."

Matty Pierce slumped against the wall and made a face. *Matty is his wife's name.* All of a sudden it all made sense. He'd been pronouncing her name out of habit. The familiarity in his voice was no kindred soul reaching out. It was routine verbiage. The warmth, the easiness, the flicker of it all. It was all a foolish duplication of old patterns. No more warm or personal than the way he ate his lunch.

Emmitt Frank sat upright in his chair with his hands folded in front of him and thought about a cross-referencing computer program he'd like to have.

Matty sat back down at her desk and tried to get a grip on what she was feeling. Sadness? Reaction? Realization?

"Matty," Emmitt called from his office.

There it was, she had it. She was *bored*.

ED'S KIDS

ED didn't have much patience for Emily's complaints. When she tried to explain to him why she needed to go take a week-long personal-insight seminar, he got testy, even cruel, with her.

"What are you going to do? Crawl around a gym floor with a bunch of strangers until you throw up or forgive your mother for cutting your hair when you were six?"

"It's not like that, Ed." Emily hadn't been looking forward to this discussion. "It's a world-renowned program designed to let people rediscover their self-confidence and worth. I need a big shot of that."

Ed Flannigan wasn't a stupid person or a mean person. He just didn't know a lot of things. So it was this ignorance that prevented him from having much sympathy for his wife. "Why all of a sudden do you have to spend a week and five hundred dollars to feel good about yourself? Is it that bad around here?"

Emily was ready for this. She got up from the kitchen table and leaned on a chair back to give the speech. "Yes, Ed, it is that bad around here. For ten years all I've done is raise kids and keep house. I was on the dean's list at Radcliffe, with a degree in anthropology, and the most significant human studies I've made since then have been why kids put corn and peas up their noses. Three children and a husband with a greasy job. I see dirty laundry in my sleep!" Emily sat back down and grabbed her husband's hand. "Ed, I'm going crazy. I have to get the hell out of here. I love you and I love the kids, but . . ."

The emphatic *but* has done more for the art of marital threats than any other element. The *but* was not lost on Ed, even though he couldn't come completely clean on the issue. "Well, driving a road grader for ten years is no spiritual picnic either, but if you gotta go, you gotta go. Me and the kids'll be fine."

It was the right thing to do. Ed knew that. He understood Emily enough to know when the proverbial poop was about to hit the fan, and he owed it to everybody involved to turn off the fan. He squeezed his wife's hand and smiled a real smile. "Don't forget to come home."

The Flannigans drew close in the kitchen. Emily's spirits soared with the certainty of a break from her domestic routine, and Ed's soared mostly because it was so seldom he got to be the good guy.

Ed *was* a good guy. Everybody thought so. He was reliable, hardworking, good-looking, and fun-loving. But (there's that *but* again) Ed was from the old school. He figured that working all the time and not complaining was what being a husband and a father was all about. He loved his kids, was proud of them, even bragged about them around the coffeepot at the maintenance shop, but Emily did the dirty work. That's just the way it went. Ed wrestled with the kids in the living room until he had them whipped into a lather, then it was Emily's job to organize them, brush teeth, find pajamas, and read stories.

In the meantime Ed would rifle through the TV channels, maybe pop some popcorn, and pour a couple of beers for them. The whole while he'd wonder and fret why she was taking so long with the kids when they could be together having fun. Ed would never think of himself as a sexist, but only because he had never really considered the term.

Emily left for Anchorage on Sunday afternoon. Ed brushed off any offers of support. "Call Kirsten if you need anything. Tiffany is available to sit on Wednesday if you need a break, and there's always Sissy Tuttle—I know you hate her, but she's great with kids."

"Hey, they're my kids too," Ed said, hauling Emily's suitcase out to the station wagon. "How much trouble can they be?"

Emily didn't feel driven at the moment to answer that question. She'd left a six-page note on the kitchen table, and Ed would learn the cold, hard truth of the matter soon enough.

Ed had a storybook romance with the kids on Sunday night. Right out of a Disney family documentary. They had hot dogs and chips, drank pop, and watched cartoons and movies. Ed had taken the kids down to Ruby's Video Roundup and let each one pick out any movie.

Ten-year-old Ed junior had taken advantage of his mother's absence and picked *Mutant Killer Nuns from Mars*. Emily would not allow violent movies in the house. Ed knew this but thought in the spirit of things, they could wink at the rules one time. Missy picked out *Swiss Family Robinson*, causing Ed junior to complain, "That's the only movie she ever picks. We've watched it a hundred times. Mom always makes her pick another one."

"Missy's six years old, and she can watch whatever she wants." Ed was holding on to his youngest boy, Corey who, for reasons known only to his four-year-old mind, had selected the animated masterpiece classic of Dante's *Inferno*.

Ed junior sat next to the TV lip-syncing all the dialogue in *Swiss Family Robinson* just to irritate Missy, who had pretended to be sick to her stomach when the mutant nuns from Mars ate the Vienna Boys' Choir.

Everything was going smoothly and Corey was nodding off at about the seventh level of Dante's *Inferno* when Missy slapped Ed in the face with a cold, hard truth.

"Are you taking us to school tomorrow, Daddy?"

Ed snapped to attention. "School! Oh my gosh, what time is it? Eleven o'clock. What are you kids still doing up? Missy, Ed, go get your pajamas on."

"Mommy gives us baths on Sunday night."

"No baths, get movin'." Ed shut the TV off, which put young Corey in a righteous snit that quickly turned tantrum, fueled by sugar, potato chips, and fatigue.

Ed soon found himself surrounded by unhappy children in three stages of disrepair ingeniously inventing doomsday scenarios to prolong the evening.

"You have to iron my blue dress 'cause Nicole's having a birthday party."

"Dad, I can't find where Mom put my homework. I'm going to get a D in math if I don't hand it in."

"I don' wanna brush my teeth. It's yucky!"

Like the screams of the damned, the children whined on while Ed bit his lip and forged ahead. He'd heard this din before, but always from afar. This was the part of the program where he was usually down in the living room looking for a late show and wondering, not always to himself, why Emily couldn't keep those darn kids quiet.

Corey cried for half an hour because Ed couldn't remember the words to the second verse of "Twinkle Twinkle, Little Star." He finally had to wake up Missy to teach him, and then she couldn't get back to sleep, worried that killer nuns were coming to get her. Ed junior was reading something under his covers with a flashlight, but Ed didn't want to know about it. As long as he was quiet, he didn't care if he was plotting to overthrow the crown.

Ed looked at his watch and the sight of midnight drained all the last energy from his legs. He was supposed to go in early tomorrow and grade Flat Back Ridge Road before the school buses had to travel it. He wondered how he was going to be able to do that and get the kids ready for school and day care in the morning. Ed felt very heavy and suddenly began to miss his wife.

But Emily, even in her absence, was not about to settle for just quiet admiration of her worth. The epic note she'd left for Ed finally caught his eye, and he reached across the table for it. An action that would catapult him into the Inferno several levels lower than where Dante left off.

"To my wonderful man," it began.

"Uh-oh," Ed said out loud. She always greased him like that before the bad news.

Thank you ever so much for letting me go. One week to be with just myself, and I'll be a new woman. Now there's a few things you should remember while I'm gone.

The kids' lunch boxes are in the cupboard under the sink. Ed takes baloney with a little mayonnaise. Missy eats only peanut butter and jelly, and you have to cut the crusts off. Corey gets lunch at day care but likes to pretend, so I always send a Ding Dong with him in Missy's old Barbie doll box. The Ding Dongs are in the cupboard above the refrigerator, and don't eat any. There's just enough.

Missy has ballet after school on Monday, so you'll have to pick her up and take her to Nicole Bindel's birthday party. Little Ed rides the bus home, but you need to take him around in the car to get pledges for his Popeye Wrestling Tournament. Kirsten will pick up Corey at day care at three, but you should go get him right after work so they can eat dinner.

On Tuesday Ed has swimming after school and can't take the bus, but you can pick him up when you get Missy from her piano lesson. Corey has a doctor's appointment at four-thirty. You'll have to leave work early. It's about his ear infection.

For dinner on Monday there's still stew left in the orange Tupperware and . . .

. . . the note went on and on, and Ed's posture at the table went from poor to worse as every page was turned to reveal yet another endless roll of chores. All of it listed in Emily's offhanded voice and precise penmanship. Ed could not believe it all. Everything was in there. When to water the plants. Where the plants were. To use the coupons on the fridge for the dog food. How much soap to use in the wash. Where the bags to the vacuum cleaner are. When the kids should do their homework. Keep little Ed out of her styling mousse. Line after line of things to remember, things to consider, and things to do.

Ed decided it couldn't be done. There was no way a mortal person could accomplish all of it in a week. Emily must be pulling his leg, he thought. Really pouring it on to justify why she wimped out on him. *Needs a week to herself to recover.* Ed chuckled to himself. "Pretty tricky little lady."

Ed walked out into the living room to turn the lights off and focused for the first time on the mess. There were potato chips ground into the carpet. Corey had stuffed some cheese slices into one of the rented videos. He found Little Ed's math assignment under the table with orange pop spilled on it, and Missy had colored in all the letters on his textbook cover.

As he wearily bent to the task at hand, all the things in Emily's note started circling in his head. The lunches, the laundry, the errands and appointments and groceries and dinner and plants and dogs and vacuum sweepers. It was all real. It did all get done. Every day of the week.

It made him so tired his knees ached. And he thought of his wife. Off to some kooky seminar to find some time for herself and recover. Leaving him here to deal with it all for an entire week. He was amazed. Shocked, really. Not that she'd do it to him. No, that was understandable. What he didn't understand, though, was that if everything in that note is true and that's what's been going on around here, then how in the world did she ever expect to recover from it in just a week?

It is fairly safe to say that while Emily Flannigan is away discovering her worth, Ed will be home discovering some of it too.

part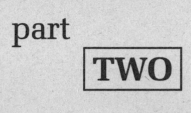

FRITZ'S FAREWELL

FRITZ Ferguson leaned against his old car in the turnout at the top of the hill and looked one last time at the beautiful bay that stretched before him.

It was a gray sort of day. Not rainy, but not the most flattering light for this parting shot. The overcast was high, but it still clipped the tops off his mountains across the water. It was a level gray line so clean you wouldn't believe the mountains even had tops if you didn't know better.

But Fritz knew better. Not only did he know the mountains had tops, but he'd been to the top of more than a few of them. And he'd skied the glaciers, hunted the hills, fished the bays, clammed the coves, and so much more in his fifty-three intimate years with this magnificent country.

When he'd come, there was nothing here *but* this. The fine little town that now lay below him nestled around and along that peculiar spit of land was only a wish and a prayer for himself and a few others to come—Argus Winslow, Bud Koenig, Ruby McClay. Good friends and good people. Oh, he'd known the best of people here.

He thought of Meredith, his native wife of fifty years, only two years passed on now. He automatically looked to their special place, Eden Cove, where they'd met and where they'd eventually fallen in love. He closed his eyes and a much younger Fritz Ferguson stepped onto a quiet little beach across the bay.

He'd rowed his dory over just to get a little time away from his homestead and all its endless improvements, and the other homesteaders and all their endless impoverishments. He lay back in the sand and gravel, still breathing hard, and looked up to the spruce trees towering around. He listened to the silence and smelled the sweet air and dug his fingers into the rocky sand.

What he felt in his hands caught his attention and he raised up like he'd been shocked. In each of his sandy palms he held a half dozen sweet little butter clams, the cuisine exemplary of the low-tide set. He dug his hands in again and came up with a dozen more. They virtually boiled from the sand. Fritz had seen some pretty darn nice clammin' beaches, but he'd never seen anything like this.

He was soon on his knees digging like a gold-struck prospector, and laughin' like one too, dredging what would prove to be several buckets full of delectable steamers, when he heard something from the woods.

He stopped his digging, tensed, and listened. This seemed to make the noise even louder. A noise he couldn't identify until he looked up and saw the refreshing, round, and giggling brown young face of a native girl just inside the tree line. She had a basket of fresh blueberries on her arm, and the smile that remained on her face even after her laughter had stopped is what captured Fritz's heart and what would eventually prove to hold it for five decades to come.

Fritz opened his eyes to shake off the memory and looked across the bay once more for Eden Cove. His eyes weren't as good as they used to be, so it was hard to tell from this distance, but it looked like Eden Cove lay just about where the group of boats was centered out on the gray water. They were oil-skimmer boats, a common sight lately, and they looked to be working his cove over.

A deadly rage, a rage all too common in these days since the oil spill, built again in his seventy-five-year-old frame and he forced himself to look away. He looked to that quiet little town and thought of the others, those who would stay to help clean this up and who would live here happily—as he no longer could. And he remembered back to that meeting, the first one, the one that changed everything, and everybody, the one that let all of us know why Fritz Ferguson couldn't live at the End of the Road anymore.

It was at the Big Garage on Clear Shot about a month ago. The oil company had put it together to let the local people have their say. The spill was three weeks old, and not only had very little of it been recovered, but nobody really seemed to know where it all was. All anybody knew for sure was that it was starting to show up here. The townspeople themselves, tired of waiting for the officials to do anything, had started the construction of emergency protection booms all on their own. The arrival of these officials did little to calm anyone's anxieties and only seemed to raise the hackles of most.

The visiting experts sat at long folding tables in the front. There was a coast guard officer, looking solemn and competent. There were two bearded biologists from state and federal wildlife agencies. There were open-collared representatives from the DEC, EPA, DOT, and every other jumbled combination of three-letter agencies they could find.

But all the real attention was focused on one hangdog and rather tense-looking oil-company representative in the middle. There was no doubt he was tired. He'd just arrived from similar town meetings farther up the way, and Fritz could tell he pretty much knew what he was in for.

The room was full of many dozen deadly serious people. In the front row with Fritz was Lars Luger, his huge meaty fisherman's hands working their palms together in his lap. Emily Flannigan sat beside him literally huffing as she continually blew a strand of loose hair out of her face. Argus Winslow was there, his big arms folded across his barrel chest, looking satisfied in some sort of murderous way. He was looking to fight with someone. Fritz had seen Argus look that way too many times. Ruby McClay was with Argus, looking every bit as ornery as he did.

Tamara Dupree sat next to Fritz, and when she made eye contact with the oilman, he saw a visible shiver go through the poor man's frame. Bud Koenig sat on the outside chatting amiably with Pastor Frank. Bud never seemed to get rattled by anything, and Fritz was glad to see him here. It calmed him and made him feel better about what he was there for.

The oilman began the meeting by introducing all the agency people, and they in turn gave reports on the cleanup operation—where the slick had been last sighted, where the skimmer boats were, the bird, otter, seal, bear, deer, and fish reports, and generally outlined in some detail everything they were preparing to do.

It all appeared so impotent in the mammoth face of this disaster that it only seemed to rile everybody even further, and finally the oilman knew the right thing to do. Which was to stop talking and listen. He took a long, deep breath of air and asked for public comment.

Lars Luger was the first to jump to his feet. "I'm Lars Luger and I'm a fisherman. At least I used to be. The oil company sent me a check to pay for all the fish I ain't catchin' 'cause o' their darn big mess. Now, what I want to know is what I'm supposed to do with myself. I've been a fisherman all my life. I fish!"

Lars sat down and a rumble of agreement went through the crowd. The oilman may have been trying to come up with a response, but Emily Flannigan didn't give him the chance.

"I'm Emily Flannigan," she said and, forgetting her credentials, she added, "I'm a mother." She blew the strand out of her face again and addressed everyone at the table: "When the pipeline was built, the oil companies and environmental agencies assured the people of Alaska that a catastrophe like this could not happen, that if a spill occurred, it could be contained before any damage was done. It is obvious that we were lied to and that lies are still being told about the severity and far-reaching impact of this spill. What I want to know is how do we teach our children responsibility and integrity when the very leaders of our free market have no more integrity than snakes!"

The oilman just seemed to get shorter in his chair, and Argus Winslow decided to enter the fray, but from an unlikely position. He stood up, turning his back on the experts, and talked to the audience directly.

"You crybabies drive me nuts! You've been livin' off this oil money for ten years. What do you think paid for that new school and hospital and all these roads you drive around on, burnin' gas like a bunch of happy fools. If you're gonna play with this messy stuff, sooner or later you're going to get some on ya'!"

There might have been a riot over that had not Tamara Dupree shot right up, "I can see how a mess like this wouldn't bother a man who lives in a junkyard!" She was cheered by the crowd into her own tirade. A tirade that lasted some fifteen minutes, designating in depressing detail the long-term environmental consequences not only of the present oil spill but of the manufacture and use of fossil fuels in general. She called for the oil companies involved to be forced to devote all of their profits to the research and development of clean energy alternatives until such time as the oil wells can be shut down for good.

Tamara was applauded long and loud. Argus tried to get back up to say something, but Ruby McClay pulled him down on her own way up. Ruby gave a long and dry report on the impact of this spill on the tourist industry and how did the oil companies expect to calculate reimbursement for those businesses that suffer. She might have gotten an answer too, but she ended her talk by pointing a finger directly at the oilman and spitting, "You, mister, are going to pay for this!"

The oilman looked more than sufficiently beaten, and as his mouth moved without words while he tried to think of something proper to say, Bud Koenig stood up to save him.

"Ruby, Ruby, let's not be so nasty. Everybody, look. There's no doubt the oil company has made a lot of mistakes here lately, but this man is here to help. Insulting or threatening isn't going to do anything but hurt people's feelings. This mess is bigger than any of us, and we can't afford to be choosing up sides right now. We gotta work this out together, because nobody wants that oil left in the water. Not you, not him, not anybody."

Bud sat down, and what he said seemed to hang like a new thought over the room for a moment. It was this quiet moment that Fritz decided to seize for his address. He stood up slowly, showing his seventy-five years, nodded politely to the oilman, then turned to his friends and neighbors, fingering his hat.

"You all know me. I've lived here over fifty years and saw most of you come to town. As you know, I sold the newspaper last year after Meredith passed away. I figured I'd retire and live out my last few years just enjoying the scenery. It's a little lonely without Meredith, but her memory was everyplace I looked, so that was okay.

"There's this clam beach over across the way you might know in Eden Cove. That's where Meri and I met and courted, and it's still the most amazing little butter-clam beach I've ever seen."

People looked at each other and nodded in agreement.

"We went over to Eden a lot, and always on our anniversary. We'd build a fire and eat clams until we couldn't anymore."

Some folks laughed a little nervously wondering what ol' Fritz was getting to here.

"Our anniversary was last week and I took the skiff over there by myself just to reminisce and such. When I come onto the beach everything looked the same at first, then I started seein' all the blobs of oil stuck around on the rocks and everything. I reached my hands down into our beach and came up with nothing but stinky, black, sticky hands. Everyplace I dug it was the same, and what happened scared me.

"I got this rage built inside of me that made me almost blind. It pounded in my chest and squeezed water out of my eyes, because I realized that no part of Meredith was left there anymore. I've waited a week and it won't go away. Every time I look over, it happens again.

"That's why I come up in front of you tonight, to tell you I'm leaving town." Fritz stopped, and a mumble of wonder went through the townspeople as, he tried to think of a way to finish.

"I'm not blaming anyone so much as just taking care of myself. I'm an old man and I can't live out my last few years being so mad. I'm going back to family in Illinois, where I might die of boredom, but at least I won't leave this world full of bitterness."

Fritz looked one last time across to Eden Cove but couldn't see it. The memory of his farewell had filled his eyes once again with tears, and all he could do was wipe at them and get in the car. He drove along the coast for a ways and couldn't help, even after all these years, but marvel at the absolute beauty of this land. He was made misty-eyed again recalling the prayer Pastor Frank had tried to offer up that same night.

Fritz's announcement had been pretty much the showstopper. Nobody wanted to hand this poor old man any more grief, and everyone grew silent. Even the panel of experts and the oilman seemed moved to solemn thought.

Pastor Frank stood and quietly cleared his throat. Addressing himself to no one in particular, he referred to some notes in his hand. "If I might leave us with a benediction," he began, and they all bowed their heads in reflex.

"Dear Lord, you have created for us a near-perfect world, one of wonder and bounty, security and beauty. You have crafted a delicate ornament that shines in your firmament like a jewel in your holy crown. And you saved your best work for what we know as Alaska. The great land, and a land like no other. From the highest of our mountains and glaciers to the bottom of our abundant seas there is nothing but treasure. In our carelessness and lust for man's desires, Lord, we have tarnished your treasure. We have killed your creatures, and fouled your golden shores and it seems larger than we are . . ."

The pastor stopped for more than a pause and many people raised their heads to look at him. What they saw was his hand reach across to Fritz Ferguson's shoulder and the tears running down his puffy cheeks. He looked at his notes but let them fall to his side as he tried to clear the emotion from his throat to go on.

And at that moment there were no oilmen in the room. Or agency experts or environmentalists or fishermen or mothers. There were only some small and worried human beings who felt with all their hearts the only words that the pastor could find to finish his prayer: "Oh, dear God," he said, looking up from his hand. "We are so sorry."

And after Fritz Ferguson took a last look at his home ground and turned his attention to the road, out across the bay the clouds were breaking up and a yellow sun pounded through to the sea, illuminating it in that mysterious color of aqua that can only come from heaven. A light as warm as forgiveness. As if a penitent prayer from one little town were being answered.

"Give Me some time to fix this," It said. "And don't let it happen again."

NORMAN'S DATE

IN spite of his nerves, Norman was enjoying getting dressed up for the big night. His dad had let him spend some of his fishing money from last summer on a brand-new suit. He looked pretty sharp even if he did go through a bowline and two clove hitches before giving up and letting his mother tie his necktie.

The grand occasion, of course, was the junior high school graduation dance and it was made even grander by the fact that Norman had a date. A real live female-type date. You may recall Norman's fascination with one young Laura Magruder of algebra class fame from a while back.

Norman and Laura had enjoyed a long and bashful courtship, made up mostly of fleeting glances and playful snowballs. Norman wasn't usually one to drag his big feet, but in matters of the heart he proceeded cautiously. Cautiously enough that it took him five months to ask her out from the time he decided it would be a pretty good idea.

When he finally did ask her, he used the traditional manner. He'd written a note and given it to his best friend, Stanley, to give to Laura's best friend, Molly, who gave it to Laura, who circled the predescribed "yes" or "no" in the affirmative and passed it back to Norman through the same proper channels. They'd had no other communication over the past three weeks except when Molly rushed up to Norman in the hallway one day and gushed, "Laura's wearing fuchsia to the dance if you're going to buy a corsage."

She giggled and dashed back around a corner to join, no doubt, Laura, who'd engineered the whole thing.

Norman stood in the hallway, flushed with the joy of contact with his betrothed, with only two things spinning through his mind, fuchsia and corsage. *What in the heck is she talking about?*

* * *

Of course, Norman's mother was able to clear up the entire fuchsia corsage quandary with one straight answer, and Norman found himself the proud owner of a big pink wrist corsage of carnations and lace. His dad had insisted he get himself a pink-carnation boutonniere as well, and it might have been this at the root of Norman's nervousness in front of the dressing mirror.

Stanley's going to have guppies when he sees me, Norman was thinking of his smirking best friend while appraising his reflection. If Norman only occurred in a vacuum he would have been a sight to behold. He had an absolutely natty looking navy double-breasted blazer over light gray slacks and black wing tips. He wore a light blue cotton oxford button-down shirt with a splash of color added by a red-black-stripe necktie. His mom had picked out the whole thing from the Sears catalog, and it all pretty much fit. Norman thought if he angled his head just right and crossed his eyes, he might even be mistaken for Prince Charles.

The problem with all this self-admiration is that Norman did not occur in a vacuum. He occurred at the End of the Road amongst friends and associates of questionable integrity, who might have a comment or two about Norman Tuttle appearing in public looking like Prince Charles with a pink flower stuck to his chest and a fuchsia female on his arm.

You see, Norman might have been a pulse or two ahead of Stanley in his adolescent development. Girls to Stanley were still mere curiosities, while they had already become an obsession to Norman. But somehow, along with the obsession, and with no little help from long talks with his dad, Norman had developed the slightest little bit of respect for taste and decency in regards to women. All of which went completely over Stanley's prehormonal head.

"You gonna kiss her, Norm?" he'd say.

"No, I mean, I don't know, I mean . . ."

"She's got those big . . . duh-huh . . . you know . . . are you gonna . . . *kiss* her?"

"Shut up, Stanley." And Norman would usually close the subject with a change of subject. He had a burning need to dismiss these ideas from his conversation because, naturally, that's all he had on his mind.

And it's all he had on his mind tonight too as his mom snapped Polaroids of him on the way out the door with his dad to pick up his date. He was going out with *Laura Magruder*. His Laura. The woman of his dreams and featured attraction of a long-playing fantasy that had developed into love, marriage, fast cars, weekend getaways—and no little bit of kissing.

Norman fingered the corsage box in his hands and thought about the idea that he was going to be face to face, so to speak, with his fantasy in a few minutes. When the reality of the matter struck him, he felt a full body-sweat coming on.

He must have sucked in his breath because suddenly his dad took brief notice of him from his driving and said a most unlikely, and unsettling, thing. "You look all grown-up in that outfit, bub. A real lady's man."

And then he laughed at some private joke, put a warm hand on Norman's bony knee, and sang a line from a song his mother had sung to him at least a thousand times, but not in years. "Normy, Normy, puddin' and pie, kissed the girls and made them cry."

His dad laughed again, and Norman clutched the corsage box in white-knuckled terror.

When Laura came around the corner into the living room, Norman had a mild cerebral hemorrhage, which triggered a sort of palsy, setting his hands and knees trembling and a cold sweat springing forth on his forehead and palms.

Laura had on a bright pink dress that was bunched and folded in such a way as to flatter the feminine lines of her budding form. Norman could only gawk. She looked like a, well, a woman, no, a queen, no—a *goddess*.

Laura blushed as bright as her dress when the elder Tuttle whistled at her as he stood off to the side with the proud father. Mrs. Magruder fussed between Norman and Laura, picking lint, smoothing ruffles, and helping with the corsage, which Norman had lost all ability to handle.

Laura and Norman were stood in front of the TV console to have their picture taken, and Laura lit off a fire in Norman's faint heart when she hooked her arm in his for the portrait.

Norman figured it was probably two thousand degrees in the Magruders' house and he welcomed the cool evening air across his face on the way to the car. His dad ceremoniously opened the rear door of his mom's big dumb sedan. Laura got in first and only slid over far enough to let Norman in close beside her. Then she had the audacity to sit there pleasantly smiling and smelling as sweet as strawberry sherbet while Norman pretty much rode the door handle all the way to the gym.

Since the theme of this year's graduation dance was New Horizons, Norman and Laura had to walk into the gym through a cardboard sunset with crepe paper streamers. All the basketball hoops had been filled with balloons and streamers for that generic gymnasium party decor. Stanley Bindel's dad was playing DJ on a raised stage at the other end and announcing the couples.

"And now arriving through the horizon's gate are graduates Norman Tuttle and Laura Magruder."

Laura and Norman heard simultaneous applause, oohs and aahs, and laughter. As Norman's eyes adjusted to the dim light he saw that the room was clearly divided into three pretty much equal factions. There were the other couples standing in the bashful shadows over by the bleachers. There were the single girls gathered around the restroom door and the single boys horsing around the punch and cookie table.

To Norman's immeasurable chagrin, the first face he chanced to focus upon was that of his friend Stanley, who jostled the boys next to him to look. Stanley mouthed "hubba-hubba" in mock admiration, while the other boys blew kisses and cackled.

The single girls were giving Laura no better treatment as they looked on with mischievous smiles, talked to each other behind their hands, and bolted in twos and threes into the bathroom to gossip and speculate.

Neither had to lead the other as our celebrated duo made their way into the throng of other timid couples in the shadows. When Norman's eyes got used to the still dimmer light by the bleachers he was made even more uneasy, as if that was possible, by the sight of unbridled hand-holding, arms on shoulders, and even one occasion of lingering-on-the-lips kissing going on a little farther up the bleachers. One more nudge of uneasiness and Norman might well rattle apart.

Laura seemed comfortable enough with the whole thing as she maintained that pleasant smile on her face and stood admiring the other dresses in the room. "Frank and Jeannette look good together, don't you think?" she said.

Norman jumped at her voice. It was the first either of them had spoken that night. He looked to where she looked and was shocked to realize that the Frank and Jeannette she was referring to were the kissing couple in the bleachers. Norman's mind raced with panicked possibilities.

Was this a hint? Was she letting him know that kissing was okay with her? Right here in the gym? Is that what she wanted him to do? All of a sudden all of Norman's bold and manly fantasies vanished from his head and were replaced by a hot anxiety. An anxiety that sent his mind reeling so hard and far that he could scarcely contain the details of the evening.

He would look back on this years later and only remember sweating buckets to big-band music and that uniquely American aroma of gymnasium mixed with fruity perfume. The smell that so many of us fall in love to. And Norman *would* fall in love that night.

It happened, he guessed, after their second or third dance at Laura's insistence, when she declined to let go of his hand after the music stopped. They walked back to the bleachers finger to palm and sat down. Everything was done in silence. It was all body language now.

Norman could see the impish Stanley making some joke and looking at them from across the gym, but it meant nothing to him. The feel of Laura's hand in his was something just short of immortal ecstasy and he would have gladly passed away on the spot if it weren't for that burning anxiety about the next step. The step he felt would propel him past boyhood and fling him headlong into life's next dimension. The kissing step.

Norman sat quietly and sweated on Laura's hand while he calculated this maneuver. He zeroed in on the location of her lips out of the corner of his eye and ran through a couple of attack scenarios. She was too far away for him to reach in one lean, so he'd have to either scoot over or trust her to meet him halfway. He couldn't risk being puckered up all by himself halfway there, so he decided that scooting over was his only alternative.

It would have to be done in one smooth motion, like Remington Steele might. Scoot over and swing the face around. Just like that. But then he wondered what side his nose should go on. If they both tried to go the same way with their noses, they could ruin everything.

He was trying to remember from television and movies if there was, like, a rule to that. Like if you're sitting to the girl's left you always keep left with your nose. That would make sense, he thought. It would be the same way he was leaning.

Okay, that's what he'd do. One quick scoot, a smooth swoop, and keep left.

Norman's pulse was pounding so hard it was making his ears wiggle. This was absolutely the hardest thing he'd ever tried to do and he had to do it now. *No, on three. One—two—no, a big breath, then on ten. One-two-three-four*, Laura scooted over toward him and squeezed his hand tight. *What's she doing? five-six-seven-* . . .

"Norman?" Laura leaned her head toward his ear, and Norman stopped the count.

"Yeah?"

Laura squeezed his hand again and said very softly, "Norman you're so nice. I could sit here and hold hands with you all night long." She turned her head away again and left Norman in the intense afterglow of his first intimate experience.

And it was a sweet wash of relief that came over him when he realized he didn't have to kiss her. That all circuits were sufficiently loaded just the way things were. And they kept them that way. Adjusting a grip now and then. Sending a reassuring squeeze at calculated moments and generally leaning back into the lap of some fascinating new episode.

There was no doubt left between them that when Laura Magruder and Norman Tuttle walked back through that cardboard sunset to start their summer, it was going to be a different sort of summer than they'd ever seen before.

ARGUS'S JUNK

RUBY McClay had mixed feelings about going out to Argus Winslow's junkyard for dinner. Ruby and Argus had been seeing each other off and on for over a month now. They'd gone to the Fishermen's Banquet. They went to a square dance at the Senior Center once, and they'd also gone to a couple of town meetings about the oil spill to yell and scream a little. All fun stuff, all public, and all pretty harmless.

But going to a gentleman's house for dinner, well, that was the threshold of something more in earnest. What, she didn't know, but Ruby had been around the block enough times to understand the way traffic moves.

It's not that she wasn't interested in something *more earnest* with Argus Winslow, because she knew she was. What she didn't know was *what* she didn't know and what she didn't know about Argus is what was bothering her. She'd lived around the man for over twenty years and there were still some big holes in the picture.

She knew that he was one of the original homesteaders here. That he'd gone into the salvage business and buried himself in an unsightly pile of rust and junk out Far Road way. She knew from rumors that he had amassed a personal fortune in quiet land dealings over the years and anonymously owned the controlling stock in the Fair Deal Bank and Trust. A position he has used to serve as benefactor to almost any troubled family in the area needing legitimate help. And as generous and caring as he was secretly, right out in the open he presented himself as a gnarly old goat with no one to serve but himself. Argus was a legitimate paradox.

He was a lifelong bachelor with a very sketchy history of women. Sketchy because, above all, Argus was a man who offered little about himself and welcomed few solicitors.

74

Ruby was not a junkyard sort of person, and in twenty years she'd never set foot on Argus's establishment. This is pretty unusual, because around here there aren't too many of us that don't have some little deal or doodad nailed around someplace that didn't come from Argus Salvage and Sales. Ruby knew this, and relied on faith that as far as junkyards go, Argus probably ran a pretty good one. But it seems like no matter how good a junkyard gets, it's still mostly a lot of junk.

This is what Ruby was thinking as she wound her little truck through and around the random piles of junk marking the way into the nerve center of Argus Salvage and Sales. She had a sense of crawling into the lair of the beast.

There was a fine weathered log cabin, which must have been the heart of the original homestead, and alongside it on blocks of wood sat a small aluminum house trailer.

It was in the door of the trailer that Argus appeared with his black Lab, Barney, squeezing out to greet her.

"It's just Ruby, boy," Argus called after him. "Try not to get 'er dirty."

Ruby bent down to scratch Barney's ears and looked up with a smile for Argus. Argus returned it as best as his rutted face would allow and said, "I just put dinner in the oven. Whyn't I show ya around while she cooks."

It was then for the first time it struck Ruby as odd that Argus would be cooking dinner for her. She couldn't recall ever being the dinner guest of a man before. But she remembered he had insisted. She'd been trying to invite him to dinner, but somehow he'd managed to turn the tables and coax her out here. Ruby looked at her host coming toward her around a couple of cockeyed washing machines, and wondered why.

"Welcome, Miss McClay," Argus said formally, offering a hand the same basic size, shape, and color of a catcher's mitt.

"Charmed, I'm sure, Mr. Winslow." Ruby touched the hand, curtsied, and they both laughed.

"We got thirty-five minutes till supper. Let me show ya my operation here." Ruby grabbed one of Argus's big arms and they walked easily together toward some back corner of the jumble of incomprehensible debris. Argus seemed energetic, almost boyish, and more relaxed beside her than she'd seen so far.

He led her to a pile of small metal parts near a place where the wooden fence had been broken down. "I keep all my littlest scrap on this pile. Kids like to sneak through that hole, grab what they can, then bring it around front to sell it back to me. I bought some of this stuff twenty times now, I bet."

"Don't you ever want to catch them?" Ruby couldn't figure the point to the whole thing.

"Oh, I might catch 'em and scare 'em someday, but not yet. I love seein' the look on a kid's face that thinks he's gettin' away with somethin'. Reminds me of myself. I was a rotten kid."

"I'll just bet you were," Ruby said playfully, and allowed herself to be led to the next attraction.

"This here's my water-heater collection. Best kept secret in the salvage trade is water heaters. Ain't nothin' can go wrong with a water heater 'cept an element go out now and again, but people keep throwin' 'em away like they was broken. I put a ten-dollar element in 'em and sell 'em back for fifty bucks 'cept those few that might be rusted, and I make wood stoves out of them. I tell ya, Ruby, there's a gold mine in water heaters."

Argus led on and it began to dawn on Ruby what was going on here. This junk was Argus Winslow's life. Argus wanted to impress her, and this was his way of going about it. Suddenly two old folks tripping through a dusty junkyard became an intimate thing for Ruby, and she decided to take part. Noticing a large collection of old refrigerators, she pointed. "Now, what would the value of those things be?"

Argus grew visibly more animated at the question. "Refrigerators? Boy I'll tell ya, it's just about like those water heaters. People throw out perfectly good refrigerators all the time. Usually they just lose their Freon, but sometimes the compressors go. I can fix two thirds of what comes in here and sell 'em again. The rest I make into smokers. A refrigerator makes a darn fine smokehouse if you know what you're doin'."

They walked passed an old rusted hulk of a crane. "That's Lorraine the Crane. Ain't run in thirty years, but she's worth a fortune in scrap if I ever get around to cuttin' it apart. Ten ton solid iron counterweight in her rear end."

It went on and on. Past the mountains of wheel rims, formations of car bodies, pyramids of engine blocks, and row upon endless row of unrecognizable appendages of heavy equipment, construction materials, and pipe.

"See that big piece o' pipe there?" Argus pointed in the general direction of something that interested him. "Guy came in here twelve years ago with that. Said it was a hunk of the Trans-Alaska Pipeline he stoled and was going to make his fortune with it in souvenirs. I shared a bottle of whiskey with him and bought it for three dollars."

Argus looked pleased with himself over everything. He was proud of his establishment, and he was proud of his unorthodox business acumen. What Ruby couldn't figure was how a man of his reported wealth could continue to take such an active interest in rubble. Argus was becoming more than a paradox. He was bordering on a dilemma.

"This here's my *archive*." Argus was grandly presenting the open door to the log cabin. He turned on the single bare bulb overhead and Ruby saw an impossible mess of books, catalogs, magazines, maps, and manuals. He waved her onto a dusty car seat on the floor. "That's the rear seat out of a 'forty-eight Nash. Ain't a rip in it. Some o' these magazines go back thirty years, and there's books there on every subject under the sun. I've read every one of 'em too. Even the seed catalogs. There used to be less to do around here than there is now." Argus sat himself down on a wired-up old stool and waited quietly for Ruby's reaction to what was obviously his most prized collection.

Ruby didn't know what to say. As she scanned the stacks for something to comment on, nothing drew her attention particularly except the walls. The walls were completely covered with baseball paraphernalia. There were bats and gloves and caps and helmets. There were curling yellow baseball cards with grinning players, and even a big white home plate nailed above the door. She saw an opportunity to turn the subject away from salvage for a while.

"You're a baseball fan, I see."

Argus brightened considerably. He sat up straight on his rickety stool, and Ruby knew for sure she had noticed the right thing. "Baseball," he said, changing his voice to near reverence, "is the most beautiful game in the world. Probably the most boring too. I can't stand to watch it, but I love the idea of it."

Ruby looked puzzled, and Argus turned to the dirty window beside him and started drawing with his finger. "You see, a baseball diamond looks like this." He smeared a rough outline of a diamond on the windowpane. "But you know these two lines here, the left- and right-field foul lines." He continued the two lines out to the edge of the window, then waved his hand in the air expansively. "Those two lines go on forever. There's no real end to a ball diamond. You can hit a home run to the moon. No limits. They play baseball in a bitty little park, but it's as big as the universe." Argus let his weight rest back on the stool and he looked thoughtful, enthralled with his idea all over again.

Ruby sat looking at this peculiar old man and she understood something. She saw that if Argus could see poetry in baseball that he must see it in his work. Everything was equally important to him, and it didn't matter how small his world was because the boundaries went on forever.

Suddenly a lot of the things she knew about Argus Winslow before tonight meant less to her. Tonight she saw the whole man, and that's why he'd brought her out here. Everybody in this world comes with a junkyard of some sort or another. The difference with Argus is that he leaves all his junk right out where you can see it. All she could do was smile up at him like she knew, and he smiled down like he knew she knew, and they went back to the trailer for dinner.

"Oooh, that smells good." Ruby sat down at the dinette table as Argus cracked the ceiling vent and opened the oven, using his hat as a hotpad. "What is it?"

"Birds Eye." Argus pulled out two foil-topped TV dinners with a flourish. "I got turkey and gravy for you 'cause you're special, but I always eat the Salisbury steak." He tossed them both onto the table and sat down across from her. "I didn't pull the foil back from the strudel part, so it might be soggy, but I usually let Barney have it anyway."

Ruby sat back, a little surprised but not really knowing what else she might have expected, and she smiled across the table as she thought, *Argus Winslow, you certainly do leave all your junk out where people can see it*.

And two better friends than came before picked at the foil on their dinners. The steam rose up between them and straight to the ceiling and out the vent and into the evening like it knew no boundaries and would just go on forever.

RUNOVER JOE

THE End of the Road, as you're well aware by now, gets more than its fair share of novel individuals. It's always been that way. From Argus Winslow to Doug McDoogan, this place has for years served as refuge to those characters who never found what suited them farther up the road. The End of the Road might be sort of the grease trap of America that way.

All this week Ed Flannigan has been telling the story of our newest arrival. Joe Miller is his name, but already he's gotten a nickname, courtesy of Ed, and Runover Joe is what he's doomed to be known as around here.

Joe was first spied a week ago last Thursday. Ed was cruising the highway in the maintenance department pickup looking for clogged-up culverts when, over in the alder bushes, he spied what appeared to be a human hand sticking out. Curious, Ed stopped the truck and got out to investigate.

Before he could reach the spot, out of the trees walked the sorriest excuse for a twenty-year-old man that Ed had ever seen.

"Glad you stopped, mister. Didn't think you'd see me." Joe Miller, soon to be Runover Joe, walked forward with the mortal remains of what looked to be a frame backpack in his arms.

"Mind if I grab a ride to the End of the Road?"

Ed, of course, was glad to help the kid out, but he couldn't tell if he should be taking Joe just to town or directly to the hospital. The young man who stood before him, wide-eyed and dirty-faced, reeked of peanut butter and appeared to be put together mostly with duct tape.

His down vest was crisscrossed with the silver tape but still continued to spray white feathers into the air with every move he made. His dirty blue jeans were ringed with it at the knees and butt. And even his hiking boots had it wrapped continuously around the toes.

"What in the heck happened to you?" was all Ed could say as he and Joe climbed back into the utility truck. Ed had to finish his reconnaissance of the stopped-up culverts along the way to town, which gave him a lot of time to hear Joe's explanation of why he was hitchhiking from a tree.

It all started a week or so earlier in Madison, Wisconsin. Joe Miller was coming to Alaska to volunteer on the oil spill cleanup for the summer. He'd always dreamed of someday hitchhiking to the End of the Road just for the sheer joy of it and now he had a legitimate reason. Little did Joe know at the outset that this dream of his would, off and on for the rest of his life, wake him up in a cold sweat.

The first indication that there was going to be little sheer joy to this adventure happened just across the border in Canada his second day out. He was standing beside his gear outside of Winnipeg on the shoulder of the road when a semi came along. Joe put a big friendly grin on his face, stuck an enthusiastic thumb in the air . . . and barely jumped out of the way in time. The eighteen-wheeler swerved over onto the shoulder and nine of those wheels ended up having intimate contact with Joe's backpack.

There wasn't much left of his lightweight quality camping gear but a rip-stop skidmark. The truck driver stopped and ran back, terrified that he'd killed somebody. He explained how a gust of prairie wind had blown him off course.

"Bad timing." He shrugged, helped Joe gather up the remains, and gave him a ride all the way past Regina.

Joe spent that night spread out in the back room of a youth hostel sorting through his gear. He suddenly regretted his decision to put the jar of peanut butter in his sleeping bag so it wouldn't get broken. Although the bag itself came through the thing pretty well all things considered, it had a brand-new sixteen-ounce jar of Skippy Super Chunk injection-molded into every little fold and crease. He got the biggest gobs out with his fingers, sealed the gaping holes oozing feathers with a roll of borrowed duct tape, and vowed that he wouldn't let this thing ruin his adventure.

Joe wasn't one to let things get to him and he looked on the bright side. The peanut butter pretty much kept the loose goose down from flying around, and as for the rest of the gear, well he had probably brought too much stuff anyway. His twenty-five-piece two-man arctic mountain tent always was trouble to set up, and now that it was in sixty-seven pieces, he figured it was a blessing to leave behind.

The backpack itself would live with a little help from duct tape and twine, and Joe thought it worked pretty well as a duffel bag, and maybe he should've thought of it sooner. Everything was going to be fine.

And it was fine for a while. He made it all the way across the Alaska border with little to complain about but the wisecracks. Every time he told somebody he was going to Alaska to help clean up the oil spill, they'd cast a dubious look to his gear and say, "Oh, you're takin' your own rags then, eh?"

It was coming down the pass into the Matanuska valley his second day in Alaska that Joe started to wonder if his road karma wasn't all that it might be.

He'd walked along the highway down from the lodge a little bit to get a look at the countryside. The road was cut right into the side of the mountain, with a sheer rock wall on one side and a steep shale slide on the other, going down several hundred feet to a river. It was a beautiful spot. Joe took his pack off and had just sat down to wait beside the road when he saw a Winnebago coming.

It was Frank and Vera from Peoria, according to the spare tire shroud on their twenty-eight-foot Swinger Deluxe. Frank was in the pilot seat arguing with Vera over who forgot the lawn chairs. Frank wasn't paying attention to the road and his heading was starting to drift a little.

It was a good thing that Joe sat down where he did, or Frank and Vera might have ended up in serious straits. It was probably the muffled double bump of a duffel bag being sucked under his tires that alerted Frank. He swerved back onto the road just in time to save the day, but not in time to see a pretty impressive leap on Joe's part down the rock slide.

Frank and Vera resumed their discussion while Joe took his little side trip. He went down mostly on his butt, diggin' in his heels to try to stop himself before he reached the river. It was too late for that, but Joe had to admit that the cold water felt pretty good on the ol' bottom.

He tried to climb back up and had almost made it when the shale cut loose. He went down on his hands and knees that time, which got chafed up pretty good but felt better when he fell in the river again. He made a second and third attempt but was getting too gun-shy of that river to give it much heart, so he gave up and walked downstream until he could find a place that wasn't so steep.

That place ended up being about four miles away, and by the time Joe got back to his scattered gear, he'd raised a couple of dandy blisters on his feet. Luckily, a state trooper came along, took one look at Joe's torn-up condition, and tried to rescue him. They were halfway to Palmer before Joe got him convinced he didn't need any triage and that if he'd just take him to a store for a roll of duct tape, he'd fix his pants and be okay, or at least decent.

Joe wasn't entirely dispirited, but the next day he was starting to distance himself a little from traffic. He didn't ever sit down either and his blistered feet were killing him. He decided when he got to Anchorage he'd buy some cushioned liners for his boots.

He made the city with no trouble, and although he was a little twitchy about the heavy traffic flows, he did manage to track down a shoe store on a quiet little side street. Looking forward to some relief, Joe sat out in front of the store with his new cushions and took off his boots. It turns out he got a size too big and went back in with just his socks on to exchange them.

And then the unfortunate thing that really started to push Joe to the edge happened. While he was in the store, a delivery van backed up to the front door and by some sadistic twist of fate caught both his boots by the heels and pinched the rubber soles right off them.

"One in a million chance o'that happenin'." The store owner was trying to calm Joe down enough to sell him a new pair, but Joe proved inconsolable. His hands shook as he bound his boots back together with tape. "Where you headed to, son?"

"The End of the Road," Joe said miserably, and that was the first time it had occurred to him. *The End of the Road. No Road. No traffic.*

Suddenly, Joe Miller's journey took on an urgency it didn't have the week before.

It took Joe longer than most to hitch down the peninsula from Anchorage because he was tending to shy away from the pavement a little bit. Most places, the drivers could only see his head and shoulders sticking up out of the ditch, but in some ways that worked to his advantage. His being in the ditch, coupled with the condition of his wardrobe, had some drivers concerned that he might have been thrown clear of a wreck they'd happened upon. It worked well enough that Joe made it all the way to Anchor Point, just twenty miles from the end, before one more incident, as frightening as it was uncanny, finally put Joe into the bushes.

He was sitting out in front of the bait store at the bottom of the parking lot, taking a breather and absently picking little wads of feathers and peanut butter off of his clothes as he was prone to do in idle moments.

Joe could no longer bear to turn his back on moving vehicles, so he faced the road with his back to the parking lot. It looked harmless enough; empty, with just one old Ford Falcon parked up the hill.

What Joe didn't know, and never would, was that there were over 175,000 miles on that Falcon and the rings were just about shot. Bob at the bait store usually put a rock behind the wheel, because the engine couldn't hold it against the hill anymore. One day he caught it staggering down toward the road the way cars will when they're working against their pistons. Go a little and stop, go a little and stop.

Well for some reason—and we're glad, because it goes along pretty well with this story—Bob forgot to put the rock under the wheel when he got back from lunch.

Joe didn't get suspicious right away. He looked back once and could've sworn that car had been parked right up next to the building, but didn't pay it much attention. Another car pulled in and Joe kept his eye on it as it went around to the store. This time he could see for sure that Falcon was gettin' closer, but it didn't make any sense. He just sat and stared at it, but nothing happened. Finally, the other car left and Joe followed it out to the road with his attention.

When he turned back around the old Falcon wasn't really moving, it was just sort of rocking back and forth on its springs, like it'd been caught at something.

It's incredible how the human mind works sometimes. It takes a situation at hand, evaluates the data, judges it along a series of guidelines established by prior experiences, and decides on an action to take. All this in a manner of nanoseconds.

And that's about as long as it took for Joe to grab hold of his bundle, jump a fence, and disappear down into the alders. A place he'd stay hidden all the rest of that day and night, until he finally mustered courage to stick a thumb out to Ed the next morning.

Ed says Joe seems like a nice enough kid and we should be looking out for him. He says you'll find him mostly hanging around the boat harbor these days, looking for a job on a boat. Any boat. Rumor has it Lars Luger is considering him for his flounder dragging crew. Lars was impressed that even though Joe didn't have any experience, he'd never met a man who seemed more ambitious about dedicating himself to a life at sea.

EMILY'S JOB

WHEN Emily first went to work on the oil-spill cleanup, Ed thought it was a pretty good idea. Like everybody else, Ed felt like they should be doing something about the spill and his job with the highway crew kept him from being able to do very much but fret and complain.

He was proud of Emily, and it made him feel a little better too that she was able to hire on with a beach-cleaning crew and really lend some personal effort to this disaster. Besides, Ed had to admit, the Flannigans really could use the extra money.

Emily was getting paid nearly what he made driving the road grader, and if this kept up through the summer, they'd have enough put away to take the kids to Disneyland *and* maybe replace that old station wagon of Emily's with something respectable. It would be a lot of work, but it would be worth it.

It all started off just fine. Ed junior and Missy went to school every day, and they dropped little Corey next door at the Storbocks'. Ed and Emily got home about the same time every afternoon and they'd be a family again. The idea that they were both working was even kind of fun.

Ed was used to coming home covered with dust, mud, grease, and sweat, stripping in the utility room, walking through the thick, delicious smell of dinner cooking, and going right upstairs to take a shower.

Now when he came home he'd often meet Emily in the utility room stripping down herself. She'd have black smudges on her cheeks and reek of spilled crude oil, a peculiar blend of odors that ended up somewhere between unleaded gasoline and low tide on a warm day. On the way through the kitchen in their shorts, one of them would chuck some frozen dinners in the oven, put a cartoon on for the kids, and they'd shower upstairs together. It was a refreshing break from routine, often crossing the line into romance.

Ed had never thought his wife was anything less than vital and competent, but he continued to marvel at how good she looked in a veil of employment. She seemed so vigorous and alive. As they sat over their pot pies, they regularly talked about things outside their family for the first time Ed could remember. Emily always had great new oil-company gossip to add to Ed's road-crew stories and there were many moments where they could've been confused for buddies.

Ed wasn't quite sure where it stopped being fun. It might have been when the kids got off for summer vacation and had to be farmed out all over town during the day while Ed and Emily worked. They felt lonely and ripped off and stole what attention they could with sheer orneriness.

Their home was turned into a whiners' convention every night after dinner, with three kids demanding impossible things from two exhausted parents. It seemed to Ed that all he'd done with his children in three weeks was yell at them. When he wasn't yelling at them, he was driving them over to yet another friend's house to do what he and Emily had no time for, which was raise a family.

It might have stopped being fun when Ed realized the closest thing he'd had to a home-cooked meal in a whole month was when they'd all gone down to Clara's Coffee Cup for the meat-loaf special to celebrate Emily's first paycheck.

Or it might have been when Emily stopped asking about his day at work and only talked about hers. The oil was getting to her. She worked hard eight hours every day. She and twenty other people on her crew. They'd shovel up the scattered rocks, kelp, wood, and debris that had oil on it, put them in bags, and go home. The next morning they'd go back to the same beach and it would look like they'd never touched it. Every tide brought in more, and it just seemed to get bigger and worse, and the hopeful idea that the job would be finished and everything would be as it was grew dimmer and dimmer and showed in dark lines under her eyes and teeth, which she ground while she slept.

Ed could see Emily gradually becoming obsessed. What had started out as a way to vent frustration and a pretty darn good job had turned into a wasteland of anger that got worse with every workday. Emily's attitude was like the beaches themselves, with each new tide heaping on more poison. Try as she might, it came too fast and stuck too well and there was little to hope for but hope itself.

"I feel like Sisyphus," she said one night over reheated frozen-chicken dinners.

"Is it contagious?"

Emily wouldn't even laugh at the remark. She put on the arrogant Radcliffe scholar face that Ed hadn't seen from her in years and explained. "Sisyphus was the legendary Greek king condemned by Zeus to roll a heavy rock up a steep hill only to watch it roll down again over and over for eternity. Haven't you ever heard of a Sisyphean task?"

"Yeah, I thought it was something you did with limp wrists."

Emily only squeezed her lips together and blew air through her nose. Ed's feeble attempts at levity were not only lost on her, they irritated her. Emily's sense of humor had been bagged and burned, like polluted kelp, a small piece at a time every day since she started that job. "Ed." She was making statements, not asking forgiveness. "You don't understand how hard this all is on me."

Ed looked at his wife glaring at him, with deep creases in her forehead and her hands knotted around each other, and being the simple soul that he was, he said the simplest thing, "Why don't you quit, then?"

Looking back on it, Ed figured that evening was pretty much where the fun started to pour out of the whole thing like an impaled supertanker with nothing to contain it but a wish that it'd never happened in the first place. Emily left the table with that frozen feminine silence that speaks volumes of foul feelings too potent for words alone, and Ed knew for sure that they weren't having fun anymore.

It was a long, chilly week that followed in the Flannigan household. Routine replaced association, and even if they reached the bathroom together, they showered separately. The overall feeling was that of a huge cold front hanging over the sea until some other fluke of nature came along to mix it into a storm.

That fluke came last Wednesday over take-out burgers and soggy fries while the kids watched the *Swiss Family Robinson* video in the other room for probably the eight hundredth time. It was one of those designer flukes. The kind that couldn't have been more readily made to order a ruckus than if you'd had seven psychiatrists and a crystal ball to invent the thing.

What it was, exactly, was that Ed had been offered to work overtime on Saturdays by his boss at the highway department the very same day that Emily's cleanup foreman had offered her the same thing.

"Who's gonna take the kids on a Saturday?" they said in harmony. They paused, looked eye to eye, and said again in harmony, "You are."

Emily started to stand to take the high ground, but Ed beat her to it.

"You sit down and listen to me, little lady." It probably wasn't the best way to gain her attention, but there was no question that he had it. "You started that job to help with the spill and earn some extra money for our family. Remember your family? The Banquet frozen-dinner all-stars? Little Ed's had four baseball games and we haven't been to any of them. Missy thinks she lives next door, and I heard Corey call your best friend Mommy yesterday. I heard you say yourself that cleaning those beaches was an endless job that'll never get done. Well, *we're not*. Instead of trying to be the Mother Teresa of the beach crew, why don't you stay home and mother your own children."

Emily sat through the whole thing coolly steaming like dry ice until Ed sat down again. If you could have added just a little bit of amperage to the electric glare she directed across the table to Ed, it would have boiled his brains right inside his thick skull.

"You listen to me, you chauvinistic, condescending, self-important, insensitive redneck motor head. You think because you work twelve years at the same dumb boring job that it makes it more important than what I'm doing. Well, if you had the environmental consciousness of an end table you'd realize that cleaning up that oil is the only thing worth doing within a thousand miles of here. 'Mother my children'—how *dare* you. Did it ever occur to you to quit your job and father your children?"

And off they went. Taking turns making impossible statements. Clouding issues. Confusing points. Ed's side was fueled by a naive passion for status quo. He was a man, a provider. His work was important because, well, it was *his work*. Men worked. They grew old, wore out and died, and then their sons worked.

Yes, men worked all right, Emily agreed. They worked and worked and built things and had great grand and greedy

ideas until something goes wrong and they make a great big
mess and then they sit back with dumb looks on their faces
wondering what to do, and asking for their supper.

She pointed out that over seven hundred miles of beaches
were contaminated by oil, nearly a third of Alaska's coastline,
and still, after all this time, not one single beach had been
signed off as cleaned by government officials. She raged on
about oil-company inefficiency. How they're obviously stall-
ing at every opportunity until it gets so far gone that the
government lets them give it up as a lost cause. She talked
about the dead birds she picks up every day and the seals and
otters that roll up bloated and drowned with lungs full of tar.

She cried and raved and ranted and roared and could not,
on top of it all, understand how in the world Ed could sit there
and not be as mad as she was.

And Ed just sat there and he didn't know why he couldn't
be as mad. He just wasn't. He used to be mad, but he got
tired of it. He had other work to do, a family to feed, kids to
raise, and being mad all the time was, well, maddening. What
he couldn't understand was how she could put all this ahead
of her family. She had responsibilities. Couldn't she see that?
There was nothing for her to see but his arrogance.

It went on for two long, bitter hours and might have continued through the night if they hadn't looked up and noticed
their three children sitting on the sofa. Little Corey was passed
out on the laps of Ed junior and Missy, who were both listening
intently to their parents and basically playing the role of tired,
frightened children pretty well.

A cease-fire was silently declared and Ed and Emily dove
into their mechanical bedtime ritual of toothpaste, eardrops,
peeing, teddy bears, stories, songs, and good-night prayers.

Ed junior thanked God for baseball and prayed for a home
run just once in his life. Missy prayed for her Barbie doll,
who was lost and probably in trouble somewhere. And a
sleepy Corey, who didn't really know what he was talking
out, prayed for his daddy and mommy to come home.

There wasn't much chatter going on in the master bathroom
that night. A lot of ungainly thoughts were being wrestled
about. Shoved up hills of reason and left to roll down obstinate
gullies.

Emily brushed her teeth and got in the shower. It was her
habit sometimes to shower at night. It calmed her somehow.

Ed stood listening to the water and studied his face in the mirror. It was a study in unhappiness. He tried to relax his set jaw and put a pleasant face on, but steam had already clouded his reflection. Without really knowing why, he stripped and climbed into the shower.

Emily was standing still under the nozzle with her arms crossed, just letting the water run over her. She opened her eyes and saw Ed standing with his arms crossed, looking cold the way you do when you're only getting splashed from someone else's shower.

She moved over and Ed stepped in without saying anything. They stood close together and eventually had to hold each other because it was too ridiculous not to.

And all the issues and ideals and demands and insecurities seemed to pour off them in clouds of steam like a problem being boiled down to the bare truth of the matter. And these battling titans of an hour ago, with their grand images and angry claims, were suddenly just two very naked little people in a shower.

And that was closer to the truth of matters than anything that had been said all night.

TONY ARRIVES

TAMARA stood outside the little wooden terminal and watched the plane taxi from the runway. She'd stood here before. We all have. Greeting relatives, receiving friends, meeting associates. Welcoming people who are strangers to our home but no strangers to ourselves. It's an edgy situation, really. Where we live speaks so much to who we are that introducing intimate acquaintances to it can be a brutal experience if we don't keep our wits about us.

Tamara, who normally gathered wits about herself as easily as clean air and sunshine, found herself suddenly in a dark and stuffy room. The intimate acquaintance who was approaching her home turf was none other than recently decommissioned major in the army Anthony Tobias M.D., her Tony, and he was coming for good. She hoped.

It was this hope that had given birth to anxieties in Tamara she'd never experienced before. Anxieties about her home, her friends, her life-style and, basically, herself. She wanted so badly for this to turn out that she'd cast a critical eye to everything around her. It'd been going on for two months now, ever since Tony told her of his decision to leave the army to join her at the End of the Road their last night together in Hawaii.

They'd been walking along the beach with the occasional wave to wet their feet when Tony said it. It seemed to come out of the blue, but it was the obvious result of a lot of thought.

"I think it's time I left the service and got into the real service of people." Tony stopped walking and addressed the blue horizon as personally as if he were looking her right in the eyes. "Tamara, I'm going to come to the End of the Road to be with you and pursue my medical practice."

91

They stood with their arms around one another's middles and waited for something to change. It was the sort of statement that altered the course of generations. The kind of grand decision that created alliances and families where none existed before and affected the lives, locations, and livelihoods of people not even privy to the ruling. You'd think there would at least be the crashing of cymbals or a flash of lightning to mark the event.

But there was nothing except a limp wave to lap at their bare toes and Tamara's quiet acceptance. She could register no surprise because she felt none. It really was the natural conclusion to their past ten days of ultrapotent romance.

They'd carried on as if everything that was missed in their eight years apart needed doing before they could continue. They'd done a pretty good job of it, and Tamara could once again stand beside this man as naturally as breathing.

It also didn't seem unusual that Tony would make such a decision without clearing it with her. For one thing, he knew it would be what she wanted him to do, and besides, it seemed his nature to be that way anyway. Tamara couldn't remember if he'd always held such command or if all those years as an officer had brought it on him, but Tony definitely exercised considerable influence on his surroundings. Including Tamara.

It was not a sign of weakness on Tamara's part, because there are few as tough as that one. Nobody could make Tamara do something she didn't want to, and that was the key to the situation. Tamara wanted everything about Tony.

He was without exception the most amazing person she had ever met. The knowledge, skills, and spiritual values he'd accumulated since Tamara last knew him captivated her attention. Not only was he an M.D. and licensed surgeon, but he'd dedicated eight years of study to holistic and alternative health techniques with the hope of one day introducing them to the armed services. Homeopathy, applied kinesiology, Rolfing, Kinlien therapy, acupuncture, dream counseling. He'd published papers in several major medical journals on diet and disease and spent two years working with malnourished refugee children in Southeast Asia. He'd lived the most spartan of existences while in the service, and with the help of some shrewd investments had amassed personal savings of almost $300,000.

He was a genius. He was committed. He was compassionate. He was rich. He was a vegetarian. And he was absolutely the best lover Tamara could ever imagine, and she has imagined a few.

Tony was such a force for Tamara that she could sit and just look at him for hours. Relish the lines of his face. The texture of his voice as it resonated through his bones. And that's all she could manage to do that night on the beach as she leaned her head against him and listened through his bones as he told how he could get an early discharge and be in Alaska by June.

Their parting the next day at the Honolulu airport was about as effortless as separating Siamese twins joined at the forehead. But they managed, and went their individual ways to manage their individual details and prepare for the melding of their lives.

Tamara did not seem herself when she returned. She was distracted, solemn, almost melancholy. Even the oil-spill effort, which should have raised her most potent ire and fierce crusade, seemed of secondary interest to her. She helped wash birds on Wednesdays and talked back to officials at the town meetings. But her heart wasn't in it, you could tell. It was sort of just sport dissent. Some mechanical will not her own.

Tamara, in fact, had misplaced a lot of her will since her return. Her typical iron-clad convictions and reckless disregard for convention had somehow lost their temper in the face of something new. Something that had placed Tamara severely off her even keel.

The first thing she started to worry about was her cabin. She was thinking maybe it was too much of a statement. No running water, no phone or electricity. Did she really not want these things, or was not wanting them just part of the image she was projecting? Tony might like to project that image as well, but then again he might want to go to the bathroom indoors. After all, he was a *doctor*. And he was coming from an environment where he was an important person. Do important people fill five-gallon water jugs with the hose at the gas station? Maybe she should at least get a phone. Doctors need phones, but she needed money for that.

Money. That really set her off. He had lots of money, didn't he? More than a quarter of a million dollars. Even Tamara couldn't help but try to fathom what having that kind of money would do to a person. She thought there must be security, freedom of movement. The privilege of deciding not to buy things rather than deciding what can be bought. She imagined it must feel great.

She wished she could get some real chairs for her table at least. The wooden wire spools she used now were fine for her and her friends, but Tony wasn't really *like* her friends. This realization really started to work her into a dither. What if he didn't like her friends?

She had to admit that some of them were a little over-done, maybe. Flag-waving new-age vegetarians with little sol-id idea of what a good diet should be. It was all taken from books, trendy periodicals, and one another. They talked a lot about food. Sometimes it seemed as though food was all they thought about. Self-righteous macho organics. They took shots of wheat grass with the same self-indulgent smugness that bar slobs did whiskey.

They would look like zealous novices in the face of Tony's unpretentious dedication to good nutrition and studied diet that had become so second nature for him it was rarely worthy of even a passing mention. Tony was going to be embarrassed by her friends. She just knew it. Tamara was bringing a lot of anxiety upon herself and she hadn't even gotten into her acquaintances yet.

Ed Flannigan would no doubt have something ill conceived and petty to say about a handsome young doctor's new holistic health clinic. Ed would infuriate Tony. She was sure of that. Tony despised nothing like he despised ignorant people with big opinions. Speaking of which, Pastor Frank Olmstead was bound to take exception to a den of secular humanism opening up shop in our little town. She could hear him screaming Satan already, and her face flushed red wondering what Tony would think of this town and what he would think of her for choosing it for her home.

While Tony had been off in the world studying his craft, practicing his trade, and centering himself, Tamara had come to this podunk at the edge of America and hidden herself behind her high ideals in lieu of doing anything useful for any-body. Tony would certainly see that, wouldn't he? Wouldn't he see how the very convictions they shared were so different? His ideals were the sickle that worked the field, while hers were hung on the barn wall for decoration.

Even her opponents couldn't be considered honored enemies, because they didn't really care. Argus Winslow would argue himself near to a coronary with her about some difference of opinion, but when it was all said and done, he would still like her. He would offer her a ride if she was walking, accept one if he was.

Everybody around this crazy place was like that. They could be diametrically opposed to every single thing a person stood for and still help you rototill your garden, just because they could. To these people, opinions were not things to be changed but to be bandied about and played with like toy sabers. Arguments were a form of recreation, and no matter how violent your attitude or proper your position, when the argument was over, you were just a part of the community. Just another person with another way of doing things.

Tony was too potent for these people. He would see the pointlessness of it all and grow bored. She was sure of it. He would grow bored with conversations. Then he would grow bored with going out at all. Then he'd be bored at home and with her, and she just knew that Tony wasn't going to like this place at all.

All these thoughts coursed through Tamara's mind and even intensified slightly as she saw her man appear in the door of the airplane. He stepped down, hefted a military duffle bag onto his shoulder, and stood there for a moment across the tarmac just looking at her.

There was something different about him. Not the way he looked, really. His jeans and denim shirt looked well and good enough. He'd even let his hair grow out to a stylish length. It was something about the way he stood. The uncertain grin on his face. He looked like, well, he looked *nervous* to her. Almost bashful.

They met halfway and became immediately rejoined at the forehead, as well as most points south, for a good long time. They peeled back only enough to allow their legs to move them around the building to Tamara's VW bus.

They sat in the front seats facing each other, and Tamara couldn't take her eyes off Tony's expression. He just kept looking at her like he was waiting for something. An order, a plan, something. Tamara was at a momentary loss. She'd been spending so much time worrying about herself lately it took a little force to pry her point of view out of her insides and onto her lover.

And when she finally did, she could see in his eyes the simplicity of it all. She saw no judgmental superman primed to criticize everything that made up her life. She saw a worried young man in a strange new land looking to his only friend in the world for help.

And a valve inside Tamara was opened and a sense of will that had poured out of her for weeks began to pour back in. She held out her hands to her man and told him as he took them, "You look great, Doctor. I can't wait to introduce you to everybody."

And the great doctor could only smile sheepishly back and unwittingly say the one thing that would relax Tamara and bring her home again. "I can't wait to meet your friends," he said, and dropped his eyes. "I sure hope they like me."

EMMITT GOES FISHING

OUR city manager, Emmitt Frank, had no idea what had come over him. It was another one of those mysterious lapses of control that had been becoming more and more frequent the longer he stayed at the End of the Road. He'd been sitting in Clara's Coffee Cup quietly reading old city budget reports and enjoying himself when Bud Koenig sat down next to him.

"Emmitt," he said, putting a hand on his shoulder in a fashion Emmitt found so hard to refuse. "Every year for the summer solstice I take a little camping trip up to my secret fishing hole along the river. I think you oughta come with me this year."

Emmitt had only been camping one time in his life. That was with a Youth Foundation field trip to the dunes on Lake Michigan when he was eleven. He'd been rolled in poison ivy, caught impetigo from the public toilet, and was carsick all the way back to Chicago on the bus. If there was one thing in this world he'd sworn he'd never do again, it was go camping.

Emmitt looked up from his budget report to Bud's friendly face, opened his mouth, and stared in wild surprise as the words tumbled out: "Sure, Bud, a little fishing sounds like fun."

Bud left satisfied while Emmitt sat terrified. Why did he do that? He didn't want to. At least he didn't think he wanted to. Emmitt was having a harder and harder time of figuring out what he wanted lately. This place was getting to him.

Eighty percent of his recommendations to the city council were either rejected or ignored. The only thing they'd showed any enthusiasm about at all during his three-month tenure as city manager was when he fixed the sewer system. All of his budgetary analysis, zoning proposals, and ordinance studies were met with cold stares and *no* votes. These people seemed prisoner to the most mundane aspects of existence. As if the wilderness were law and it was civilization that needed beating back.

Somehow this environment had set Emmitt's personal-guidance gyro askew, and he was getting prone to doing unspeakable things, such as camping.

Bud had stopped by Emmitt's office early last Friday afternoon to drop off some things. Bud figured Emmitt wouldn't have any suitable camping clothes, so he left a pile of his old ones, a pair of work boots, and an empty pack. "Just bring your essentials, Emmitt. I got the grub and tents and whatnot. Pick you up at five. And try to keep off your feet, we got a piece of walking to do tonight."

Emmitt sat in his three-piece suit, fingering his necktie with one hand and the backpack with the other. The only sound in the room was that of the copy machine and he hoped that it would explode and blow him safely into oblivion—where nobody goes camping.

At four forty-five, Emmitt was standing at the mirror looking at the reflection of an idiot. He had on a borrowed red buffalo-plaid shirt, some baggy denims, and two big dumb leather boots with yellow laces that must have weighed five pounds each.

Four years of engineering school, twenty years in the Chicago Planning Department, and I look like a homeless person. It was something less than exuberance propelling Emmitt along as he packed his *essentials* into the empty pack. Emmitt's essentials amounted to about fifteen pounds of paperwork he'd like to review over the weekend, an electric razor, toothbrush, paste, cologne, brush, comb, cuticle scissors, nostril-hair trimmer, eye, ear, nose, and throat drops, tweezers, squeezers, Q-Tips, and cotton balls.

Emmitt was feeling about as inspired as a beached bass when Bud pulled up in the pickup to get him.

"Emmitt, by golly, you look like a regular sportin' man," he said as he threw the pack into the back without ceremony. Little or nothing was said as the two men drove up the road to Bud's "secret spot." Bud guided the old truck down a rutted old side road for a mile or two, pulled it off into the bushes, and announced, "This is it, buckaroo. Bud Koenig's A-1 grade-A king salmon hole lies just a stroll away. Five miles from now, you'll be the happiest camper alive."

The terms *happy* and *camper* had never occurred in the same sentence for Emmitt before, and he was intrigued in some noxious way as he watched Bud open his pack to examine his belongings.

Bud shook his head kindly and began pitching things out. "You won't need all this paper. It hasn't rained in days and we should get a fire going no problem. Don't know what you need all this surgical equipment for. Grab your toothbrush if you want, but we need the rest of this room for your tent and sleeping bag."

Emmitt saw everything he'd brought being piled on the truck seat, but he didn't really mind. He knew it was going to be awful anyway, and one more degree of awfulness didn't seem to matter right now. He absently looked at his watch, saw that it was nearly eight o'clock, and wondered out loud if they shouldn't be going.

Bud reached across the truck bed and grabbed Emmitt's wristwatch. "I forgot to tell you the first rule of Bud Koenig's annual solstice camp-out, and that's no clocks." Bud stuffed Emmitt's watch down behind the front-seat cushion. "The solstice in Alaska is a place of constant daylight. I don't want to pollute that with a lot of odd ideas about time."

This made about as much sense to Emmitt as camping out in the first place, but he was so far out of his element by this time, he may as well have had a ring in his nose. He watched as Bud stuffed his pack full of tent parts, lashed on a sleeping bag and fishing rod, and filled the gaps full of nondescript foods wrapped in newspaper and Baggies.

"We're gonna live like kings, Emmitt." Bud helped him on with his pack and led the way down the trail. "Ain't nothin' ahead of us but big fish, daylight, and daydreams. Most men would kill for this."

Emmitt had never considered murder before, but it occurred to him more than once on the five blistering miles along the bluff to Bud's "secret fishing hole." His pack weighed at least as much as a copy machine, and Emmitt was trying to equate his misery to something in his experience, but to no avail. Even the camping trip to Lake Michigan had been done on a bus. There was no question about it. This was a new development on the misery front.

Emmitt's feet were blistered and his back was broken in at least seven places by the time Bud stretched and shed his pack alongside a particular spot on the river and announced, "This is it, Emmitt. You're the first person I've brung up here since Argus Winslow and I quit gettin' along. Consider it an honor."

Emmitt fell down with his pack and considered it everything but an honor. It was a horror. He felt like it must be midnight at the very least, but it was broad daylight. There was no way of gauging the time.

"The fishin' seems hot to me, Emmitt. Let's set camp later. I think these silvers have been waiting for us."

Emmitt watched dispassionately as Bud assembled rods, dug through tackle, and attached lures. Delirious from exhaustion, Emmitt accepted his rod from Bud and followed him to the river like a tired dog.

Bud showed him the workings of the spinning reel, demonstrated how to cast upstream and float the lure down with the current, then separated himself upriver. Emmitt was as far removed from himself as he'd ever been. There was nothing there for him to grab hold of. There was a breeze in the treetops, the gurgle of the river, and the occasional slurp of an eager fish bucking the current. Emmitt mechanically tossed the lure up into the current as Bud had instructed.

And just as Emmitt was searching through his mind for something to occupy it with, he felt a life in his fishing rod. It was like someone had tried to grab it out of his hand, and the reel started squealing that sweet song that sends chills of pleasure down the spine of anyone, including Emmitt, who's ever hooked a fish. There are few earthly pleasures that can so totally override all prejudices to the contrary, but catching a fish is at the top of the list.

Emmitt rared back on the rod in reflex as Bud hollered from upstream, "Set the hook! Set the hook!"

Emmitt couldn't hear him. He was completely immersed in what he held in his hands. He could feel the power of the fish as it swam upriver, then down. It swam toward him, and he instinctively cranked in some line. He jerked the pole again and that sent the fish streaking downstream with Emmitt's reel wailing in remorse until he tugged once more lightly, which sparked the fish to buck like a mustang into the air where Emmitt could see it.

He saw it all, like a slow-motion documentary. Drops of water spraying away, a long, sparkling king salmon thrashing about with its mouth wide open trying to spit the hook. Emmitt lashed back again with the rod and brought the fish back to water.

It went on and on for a long time. The kind of time that clocks can't count. Bud said and did little. He stood to the side, net in hand, and watched the expression on the city manager's face. A stone face suddenly turned rubber that flexed from panic to defiance, hope to despair, as the wily salmon went through its dying dance.

By the time Bud gathered up the spent catch in his net there was little left of the fish, little left of the night, and little left of its victor.

Emmitt sat deliriously looking at his prize as Bud set up camp. The spoil lay gutted on the rocks, shimmering in the gray solstice twilight like manna from heaven. It was such a delightfully unexpected development on such a miserable journey that Emmitt could only look at it as a miracle.

Emmitt lay awake the whole night long. His adrenaline had soaked too far into his tissue to allow any sleep. All he could do was continually replay the catch. He never even noticed he was lying in a cheap cotton bag inside a thin blue nylon tent within the unplanned wilderness of the country's last frontier. That was all beside the point. He'd caught a, by God, fish! It was going to take a while to get his mind off that.

For the next two days all Emmitt wanted to do was fish. He was suddenly impervious to mosquitoes. Bud's camp food of smoked salmon and boiled potatoes went unnoticed when not thoroughly enjoyed. He sat around the fire quietly listening as Bud expounded on fishing expeditions past, trophies of memory, and those that got away.

Every morning at God only knows what time, Emmitt would be at the river with his rod, calculating his cast, studying his drift, and plugged into his rod like a live wire. The scene from his first night was replayed many times, and the excitement only built, never lessened. It was probably the first time since Emmitt rolled in poison ivy that he'd lost control of his faculties. He might have stood in that river and fished until he died if Bud hadn't drug him back down the trail on Sunday.

Late that Sunday night, how late Emmitt didn't know, he stood in front of his mirror and looked at the reflection of something new. He had on a borrowed buffalo-plaid shirt, baggy denims, and two big dumb leather boots that must have weighed five pounds each.

There was fish blood on the pants, mud on the boots, and the smell of alder all over the shirt. There was a three-day growth of hair on his face and the robust odor of sweat and fatigue everywhere. His skin had the tarnished color that sun and exposure make, which put his teeth in a good light even if they did feel like they'd grown fur on them.

Emmitt stretched and felt the knots in his calves and thighs from a lot of walking and standing in cold rivers. It hurt and it felt good. Emmitt didn't know how. Emmitt didn't know a lot of things all of a sudden. He stroked his three-day-old whiskers with his hand and contemplated a beard.

He lay back on his bed without shaving or showering and wondered why he did neither. He felt his muscles congratulating him and his feet scream in relief and he thought of nothing but that. And it bothered him in a way and it kept him awake in spite of himself, because for the first time in his professional life he wasn't thinking of his profession.

And our city manager, Emmitt Frank, sat up the whole night long, not knowing what time it was or what in the world had come over him.

EMILY'S NEW CAR

EMILY wasn't so sure she wanted a new car after all. It'd been three weeks since she'd quit her job on the oil-spill cleanup crew, and the money she had made wasn't exactly burning a hole in her pocket.

She and Ed had talked about getting a new car off and on for a year now, but they'd also talked about taking the kids down to California and Disneyland. After what the family was put through with both her and Ed working full-time for most of two months, Emily had taken it upon herself to feel bad about it. The family needed some time together, and the money in the bank, she figured, could be better spent on the Magic Kingdom of Anaheim than a down payment on some fancy new car in Anchorage.

Besides, she kind of liked her big dumb old station wagon. Sure it leaned a little to starboard. Admittedly it was more rust than substance in most places, and the upholstery had been permanently scented with the smells of three growing children—mud, blood, lotion, and curdled ice cream. The dogs probably didn't help much either, and there was an undeniable sense and quality of fur about the backseat. But it ran well enough, it was her car, and she just didn't need a new one.

Ed, of course, would beg to differ. In fact he wouldn't even beg, he'd just differ. He pointed out that the car ran well enough only because he had to work on it at least three times a week. He said it was the most jerry-rigged contraption on the road, and it was a good thing the kids spilled as much stuff as they had because it's probably the only thing holding it together. Ed described in no uncertain terms how her car was well beyond proper repairs and the only thing that didn't need to be fixed on it was the speedometer, because it couldn't go fast enough to break any laws anyway.

103

Emily knew Ed was exaggerating, but that was his nature when it came to trying to convince her of something. Somehow Ed had got it into his head that she was going to get a new car, and he wasn't going to quit until she did.

So it was that the Flannigans found themselves careening up the road to Anchorage in a fur-lined station wagon, leaning to starboard, dribbling rust, and listening to the piercing din of three bored children and two pestered dogs in the back.

"For goodness' sake, leave those poor dogs alone! Missy, Spike wouldn't be drooling on you if you'd move away from him."

"But there's hair on my sucker."

"You're the one who let Buck have a lick, so you live with it." Emily looked over to Ed behind the wheel, seeming oblivious to the commotion. "Ed are you sure you wouldn't rather go to Disneyland?"

Ed smiled over in that maddeningly reassuring way that men do when they're sure they're doing the best thing for everybody, even when they ain't. "Don't worry, honey, we'll make a fun family weekend out of this. We'll take the kids to Chuck E. Cheez. They'll never know the difference."

"I'll know the difference," Ed junior mumbled from the backseat.

"No one asked you, son." And Ed turned back to his driving, doing his best to keep it between the lines and fantasizing the whole time about precision gear boxes, power steering, and brakes that didn't conspire to send the car into the ditch every time you touched the pedal.

Emily sat quietly thinking of her old car and all they'd been through together. How she'd bought it after arriving in Alaska and just before she met Ed.

She had been escaping from some new-age bohemia she and a few old college friends had fallen into in Los Angeles. She'd been living with a performance artist whose latest work in progress had been standing in a dry shower reading James Joyce's *Finnegans Wake* backward at the top of his lungs. When Emily observed that the public couldn't hear him so what was the point, he told her that a collaborator was presently in a Kansas City tenement screaming Ezra Pound verse down an incinerator shaft, and couldn't she see the magnificent irony of it all?

Emily left for Alaska a week later and bought the old station wagon the day she stepped off the plane in Anchorage. Who knows where she might be now if this grand old wagon hadn't busted down just outside of town those ten years ago just as one Ed Flannigan was making his way along the shoulder in a state highway department road grader.

He was handsome, helpful, and healthy. He towed her car for her, fixed it, and by then had pretty much garnered her keen attention. After coming from the cynical impressionism of late seventies Los Angeles, what struck Emily the most about Ed Flannigan was that everything he said and did made sense.

He saw the world for exactly what it was and read nothing between the lines. His honesty and innocence teamed up with his steady job and paycheck, and our bohemian soon found herself the willing matriarch of a small band of Flannigans living in a duplex with a pickup truck and a grand old station wagon parked out front. Almost everything had changed for Emily in the last ten years except this old car of hers.

It had been some binding tie for her. A constant reassurance that her staunch and self-important years of academia at Radcliffe and the nebulous arena of modern art in L.A. were best left where they were—far, far behind her. Each time a new child was strapped into this car or another dog loaded across the tailgate, this leaned-over old friend of a jalopy became a wholesome and righteous thing. It was large. It was heavy. It was predictable. And even when it didn't always run, everything it did made sense. The sways, bucks, shimmies, and shakes were all a part of the comfort Emily drew from this unassuming and ordinary life she'd chosen, which even after ten years seemed like a recent and good decision.

They arrived in Anchorage in the early evening. Ed cruised them around to some car lots picking up brochures, then sat reading them at Chuck E. Cheez while the clan ate pizza, drank pop, and played on the amusements.

"These Japanese make a lot of nice rigs, but I think you want an American car." Ed tossed aside one flyer for another. Each pamphlet had some smiling couple in an action setting around their new gleaming automobile. The heavier-duty vehicles were captured half underwater splashing through some river, or airborne over rocks the size of toaster ovens on a mountain range somewhere like we all drive on all the time. "You don't need anything that rugged," he said.

Emily just sat munching on a stray crust and wondered what her husband was doing. "Ed, I really don't want a new car."

Ed looked up from his reading impatiently. "Now, don't start that again, honey. You do too. Besides that old wagon being unreliable *and* unsafe, it's downright embarrassing."

"Embarrassing to whom?" Emily wasn't angry. She really was just being curious.

"Embarrassing to our family. The Flannigans are better than that old wreck. You went to work thinking you'd earn a new car and that's what you're going to get. Now, let's figure out what you want here."

And Ed proceeded to figure out what Emily wanted in a new car. He included her mostly by running color pictures of shiny and unfamiliar automobiles past her face. First at the restaurant, then later in the motel after the kids were stacked up in their sleeping bags on the floor, the dogs bedded down in the car, and the television on low for atmosphere.

Each picture in each brochure showed a handsome couple with a child or three happily unloading beach toys, camping gear, or groceries and grinning in wonder as if none of these feats could ever be possible without the car.

Emily tried to watch the late movie through Ed's interruptions. She'd gotten to where she could actually care less about this whole deal. She was simply resigned to the idea that Ed was going to buy her a new car, and didn't give a genuine whit what it turned out to be. She trusted that whatever Ed did, it would probably make sense.

Ed lay on the bed with his brochures not caring whether she listened or not. "Four-wheel drive for sure. I'm tired of pulling you out of the ditches all winter. But it's hard to tell what kind of power this little van will have over this wagon here. Won't know until we test-drive them tomorrow."

The next morning, after a messy and traumatic breakfast at a pancake house, the Flannigans bounced into their first car lot of the day. Somehow during the night, Ed had narrowed their choices down to two models. He and the first salesman talked very little. They looked under the hood of a little red van, and then Ed asked Emily if she'd wait with the kids while he took it for a test drive. The salesman stayed behind and began to approach Emily for conversation but seemed hesitant to get too near the car. It might have been the dogs holding him off or even the kids, but Emily pretty much knew he didn't want to catch whatever it was her car had and infect his lot of merchandise.

She was feeling fairly ill-at-ease by the time Ed rolled back up with a less than exuberant expression for the salesman. "Got anything with a motor in it? This thing couldn't pull a greased string out of a pig's nose."

The salesman got mad the way car salesmen do when they've been caught dead to rights, he and Ed went back and forth a little bit just for sport, and Ed was soon back in the wagon growling about how nobody knows how to make a decent car in this country anymore and heading to the next stop.

At the following lot, Ed took a little more time with the salesman, so Emily went across the street with the kids for ice cream. By the time they got back, Ed was gone on the test drive and Emily let the dogs out to run a little while the kids finished their cones in the backseat. "Watch the drips . . ." she started to say, then, "Oh, what difference does it make."

This time when Ed got back, Emily did a double take. What first caught her attention was the look on Ed's face. She'd seen it before. The look of a man who'd just bought something. But that's not what surprised her. She figured she'd be seeing that look sometime this weekend. What caught her unawares was that she couldn't take her eyes off the car. It was the prettiest little blue wagon she'd ever seen. It sat level and poised like a show dog, with a chrome grille beaming its best welcome aboard smile.

"Emily, you gotta drive this thing." Ed was fairly gushing as he walked her over to the door and stood back with the salesman, who was beaming as bright as the chrome grille.

Emily closed the door behind her and felt her ears pop the way they will when you close the door to a car with all the seals still in it. She ground the key and winced through the windshield at Ed when she realized it was already running. *It is so quiet*, she thought. She dropped it into gear and the car seemed to glide away on a cushion of air. There was no hesitant clunk or the pop of a stuck brake shoe flopping open, as she'd grown so accustomed to.

She pulled out onto the avenue, steering a little wildly with the unfamiliar touch of a steering box with all its teeth. At a stoplight, a handsome young man's attention was drawn by the sparkling car, but he turned to Emily at the end with an admiring raise of an eyebrow. It was for the car, Emily knew, but it felt as good as any.

She turned on the radio, and as the crisp notes of a completely screwed together stereo wafted through the interior, Emily settled back into the seat and surrounded herself with the sweet opiate more responsible for the broken budgets of American households than any other single item on the consumer price index—the intoxicating smell of a brand-new car.

Emily pulled back into the lot and was a little disconcerted to see her family sitting on the hood of their old wreck waiting for her. "You kids get off the car. You'll get filthy," she said on her way around the car looking for Ed, who was already inside with the salesman reading some sale papers.

She stopped and took a long look at her grand old wagon alongside the New Blue Ride. It looked diseased. This tie that had bound her life together for her all these years as the shroud around her family and a trusted old steed suddenly had no relevance that she could focus on. It was just a big sticky rig with rust on it.

And in her mind it all started to make sense and fade back into the distance, like it would in her shiny new rearview mirror all the way home. Where she'd sit by herself for the first time in ages, watching the recent memories of ten years of family and dogs, who were far too messy to ride in the new car so soon, falling farther and farther back with no way to catch up until Emily decided to let them.

HOUSE RAISING

STORMY jammed the last piece of plywood decking into place and looked toward the still empty road out front. "Maybe nobody's going to show." He called over to Kirsten, who was shoveling drain rock into a wheelbarrow with Emily Flannigan.

"Don't worry, they'll show up." Stormy took note of the excitement in her voice. An excitement he couldn't quite share with his wife this time around.

Their first house had been a labor of love. Ten years of love and all their expendable cash had gone into the place. They'd had lots of love and little cash. But they'd also had lots of friends and lots of help, and somehow the job had gotten done in that beautiful lingering way that all worthy projects do. The whole works burnt to the ground in November and left them with nothing but a smoldering and uninsured hole in the ground.

The Storbocks had spent a long, tense winter in one half of the Flannigans' duplex working overtime, cheating on financial statements, and finally securing the loan to rebuild. But this time it was going to have to be different.

They had only four months to complete the new house, because of the terms of the financing, and they'd have little time to work on it themselves owing to the fact that they both had to work at their jobs in order to keep up with the construction-loan payments. Ed Flannigan, Stormy's best friend and best helper, was also tied up all summer with overtime on the highway crew. The Storbocks had no choice but to hire somebody to do the work for them.

It worked out pretty well for a little while. After Kirsten and Stormy had finally agreed on what exactly they were going to build, the work had begun. They'd drive up to Flat Back Ridge every night after dinner with the kids and see what had gotten done that day.

One day they'd come out and the new hole would be dug. The next day there would be some form boards nailed together, then some concrete in the footings, then a few blocks. Then pretty soon a basement would take form, and a new house began to rise from the ashes and dirt.

Stormy couldn't have been more pleased. "They do good work," he'd say, peering around and under things.

Kirsten was less impressed. "It just looks like anybody's house." She'd stand away at a distance with her arms crossed, refusing to make friends with the project.

Stormy knew what the problem was, of course. Kirsten wanted this house to be like the last one—where every friend they had owned a piece of it somehow and every board and nail seemed to have a story all its own. It was a romantic venture, that was for sure, and Stormy felt the lack of warmth himself. But he also felt a certain sense of relief, because not every story of every board and nail in the old place was such a sweet tale and it might be nice to get things done right this time.

So it was with this anxiety that Stormy looked to the arrival of his friends and neighbors to help raise the walls and roof of the new house. He still wasn't quite sure how Kirsten had talked him into it, but he'd persuaded their builder that they would frame the place up themselves to save some money.

"And we're *only* going to frame it," Stormy had insisted to Kirsten.

"That's enough," she said gratefully. "I just want some *love* built into this house."

And a few varied forms of love that would be put into the place were at that moment raising a dust along Flat Back Ridge Road hell-bent for the great Storbock roof-raising party.

Leading the charge was Argus Winslow, and his dog Barney, in his old tow truck. Right on his bumper was Bud Koenig, honking his horn at Argus out of pure and habitual irritation over everything the man did.

It looked like young Norman Tuttle had hitched a ride from town in the back of Ruby McClay's little truck and his aunt, Sissy Tuttle, was riding shotgun talking the ear off Ruby, who wasn't listening to a word she said as most of us don't.

Stormy shrank a little in the face of the onslaught. He clearly imagined the turmoil that was about to ensue, took a deep breath to overcome the nerves, then shrank again when he saw

Pastor Frank and his wife, Fanny, come around the bend.

Turmoil commenced to ensue.

Everybody appeared to have brought two kids and at least one dog each, all of whom blended into a gyrating vortex of Frisbees, dirt clouds, broken hearts, and bicycles.

Sissy Tuttle jittered up to Kirsten and Emily, who had interrupted their drain-rock project long enough to greet everyone. Sissy started gabbing even before she was within earshot about why her husband, Stu, wasn't able to make it and neither was Norman's dad, Frank, because of course they were out fishing. But wasn't that always the way with men when there was something important to do, but Norman was here anyway and he'd be good help, although he is a little young yet, he was tall for his age . . . and she was well into some height comparisons of the overall Tuttle clan before she realized Kirsten and Emily had returned to their work and the only one listening was Argus Winslow's tired old dog, Barney, who had little use for kids or Frisbees and mostly wanted the sandwiches Sissy was carrying in a big brown sack.

Meanwhile, up on the deck, Stormy was trying to organize this ragtag army of volunteers into an effective fighting unit. It wasn't proving easy. There is one thing for sure about men in general, and Alaskans overall, and that is *everyone* is an expert when it comes to building something. All Stormy had to do was unroll the floor plan to prove this out.

"Cut all your headers and trimmers first, size your studs, then nail on the plates."

"Take all day, and be too heavy to lift. Whatcha do is crown all your studs and put on the top plate. Then you nail your bottom plate to the deck, stand 'er up, and toenail the bottoms. Put your headers and cripples in later. Easiest thing in the world."

"Work fine if you don't mind the house fallin' over in the first stiff wind . . ." And the debate raged on as, one by one, each would-be carpenter found a job to do in the wider scheme of things, while Stormy did his best to officiate.

The first thing he did was get Norman Tuttle on the task of nailing down the plywood deck he'd spent all morning laying. Stormy could see in a glance that he was going to have to pull out half of what Norman did, because he couldn't follow a joist and the fingers on the poor kid's left hand were going to be pounded into pudding if he didn't learn how to move them back from the nail. But it seemed to be keeping him happy for the time being, and that was worth something.

Bud Koenig and Argus Winslow were by far the most competent help on the crew and they busied themselves separately, laying out plates, figuring studs, headers, trimmers, and doorways—and bugging each other.

"My God, Koenig, where's my headers at?" Argus called across the deck. "You're as much use as two good men who stayed home."

"Well at least if I'd stayed home it'd saved me the heartbreak of having to do everything you do over again."

It was encouraging to Stormy to hear that nothing had changed between those two guys, and he was glad they were there.

Ruby McClay was carrying short stacks of two-by-sixes, marking them to length and laying them in front of Pastor Frank, who had elected himself saw man. Frank continually drove a power saw, which was clearly out of his control, through one board after another, pinching and bucking, while his devoted wife, Fanny, stood a distance away with her fingers in her ears wincing, watching, and worrying.

Ruby McClay, who'd been through more than a few construction jobs in her thirty years in Alaska, took a look through the pile of cut studs. "Pastor, I think I could chew these boards off straighter than you're cuttin' 'em."

Frank looked at Ruby in his patented patronizing way that made one wonder how he had any teeth at all left in his head and said, "Power tools aren't for women, dear Ruby. And remember, Jesus was a carpenter."

"Jesus was a carpenter all right, but He gave it up for preachin'. You'd be well advised to do the same." And she forcibly grabbed the saw out of the good pastor's hand, leaving him only to stare in wonder as the old bird started chopping off studs at a rate at least seventeen times that of his own, and straight as a ruler.

The afternoon wore on with Stormy busying himself with one little crisis after another. Things moved fast but were in control, if only just barely.

Norman Tuttle got so frustrated with bending nails and smashing fingers he threw his hammer down to the deck, which bounced it back up square between his eyes. It raised a goose egg so big he could see it in his shadow as he snuck off to the woods pretending to pee rather than let anybody see the tears in his eyes. He never came back to the house project and elected instead to haul rocks for Kirsten and Emily, who were raking out the drain field in fine fashion.

"Don't be makin' a piece of art out there," Stormy called out to his wife. "We're just going to flush a toilet into it."

Kirsten looked up in mock irritation at the remark, and Stormy could see in her eyes how pleased she was with the whole grand mess.

And messy as it seemed, it was indeed grand. Every time Bud and Argus finished nailing a wall together, the whole menagerie, Fanny and Sissy included, would jump up on the deck and hoist it into existence. After the big front and back walls were up, they took a break for beer and halibut-spread sandwiches. There was a lot of job talk, but mostly folks munched and admired the work.

There's something heavenly about erecting things taller than we are. Like little towers of Babel, every wall raised by our hands seems to bring us closer to some inexplicable reward. And all we can do is beg and build for more, and higher.

The standing white lumber cast long harsh shadows on the deck and spurred our crew onward and upward.

"Better get a move on if we're gonna raise those rafters tonight." Bud Koenig settled in to the delicate task of cutting the roof members while the rest finished banging together the end-walls. Sissy and Fanny occupied themselves with games for the kids, and a quiet determination was fueling the whole endeavor by this time.

Stormy was given the ceremonious honor of nailing a spruce bough for luck to the first rafter set in place. And before the late-summer sun had hidden itself behind the tall trees, there was the shell of what would become a home standing proud and pure in front of a dirty near-dozen good friends and their filthy children.

Ed Flannigan showed up from work just in time for the celebration toast, and the kids were soon dragging their parents off to cars and promised ice cream leaving Stormy and Kirsten in the shadow of their home.

Kirsten leaned against her husband, and that deep satisfaction that comes of a hard job finished flowed through them both.

"There's no doubt there's some personality in this place now." Kirsten had gotten what she wanted.

"They forgot to frame in the front door, you know." Stormy was just being informative, not complaining.

Kirsten hugged his waist, knowing that Stormy had been part right in his fears.

"Doesn't it look a little crooked to you too?" Stormy didn't expect an answer. He just wanted to leave things in their rightful place.

Kirsten hadn't made her point yet. "It would have taken your hired men two or three days to do all of this."

"You're right," Stormy said. He'd been waiting all day for the line. "And it'll probably only take them a week to fix it."

EMMITT'S CABIN

EMMITT Frank sat at the lunch counter at Clara's Coffee Cup and eyed the front door. Sitting in front of him beside his cleaned lunch plate was a box. He unconsciously reached out with a hand and adjusted its position for no reason, like a new mother will fuss with a baby's bonnet.

Emmitt was waiting for Bud Koenig to come in so he could show him the new spinning reel he'd bought. Ever since Emmitt caught his first fish up at Bud's secret silver salmon hole, he'd come a little off his course. He'd sought Bud out at every opportunity for more fishing trips, and Emmitt had spent every weekend since, rain, shine, or high water, somewhere in a camp with Bud, either fishing or waiting to go fishing.

Bud had given Emmitt the short school on fishing gear, and the deluxe reel he'd ordered two weeks back had arrived that day. He'd played with it in his office all morning—listening to that sexy click of a precision mechanism. He snapped the baler open and shut and polished the chrome parts with the tip of his necktie.

Over the past few weeks, Matty, his assistant, had begun having to remind him of appointments and deadlines for the first time since he hired on as city manager. Emmitt had never had to be reminded of anything, except maybe to go home or to eat.

He still was attentive enough to his responsibilities, but his mind seemed to be drifting somewhere. The *City Planner News Letter, Engineering Weekly*, and *Software Monthly* in the restroom were being lost beneath a stack of *Field and Stream, Outdoor Life*, and L. L. Bean catalogs.

Emmitt actually chuckled out loud in his office one day while reading an amusing anecdote in a sporting magazine. The sound was so foreign to Matty she rushed in, horrified that he was choking on something.

He still continued to wear his regulation three-piece suits, but they seem to be losing some of their hone. He'd grown his beard out and, because of that, seemed to be taking less care with the knot in his tie. He'd even gone so far as to loosen his top button on several late afternoons. Emmitt Frank, in his wavering way, was taking a walk on the wild side.

When Bud Koenig walked through the door, Emmitt's eyes lit up like a number-three Mepp's in the midday sun.

"Bud, look at this beauty, would you?" Emmitt pressed the box into his surprised friend's hands. "The rod was back-ordered but should be here before they close us down up at your secret hole."

Bud flinched a little and glanced around the room at the mention of his private fishing spot. But he saw that nobody was paying any attention to Emmitt or anything he said, just like they always didn't.

Bud took the reel out of the box and turned it over in his hands. "Yes sir, Emmitt, looks like you're puttin' together a first-rate outfit for yourself."

Bud took another long polite look at the rig, handed it back to Emmitt, and sat down on the next stool. He turned his attention to his hands and Emmitt could see he had a piece of business on his mind. Bud Koenig sat on the city council and was frequently the one to communicate council directives to Emmitt.

Emmitt sobered with the realization that Bud had some official matter to discuss and slipped on his stock professional veneer of alert posture, sharp focus, and a half grin like a gas attack was coming on.

"I'm afraid I've got some bad news for you, Emmitt." Bud's serious tone set Emmitt's heart to pounding, but he waited.

"Emmitt, you've been working for us for over four months now and living in the city's apartment across the street. Well, the council feels it's time you found your own place. We need that space for visiting consultants and all the big mucky-mucks coming through here on this oil-spill business. Hate to do it to you on such short notice, but we got no choice." Bud put his hand on Emmitt's shoulder, a mannerism the middle-aged manager had grown used to from his elderly mentor.

Emmitt took some time to think before he responded. "Well, Bud, if that's the council's wishes, then so be it. I hope I can have a week at least. You know how tight housing is around town with the oil-spill workers and summer transients."

Bud was able to hide his mischievous grin as he delivered the information he'd come to. "I hear that old goat Argus Winslow is looking to rent the cabin he's got sitting back in the woods behind his junkyard. Used to be the original homestead until he built the big one, then moved into the house trailer."

Bud watched Emmitt's face brighten a little with interest. "It's not very modern, you know. The water comes from rain barrels, and there's no plumbing indoors. There's no electricity, but I suppose it could be hooked up. But there's a real good wood stove in it. Argus makes 'em out of old water heaters. Best around." Bud paused a bit to let Emmitt digest it all, then added, "It wouldn't be what you're used to, of course. Be real Alaska living. Maybe you ain't interested, but it's someplace anyway."

Bud patted his shoulder one more time as he got up to leave. "You think it over, Emmitt, and give ol' Argus a call if you decide on something." Bud walked out the front door grinning, but feeling just the slightest bit guilty over the whole thing.

Bud, of course, had planned it from the start. He'd convinced the rest of the council that they needed the apartment back, but only after he'd worked things out with Argus and checked on the old cabin. He'd replaced some windows, redug the outhouse, and chinked some of the cracks in the old log walls. He'd cleaned the inside, hacked down the tall weeds outside, and laid in a short supply of firewood. He wanted Emmitt to have a rustic experience, but not enough to kill him.

There was something about this Emmitt Frank that had intrigued Bud from the first day he met him. He'd never come across a man as uncomfortable with the world as Emmitt was and acting so in control of it at the same time. But there was some kind of spirit in there too. It was deep and it was bashful, but it was there.

There was something that drove this Midwestern bureaucrat to the End of the Road to make his last stand. People don't just show up here by accident, even if they think they did. Bud intended to help Emmitt find his reason for being here. That's why he befriended him from the start. That's why he took him fishing. And that's why he booted him out of his apartment.

Emmitt went back to the office that afternoon but couldn't concentrate on anything. He hadn't been this thrilled since he'd been named Municipality of Chicago Assistant Planner of the Month, and that was over ten years ago.

He couldn't really explain the excitement. In fact, at closer look it could easily be mistaken for terror, but it felt good somehow. Vital in some strange way he'd only recently discovered. It was all fairly fresh for Emmitt. These last few weekends fishing with Bud did it.

You see, fishing only takes up a certain amount of brain and leaves the rest of it roaming around wherever it wants. Where Emmitt's decided to roam was new territory for him. It wandered up to the tops of the hills holding the river and down around the spruce forests rocking with the wind and creaking in the faded summer nights. And it followed moose across creeks, bears down beaches, and eagles riding currents of clean air that gulped down from the mountains in a way a man could swear he smelled ice and snow in July.

This land had worked its magic on probably one of its toughest cases, but eventually we all go down—or we leave. And Emmitt wasn't leaving. The End of the Road was his last stop, for better or for worse.

For worse appeared through the tall trees as Argus led Emmitt down the two-rut road, past the junkyard, and into the quiet of a Sunday wood.

"There she be, Frank, but I don't see why you'd want it. I worked my big behind off thirty years so's I didn't have to live like that. A house trailer, now that's what you need."

It should be noted here that Argus Winslow in no way, shape, or form shared Bud Koenig's reverence for the wilderness. Nothing Mother Nature did impressed Argus near as much as what mankind has pieced together from her. He collected junk like fine art, and the wilderness to Argus was just raw materials with no present function. He agreed to make the cabin available to this goofy guy, but as a favor to Bud, not because he thought it was a good idea.

As they walked up on the porch, Argus spit a stream of tobacco juice on the doorpost. "Yer gonna hafta go t'bathroom outdoors, ya know."

"Yes, Bud told me there was no plumbing." Emmitt held his hand against the weather-worn logs and smelled the rugged flavor of wood burning as Argus pushed the door open.

"I started a little fire for ya s'mornin'. Keeps the snakes out."

"There are no reptiles in Alaska." Emmitt was unaffected.

Argus, a little disappointed he couldn't rattle Emmitt right off, kept on. "The outhouse needs a seat, ya know."

"I'll get one."

"You'll have to chink these holes. Koenig did a sloppy job. Look, you could throw a cat through some of these cracks."

"I can manage that."

"You gotta check your water barrel for dead shrews, or you'll git sick."

"I'll bring drinking water from town."

"The squirrels get up in the attic and make a hell of a chatter all night."

"They'll keep me company."

Argus could see Bud had already primed this guy, so he pulled out his big guns. "If the moose come around, don't go outside. A mama moose'll kick a hole right through you if she wants to."

Emmitt hesitated a beat. "Well . . . I'll certainly be cautious of them."

"And if that big bear comes back scratchin' at the door, just lie real still. He usually goes away."

Emmitt's competently furrowed eyebrows shot up. "Wait a minute. Nobody said there were bears out here."

Argus breathed a sigh of relief. He couldn't leave until he'd struck some fear into this fella, and it'd taken longer than he figured it would. Bud must have really prepped him, Argus was thinking as he turned to head back out the door. "Oh, those bears hardly ever eat people. Only heard of six or seven cases of it myself, but there might be more nobody told me about. Bear poop don't talk too much." And with that, Emmitt's new landlord took his leave.

Very late that night, Bud Koenig stalked up the two-rut road to where he could see the dim warm light of oil lanterns blushing evenly out of the cabin windows. It pleased him no end to see, and he leaned back against a tree just to ponder it.

It was about then he saw the familiar stocky form of one old friend and nemesis sneak by a window up to the front porch and spit a stream of tobacco juice on the rail. He carried a long branch in his hands and, while squatting in the shadows, he reached out with the stick and started scratching at the front door.

Bud could hardly contain the snigger that bubbled up in him at the scene, but he did, and stayed where he was. And Bud knew then for sure that somewhere inside that old rustic cabin was one incredibly alert city planner from Chicago who was at that moment coming to grips with his real reasons for being here—for better or for worse.

TAMARA'S MAN

TAMARA'S man, Tony, seemed to be working out pretty well around the End of the Road. At least by all appearances. He blended in as well as anybody here did in this busy summer of the oil spill. In fact he looked to be making great strides at becoming an active part of the community.

Dr. Anthony Tobias had joined a softball team, established himself as a formidable pool player over at the Lame Moose Saloon, and had developed an uncanny hand at horseshoes up at the park on Sunday evenings.

All the requisites of becoming an exemplary citizen of the End of the Road were falling firmly into place. You wouldn't figure anybody could find a beef with that. But then you wouldn't have figured in Tamara Dupree, and Tamara Dupree hates beef.

Tamara and Tony had settled nicely into her small cabin out on Far Road. Her fears that her rediscovered beau might find her house and home inadequate were put quickly to rest. The idea of having an outhouse not only failed to insult him, it charmed him. After nearly ten years as an officer in the army and a highly acclaimed military heart specialist, Tony was drawn to the rural accoutrements of Tamara's life in some way he'd never considered before.

Tamara loved to watch him chop wood. He had a natural dexterity that enabled him to do almost any physical task with finesse. The sight of him splitting rounds of spruce with deft swings of the heavy ax seemed almost like dance to her.

He took to her garden with the same amount of panache. His unfailing surgeon's hands worked through the rows of vegetables, pinching and pruning, smoothing and touching. He'd sometimes pause to hold a lettuce leaf or carrot top

121

between his fingers as if he were taking its pulse. They were serious, caring hands. And hands that could love.

This she knew for sure, and a good portion of Tony's first few weeks in town was spent alone with Tamara, loving, laughing, and talking.

They talked of grand things. Finally, Tamara Dupree had someone who could match her ideal for ideal, cause for cause. A man who means things *and* a man of means. He and Tamara yammered endlessly of the holistic health clinic they were to open soon.

Tony had devoted all his spare time while in the Army Medical Corps exploring alternatives to modern Western medical practices, including the surgery that was his stock in trade.

He was also what he called a theoretical dietician. Tony firmly believed that most illnesses are caused by improper diet. Late into many nights Tamara would listen intently as Tony spouted angrily about how modern medicine continues to drug and slice apart sick people instead of making them well. He pointed to studies confirming that 99 percent of Americans are malnourished, and it's no wonder everybody's so sick all the time.

Tamara could have died and gone to heaven, well, at least to her next incarnation. After all these years of being the lone crusader of the new age around this obstinate little town, she now had a partner. Dr. Anthony Tobias and Tamara Dupree would make themselves a force to be reckoned with. She was sure of that.

She told Tony how they would make it a nonprofit clinic, charging only what people could afford. And that if they did accidentally make money, it would be donated to worthy environmental causes to get the very poisons out of the world that were making everybody sick in the first place. She couldn't wait to get started. Actually, she couldn't wait for Tony to get started.

All she had was energy and a good idea. Tony had all the cash and licenses. As the weeks waltzed by, the grand talk and idling dreams started to nag at Tamara's "go" button a little bit, and consequently she started to nag at Tony's.

Tamara was making tea one morning while Tony lay in bed absently picking at her old mandolin and staring out the window. He hadn't worked in the garden in over a week and appeared to be contenting himself with their listless speculation of the future. She decided to force the issue.

"Did you talk to any realtors about leasing space for the clinic yet?"

Tony took a moment to pull himself into the room from wherever he had been. "Oh . . . I did last week. Doesn't look so hot. The oil company has just about every available space leased for the spill cleanup. They said they'd get in touch if anything turned up."

"It wouldn't hurt to do a little looking on our own."

Tony took note of the edge to Tamara's voice and snapped to. "You're right." He swung out of bed and stood in a crisp military manner. It was done out of habit, but Tamara took it as sarcasm.

"I don't mean to badger you, sweetie." She went to hand him his tea, and all was forgiven as soon as they touched.

Tony rode his mountain bike into town that day. Tamara stayed at the cabin to work on her latest project—arranging rocks around the pond in the signs of the zodiac. The day before, she'd discovered the outhouse sat right in the middle of Gemini and she was puzzling over whether to dig another latrine or alter the astrological charts.

Tony was gone all that day and returned with the early evening. As soon as he walked through the door, Tamara could sense that something was changed. He wasn't drunk, exactly, but he smelled a little of beer. He also smelled of sweat and grass, and he had a look on his face that made Tamara shudder.

It was a look she'd seen far too much of on the faces of men around here. It was something she'd come to detest more than the men themselves. It was that foul, flippant look of a mature person who thinks he's a little boy. *How is it men so easily turn to boys*, Tamara was thinking. And Tony unwittingly answered her question.

"I ran into your old friend Ed Flannigan this afternoon."

It was worse than Tamara had imagined.

"Yeah, ol' Ed's a nice guy. Him and his buddy Stormy invited me up to the softball game. I told 'em I used to pitch with our inner-battalion league at Fort Lewis, and guess what?"

Tamara didn't want to guess. She didn't even want to listen. She was busying herself with her juicer, squeezing out a shot of wheat grass, and she decided to make it a double.

Tony continued on about how they'd let him pitch a couple

innings and he'd struck out five batters. They invited him to play second base the rest of the season and relief-pitch for Stormy. Then they'd all gone down to the Lame Moose for a beer and some pool. Had he ever told her he was the C Company nine-ball champ four years in a row until they promoted him out?

No he hadn't, she allowed. And for the first time since their reunion, Tamara could see that Tony wasn't altogether with her. Part of him had gone on to other people. And of all people, *Ed Flannigan and Stormy Storbock*, spiritual dweebs if ever there were some. The Bert and Ernie of the cosmos. Enlightenment to them were the jokes in *Reader's Digest*. Tamara panicked and flushed at the thought of a potential submission to *Humor in Uniform*:

I had just taken early retirement from the Army Medical Corps and gone to live with my hyperorganic girlfriend in Alaska . . .

Oh God, was this how it was going to end? My Tony swept off to idiocy with the barbarian horde?

Tamara held her doctor close that night in bed. The masculine smell of him stirred her at the same time it set her to worry.

It was a worry she would carry quietly for the next couple of weeks. She sat silent and forced a smile of good luck when Tony headed out the door to softball practice three times a week. She didn't say anything when he wanted to go to the horseshoe tournament Sunday night rather than the Environmental Poetry Recital and Earth Healing Chant at the Coop.

She even went to one of his softball games to watch. She sat horrified in the bleachers with the other wives and girlfriends. They wore tight pants on their big butts, jammed candy of every noxious description into their rowdy children's mouths, and shouted obscene things to the players.

Tamara watched her man and wanted to cry. There on this shallow mound stood one of the most papered young medical professionals and skilled surgeons in the Northwest, appearing to devote his ample mental capabilities and unmatched manual dexterity to flinging a white ball past a beer belly holding a baseball bat.

With every pitch. With every hoot, holler, or curse of her bleacher buddies Tamara's vision of her and Tony's future together grew dimmer.

It was just a faint light in the distance by the time they pulled up to her cabin in the van that evening. He'd been here six weeks, and the only thing he'd accomplished by way of paving the road to his local medical career was showing Kirsten Storbock how to make a mustard-and-herb compress for Stormy's pitching arm.

Tamara was getting near her breaking point, but she probably would have lasted a few weeks longer had not Tony laid one last intolerable straw on her back.

"Guess what?" he said.

Tamara was rapidly growing to hate those two words.

Tony kicked off his shoes on the porch and went cheerily on. "Ed and Stormy asked me to bowl on their team when the leagues start up this fall. Did I ever tell you that when I was with the Third Battalion . . ."

That was it. Tamara whirled, placed her hands solidly on her hips, and opened fire.

"What in the world has come over you, Tony? You're one of the most intelligent, enlightened, and skilled people I know. You could be helping hundreds of people here, but instead you're trading one-liners with those cretins at the ballpark. You haven't done a thing around here in weeks except talk to the garden when you're bored, and you haven't taken a single step toward opening our clinic. You left the army to start a health practice, remember?" Tamara brought her arms up across her chest and glared at her man, demanding a response.

Tony had stood calmly through her speech, and then while keeping her eyes in his he sat down on a stool beside the counter. When he started to talk, his voice was soft and strong and pitched in such a way that demanded attention. It was the voice of healers.

"To start with, Tamara, I didn't leave the army to start a health practice. I left the army to be with you. I'll start the clinic just like I said I was going to, but I'm not in such a hurry as you are."

Tamara's arms relaxed and she sat at the table facing her man. Waiting. She wouldn't have looked away from his gaze if the moon itself crashed in the backyard.

"Tamara, I went to school for eight years, four of those in the army because my family couldn't afford medical school.

I've worked with starving and dying refugees from Thailand to Lebanon. In the last ten years I've had more surgical experience than doctors twice my age. I've learned techniques and developed variations that have saved lives all over the world. I've also had the hearts of small children stop beating while I held them in my hand, and gone out to dash the hopes of waiting parents with blood still on my gown.

"I've been busy, and I'm tired. These last few weeks have been the first time since I was a little boy that I've been allowed to do nothing but have fun for fun's sake instead of as a relief from horrible things. I'm going to play softball and I'm going to go bowling and play horseshoes and I'm going to practice medicine and I'm going to love you, and I'm going to do them all in good time. There is only good time now."

Tamara sat still and quiet and continued to look deep into her man's eyes. She saw down inside him where nobody else goes. And what she saw awakened her and seduced her and scared her all at once. For in those eyes was the brazen reality that the great and undisputed champion of the cause supreme, Tamara Dupree, had met her match.

NORMAN
CAUGHT DEAD

NORMAN Tuttle tasted the sweet cut grass of Stanley Bindel's front yard and he knew he was dead. He'd taken a full burst of what seemed to be light automatic weapons fire from Stanley's younger cousin, Fred, hiding behind the trash cans by the garage.

Norman loved to die. As he counted slowly to a hundred waiting for his next life, he replayed his excellent death once more to himself.

He'd been running full-tilt across the yard in a suicide charge at the enemy's position. He hadn't seen Freddy laying for him by the garage, so he was a little surprised to hear the voice of gunfire and the inevitable, "You're dead, Tuttle!" just as he got on his full attack stride.

Norman had let himself leap from his feet and lose his grip on the plywood Thompson submachine gun in his hand. He approached the ground facedown, spread-eagle, but tucked and rolled at the last possible instant, tumbling over and over in the grass and finally coming to a halt with an agonized, if not melodramatic, quiver of arms and legs.

Freddy came over holding a plastic model AK-47 behind his head, enjoying the look of it in the shadow he cast across his victim. He said, "You've only got one life left, Norman." Then he disappeared around the house to a new ambush position.

Norman finished counting, gathered up his weapon, and stalked off into the weeds, looking for enemy movement and not really thinking about what he was doing. The rules of the game gave him two lives, and he'd only spent one. It was an exceptionally lighthearted afternoon for Norman in this heaviest of his thirteen summers so far.

Ever since he and Laura Magruder had started going steady after graduation from junior high, Norman's life had taken on pretty sober proportions. He and Stanley hadn't done much goofing around together this summer. It was just happenstance that he'd gotten into this game of play army.

He'd been expecting Laura to pick him up for their date to watch the dirt-bike races on the Spit with her older brother, Burt, and his girlfriend. He grew bored waiting, and started to walk up the road past the Bindel place to meet them. Norman saw the gang of kids running around with toy guns and stopped to watch while he waited for his date.

He'd gotten caught up in the process of naming the armies that turned into a political discussion eventually leading to war. Stanley had told the younger kids that contras were bad guys, and they wouldn't believe him. They wanted the Palestinians to be bad guys and the contras be the good guys. When Norman appeared on the road, the gang went to him with their debate.

Norman didn't really know a Palestinian from a canned peach or a contra from Kool-Aid, but that didn't keep him from expounding on the world of foreign affairs anyway.

"Palestinians and contras are the same thing. They're all fighting for freedom in Africa against the communists. Communists are always bad guys."

It sounded good enough to the younger kids, but Stanley, not liking Norman's self-important manner, wasn't buying it. Pretty soon the two recently best friends were caught up in a heated argument over the political overview of the world, which made less sense than the truth, if that's possible. Before either one of them knew it, they were each captain of their own fighting unit struggling for political recognition in the world of Stanley Bindel's front yard.

Norman went at his play with a fierce determination like he hadn't felt in months. His summer romance with Laura Magruder had boosted his experience a little bit out of reach of his friend Stanley. Stanley was still an undeveloped third-world country of a boy. But somehow the magic of a summer's day had placed them together once again on the battleground of boyhood.

It felt good without thinking about it, and it was such an overpowering relief from growing up that Norman forgot all about Laura and her brother. This was much more remarkable than it might at first appear, because Norman had thought of very little else *but* Laura and her brother for over two months.

*   *   *

Having Laura Magruder to call his girlfriend would have been enough to let Norman die a happy young man all by itself, but getting to know her brother, Burt, and his girlfriend, Jackie, was almost too much to take in.

You see, Burt Magruder was probably the most popular guy in the whole school. He was the captain or president of just about everything that moved. Burt was going to be a senior this year, and his girlfriend, Jackie, who was a past two-time homecoming queen, had graduated last year and was already a legend. All this coupled with the fact that Burt had his own high-rider pickup truck put him on near equal footing with God in the world of soon-to-be freshman Norman Tuttle.

Burt walked with a cocksure stride and wore a perpetual smirk insinuating that the world at large was nothing more than a major inconvenience to him. But of course not as big an inconvenience as his little sister, Laura, and her nerdy boyfriend, Norman Tuttle, seemed to be.

Norman was shocked, delighted, and terrified all at the same time the night Laura's dad had suggested that Burt and Jackie take Laura and him along on their date. Burt and Mr. Magruder got into a huge yelling match in the kitchen while Norman and Laura squirmed in the living room. Eventually, Burt's vicious tones turned into whines and almost whimpers before he reappeared red-faced and angry and stormed past them to the front door. "I guess you two punks are coming with us."

In spite of Burt's ugly mood, it had been a magical night for Norman. Jackie sat so close to Burt in the cab of his truck that Norman was amazed he could still drive. Norman and Laura sat a little more loosely on the other side of the cab, and nobody said very much. Burt put on a rock 'n' roll tape and turned it up louder than Norman had ever heard music before.

They cruised the loop from the bowling alley down through town and around the parking lot at the Big Garage on Clearshot about twenty-nine times and Norman couldn't believe that all of this was really happening to him.

To actually be seen in the truck of Burt Magruder, and with his own date to boot, why, a ticker-tape parade down Fifth Avenue couldn't feel so good.

Burt and Jackie seemed anxious to be alone, so when they stopped at the bowling alley for sodas, Laura and Norman stayed inside to watch the bowlers and play video games. Later on, when they went back out to the truck to check in, they didn't see anybody in the cab at first and they got a little worried. But a closer inspection revealed, much to their embarrassment, why Mr. Magruder had been so insistent that Burt bring Laura and Norman along on that date.

And there had been many dates since then. Norman had probably been around the cruise over five hundred times so far this summer. But there had also been softball games, movies, dances, and even one bonfire on the Spit beach, when Burt drove his truck right up to the fire with the stereo playing while they all climbed out.

Norman and Laura were almost universally ignored by the older kids, but they were perfectly content just to be along and to be together. They were perpetually holding hands off by themselves in some shadow or corner, overhearing conversations and absorbing vital information, like two sly spies in the enemy camp.

The most important thing to keep straight was the hierarchy of vehicles. Burt's big-wheeled truck ranked right up near the top, but there were several other cars and trucks that fell in and out of grace depending on the mood of the gang.

Laura and Norman soon learned which cars it was cool to admire and which ones to ignore. Anything with tinted windows was safe territory, Norman discovered, but complimenting somebody on his parents' borrowed Subaru was a social gaffe of deadly proportions.

They kept the who's who of dates and steadies current, memorized the names of rock bands of choice, and were slowly learning not to giggle so much.

Overall, Norman and Laura were learning the necessary rules of getting older. Because of Burt and Jackie's rather unnerving habit of wandering off by themselves, the younger couple had ample time to rehearse their grown-up talk as well as sparkle with the innocent opportunities of adolescence.

All of this had the effect of drawing Norman into a world away from the one he had grown up in. It was a world he didn't understand well enough yet to explain and it had made him quiet at home and absent in the neighborhood. He still worked for his dad on the fishing boat, but there was less of that this summer because of the oil spill, and Norman spent most of his days doing chores around the house and the boat, then retreating to his room.

He saw Laura at least two or three times a week and talked to her on the phone every day. More and more Laura was becoming Norman's only friend in the world, at the unjustified expense of all others.

One sunny Saturday they'd been riding around with Burt when Norman spotted Stanley Bindel, with a group of other classmates, skateboarding on a side street. Norman was glad to get this opportunity to be seen in such a heady circumstance by his peers and he let his frame droop a little into the seat in order to deliver his most nonchalant wave.

He never made the delivery, though, because just as he was about to, Laura straightened up next to him and sniffed with rare viciousness, "Oh, there's that Stanley Bindel and his friends. They are so immature."

Laura looked away with such a purpose that it distracted Norman and left him in a helpless moment of confusion. And a moment was all it took for the truck to roll by his friend. There was nothing Norman could do but memorize the look on Stanley's passing face.

It was a look like surprise all mixed up with hope and mercy. It was a look that wanted something, that needed something. The simplest thing. Like a friendly wave from an old buddy.

But Norman just looked back and did nothing. He sat numb, looking straight ahead, and let Stanley disappear behind him. Laura relaxed again beside him, and Norman was pulled back into his present company by her touch.

He looked at Burt's irritated smirk and Laura's indifferent reserve and he recovered himself. He was riding in one of the hottest rigs in town with the soon-to-be president of the senior class, going to pick up the legendary Jackie, while in the company of his very own steady girlfriend. Did he have anything to be unhappy about? Nothing he could remember.

Forgetting things is a necessary privilege of youth that often serves us well on the way up. It's easier to disregard some things than it is to do anything about them, but Norman's selective memory was about to have its revenge on him.

He was crouched in the tall weeds eyeing three of Stanley's cousins, who were defending the tractor-tire sandbox that served as enemy headquarters. Norman had lost the rest of his platoon already. He'd made poor choices from the beginning, and the little kids he had on his flanks were quickly and mercilessly ambushed out of their two lives apiece.

It was just him now, and he thought he could try another suicide run at Stanley's troops. They wouldn't expect it twice from the same place. He didn't see Stanley anywhere but figured he was out back looking for him. Norman had put some thought into this, and he felt cocky enough to try it. The three defenders were looking the other way, and it was now or never.

Norman gripped his plywood machine gun, took three deep breaths, and burst from the edge of the weeds in a silent streak toward the sandbox. His heart pounded with blood lust and the revenge that was to be his.

Just as he was about to open his mouth with deadly fire, his attention was caught by something on the road. But before he could look over, he heard a staccato burst of verbal gunfire. It was Stanley from behind the front stairs. He'd been ambushed again.

Norman knew it was his last life, and wanted to put everything he had into it. This time he decided to clutch his chest and turn around. He'd stagger, land on his back, and roll. And as he turned, he looked up and suddenly remembered something he'd forgotten.

Standing stock-still on the road in front of him was the hottest rig in town, with the soon-to-be president of the senior class, the legendary Jackie, and his very own steady girlfriend. Three heads turned precisely toward him with the deadly aim of a firing squad.

He caught a round each of Burt's irritated smirk, Jackie's bored amusement, and Laura's indifferent reserve before he turned and fell face-first into the lawn.

Norman Tuttle tasted the sweet cut grass of Stanley Bindel's front yard for the second time that day. And this time he knew for sure that he was dead.

EMMITT GETS LOST

EMMITT Frank and Bud Koenig had been fishing all afternoon, but it was slow. They'd walked in from the road a mile or so to one of Bud's secret fishing spots. He had a different secret spot for every kind of fish around. Most of them were tucked back in the trees and weeds pretty good, but this one wasn't so bad to get to. There was even a partial trail out to it.

"Me and Argus Winslow first hacked this trail in here thirty years ago, but nobody comes out here much these days." Bud was maneuvering over and around fallen trees with the ease of a man who had been in the woods more than a time or two. Emmitt stumbled along behind him. "We oughta bring my chain saw out here and cut these windfall out of the way. You can't beat the trout fishing at this place in the river." Bud really seemed to enjoy showing Emmitt around his old stomping grounds and he always seemed to be right about the fishing, with the exception of possibly this time.

Emmitt had hooked into one nice trout but lost it under a logjam. Bud eventually wandered upstream looking for some new holes and left Emmitt alone to his rhythmic ritual of cast and drift, reel and cast, and drift . . . a state of mind that Emmitt was growing more and more accustomed to.

Ever since Bud Koenig had befriended Emmitt, his life had taken many pleasant and interesting turns such as this. With the help of a little manipulating on Bud's part, Emmitt had moved from his modern apartment to a plain log cabin in the trees. That in itself was probably the biggest step in the rebuilding of Emmitt Frank. But learning how to fish was a close second.

The cabin was teaching Emmitt a new perspective on the world, and fishing was teaching him to stop thinking so much. Bud taught Emmitt that thinking too much about fishing gives the advantage to the fish. "You gotta feel for them," he told him, "just like they're feeling for you."

Emmitt wasn't sure why this fine old frontier gentleman had taken it upon himself to be his guide and mentor. When Bud first took Emmitt fishing he suspected it was just to torment him, but there'd been no torment, only pleasure. Whatever Bud's motives were, it had a good feeling about it.

Bud appeared through the brush across the little river. "I'm going to go look around over the ridge there a little while, Emmitt. I'll meet you back at the truck."

Emmitt just nodded, waved, and felt just a twitch of anxiety. It was so unlike him to agree to such a loose agenda. There were concerns that popped into Emmitt's head, and it surprised him only a little that he didn't voice them. *What ridge? What are you going to look for? What if you're late?*

He continued to drift and reel and cast and didn't think about it too much. If his mind was doing anything, it was pondering the notion of how long "a little while" was, and he was pleased that he sort of knew. "A little while" was a lot longer than "just a bit" but not near as long as "after a while" and, depending on how it was said, made "a little while" a little longer or shorter. It was confusing to think about, but Emmitt knew it. There were so many things he knew these days but didn't know why.

Emmitt was getting to know when there were fish around and when there weren't. Even when he couldn't see in the water. It would "feel fishy," as Bud would say. Emmitt's line would drift down in front of him, and if fish were there he could tell it somehow, as if his whole body were wired to the river. It was uncanny. He described it to Bud one time and the old sportsman had only smiled in that knowing way of his. "You got good instincts," he told him.

As Emmitt stood on the bank watching his line drift by undisturbed for the hundredth time, it didn't take his good instincts to know he'd better make his dinner plans around something other than fresh trout. He cast and drifted for just a little while more, then wrapped up his gear for the day.

Emmitt headed back through the thick trees on the crooked little trail that roughly followed the river and the ridge. The trail appeared to be maintained mostly by small forest animals. As he ducked around and tripped over the fallen logs, he was paying pretty close attention to what he was doing but not so much to where he was going.

He listened to the busy sound of his feet popping twigs and scuffing spruce needles and thought the idle thoughts of a satisfied man. It had been another fine day in a long line of fine days this glorious summer. He and Bud had gone fishing at least two dozen times in the last couple of months and that was exactly twenty-four times more than he'd ever been fishing in his life.

The only outdoor activity Emmitt used to do back in Chicago was mow his lawn. The outdoors bothered Emmitt. It was always *doing* something, and it couldn't be regulated. It would rain whenever it wanted to or be too hot or too windy. It was always too something and never seemed to be just right when you needed it to be. It was impossible to make firm plans that involved the outdoors, and as you know, Emmitt Frank lived by firm plans.

When he lost his wife and job of twenty years to the same young man in Chicago, he was set adrift for only a few miserable and uncertain hours before he had another plan. That's the one that brought him to us at the End of the Road.

Emmitt climbed over another log and took a moment to gather his breath. He took in the sweet, cool air of the great outdoors and looked around at the magnificence of it all.

He looked at the tall and untouched spruce standing straight and almost ordered, it seemed, over the quiet world underneath it. *Almost like a temple*, Emmitt was thinking as he looked through the trees and into a bright meadow alive with fireweed and long shadows. And beyond that there was nothing but the endless blue of a clear Northern horizon. The look of it made him proud, almost as if it were all his.

Emmitt took a long, thoughtful look around him and his face suddenly went white. He had another sharp look around at this quiet forest underworld with nothing beyond but the endless blue of a clear Northern horizon and he realized he didn't have the faintest idea where he was.

His mind was doing back flips as he looked ahead and behind him to discover he was not on any kind of trail anymore. He'd been spending so much time looking at his feet, he'd just wandered off into the woods without knowing it.

He started to walk back the way he came with a little more spark to his step than before, but he soon pulled up short. There was no evidence of his tracks in the thick blanket of spruce needles, and nothing looked familiar to him. He admitted that he couldn't really tell one rotten log or tall tree from another, but he knew foreign territory when he saw it.

He was paralyzed for an instant, and as his heart hammered in his ears his mind was racing with possibilities, groping for answers.

He saw the ridge he'd seen from the river over to his right, and he turned and walked toward it. He walked for "a little while," paying keen attention like he wished he had when he followed Bud in this afternoon.

He thought he should be reaching the river again pretty soon, and when he didn't . . . and didn't . . . and *didn't*, he walked slower and slower until he came to a gradual halt, like a spent wind-up toy.

The sun was finding its way down behind the ridge and an anemic light was surrounding Emmitt. The fading sort of light that might be prone to instill a little bit of anxiety and self-doubt into the likes of misplaced city managers from Chicago.

Emmitt tried to pull himself together and think this thing through. He thought there had to be some logical way out of this, and his mind began to devise a plan. A plan that wouldn't begin to work, but it was still a plan.

He decided that he'd pick a direction and walk toward it for exactly ten minutes. If he didn't run into the trail or the river by then, he'd turn around and walk the other way exactly ten minutes and he'd be back where he started. If he did this in four different directions, he'd have to run into something familiar.

It took some of the hardest and most sincere walking he had ever done, but thirty minutes later Emmitt Frank had succeeded without question in getting himself irrefutably and hopelessly lost. He'd roamed into a denser section of trees and couldn't even see the ridge anymore.

A person can only sustain panic for so long, and once it goes, it leaves behind the most potent of exhaustion. The kind of exhaustion that buzzes in your head. Emmitt sat on a log with his buzzing head in his hands and wondered how this had happened.

It happened because he hadn't paid attention to where he was going, he was thinking. No, it wouldn't have made any difference, because he hadn't paid attention to how Bud brought him in here, so even if he had seen the trail peter out, he wouldn't have known what to do. Emmitt looked at his sore feet, getting dimmer and dimmer in the twilight, and thought how this would have never happened if Bud hadn't left him alone. In fact, it wouldn't have happened if he hadn't brought him up here in the first place.

Why did he bring him up here? Why did Bud do anything? He always had that sneaky smile on his face like he knew something. Like when he booted him out of his apartment and arranged for that cabin. What'd he do that for? Why'd he teach him how to fish in the first place? Emmitt had lived perfectly happy for forty-two years without fishing. Why did Bud figure it was something he'd want to do now? *Feel for a fish. Holy smokes.* A highly experienced municipal-planning engineer feeling for fishes and then getting left in the woods to die. It was embarrassing.

Suddenly Emmitt Frank didn't feel just lost in the woods. He felt lost period. He knew everything he'd done, every dumb move he'd made since his life fell apart in Chicago, had led up to him sitting on that log in the faint light of day waiting for something to come along and eat his head off. He should have never come to the End of the Road. That was the only thing he knew for sure.

Emmitt sat and wallowed in the pitiful little bog of emotion he'd walked himself into, and wondered over and over again how he could have gone so far astray from where he was supposed to be.

He'd been doing this for "just a bit," although it could have been "a little while," he wasn't really certain of anything anymore, when he heard a noise behind him through the trees. It made him leap to his feet with a mixture of shock, joy, and a dizzying change of perspective, like vertigo; a sound as sweet as Gabriel's horn. It was the sound of a truck door being slammed about as far away as a person could cast a fishing line. Emmitt heard an engine start, and when the headlamps came on he drifted toward the light, stunned and dumb as a big bug.

Bud Koenig was sitting behind the wheel of his old truck, and Emmitt climbed in beside him without a word.

"I thought you was lost for a little while there, Emmitt."

Emmitt looked over at Bud and didn't know what to say except the truth. "I *was* lost."

"Ah, you just thought you were, and here you are right where you're supposed to be." The old sportsman looked over at Emmitt with that sly smile of his. "You got good instincts," he told him.

Emmitt relaxed back into the seat trying not to think about it too much as Bud ground the old truck into gear to take him home.

part
THREE

ED'S ACCIDENT

THE better part of Ed Flannigan jumped and woke up. He couldn't tell if he'd shouted out loud, but he might have. He focused his eyes on the pale green walls and the colorless furnishings of his hospital room as the morning light came in strips through the window blinds. He reached over with his left hand to rub the throbbing pain in his right arm for the thousandth time that week, and there was still nothing to comfort. He'd been dreaming about the accident again.

He wasn't even supposed to be working that day. The highway crew never worked on Sundays unless they were on winter snowplow duty, but Ed had gone in as a favor to his boss. Jack had asked him if he'd come help clean up the gravel pit for the big Labor Day Bazaar this weekend. It was the state's rock pit, but the city always used it for any outdoor activities that required a little room on a flat spot.

Even though he'd rather have been fishing, it was sort of a rainy weekend and Ed was glad to get the overtime. The pit had a lot of loose shot-rock and gravel lying around that had dribbled away from the dump trucks. Jack wanted to tidy it up with the loader so the folks had a place for the beer tent and pistol range. Ed had the great idea that as long as they were going to bother to push rocks around, why don't they load them in a truck? They were planning to fill the big sinkhole behind the Big Garage on Clear Shot anyway, and a load of rock is a load of rock, Sunday, beer tent, or otherwise.

It was this great idea that had Ed Flannigan by himself at the garage warming up the big orange end dump. It was parked outside with the dump bed tilted back like they leave them so they don't fill up with water when it rains. Ed sat listening to the throaty rattle of the big V-8 diesel, waiting for the edge to come out of it and the black smoke to quit. "Making up its mind," as Ed would say. It always took it a little longer to make up its mind when the weather was damp.

Ed knew this truck well. He'd been working with it for over ten years. It was temperamental, sometimes even cantankerous. But mostly reliable, and as sturdy as they come. It had some hard miles on it, but lots left to go, and even if it was missing a few parts, there was still hardly anything it wouldn't do.

When Ed heard the motor even out, he threw the dump lever down to lower the bed. It creaked down slow with that sort of creepy mechanical ease, but when it was about two feet short of being all the way down, it stopped.

The truck bobbed around on its springs and Ed blew air out his nose. "You wanna play that game again, eh?" Ed grabbed a pipe wrench lying next to the seat and jumped out of the cab. This had happened before. Ed reluctantly lay down in the mud under the truck and started banging on the hydraulic pump bolted to the frame. It had a sticky valve that did this sometimes. He thought he heard it engage and crawled back out, feeling the wet come through the back of his coverall.

Ed climbed back to his seat and tried the lever. He pushed down hard, and only got hissed at by the pump. He pulled up, and got the same treatment. "Damn-dead-stuck-bucket-a-rust."

Ed remembered climbing back down and looking at the hydraulic pump over the top of the truck frame. He didn't recall making the decision not to, but somehow he didn't want to lie back down in the mud again. He couldn't remember if he was thinking about it at all. He couldn't have been or he wouldn't have done it. But what he could remember, and what his dreams would never let him forget, was watching his hand reach out with the pipe wrench between the frame and the stuck dump bed, and how it was the last time he would ever see his right arm.

Ed's memory was at least merciful in that he remembered nothing more about the accident except waking up in this Anchorage hospital four days ago. His doctors told him the EMTs had sent the arm up with him in the medevac, but it had been too rough of a separation to put back together. "Pinched it off above the elbow," as Ed would put it.

He kept a humor about him when there were people around, but it was hard on him. Especially with Emily. He hadn't seen the kids yet. In fact, Emily and a bunch of doctors and nurses were the only people he'd seen at all since Sunday. It was bad enough just watching them through the pain sometimes.

Every once in a while it hurt so bad he couldn't breathe. It would boil tears up out of him, and his teeth would grind together. He'd already lost one filling and cracked another. He didn't want anybody to see him like that.

The pain would come and go. The nurses would give him a shot almost anytime he wanted one, but he tried not to take too many. They'd make him sleep, and then he'd dream that dream. Ed knew it wasn't the dream that bothered him so much as waking up and seeing his arm gone.

One time he woke up without the dream and it took him a little while to put things back together in his head, like you do sometimes when you wake up away from home. For one long glorious minute Ed had two arms again. He didn't remember two arms feeling so good when he really did have them.

He used to watch them work. If he was pulling on something, he used to like the way the muscles cinched up and pushed his big blue veins out under the skin. They were reliable arms. As sturdy as they came. And the right one was the better of the two. He couldn't stop counting how many things he did with his right arm.

Throwing softballs, pounding nails, turning wrenches, unscrewing jars, writing notes, brushing his teeth, brushing the kids' teeth, driving a stick. *Oh God*, he thought. *How will I ever drive equipment again*? You can drive a car with one hand, but they don't make automatic road graders. There's so much going on inside a road grader, two arms are barely enough to do it right.

Ed was afraid to look at what lay ahead. It was all confusion to him. He'd do anything to have it all the same as it was. He would lie on his back in the mud for five years beating on stubborn machinery until it all started over if he could take back what he did. He thought of how many times he'd said, "I'd give my good right arm for . . ." whatever. And he knew there was nothing worth it. Not nothing in this whole big world was worth it.

"You've got some visitors today." Ed's morning nurse was cheerful in that sweet, synthetic way that always made him want to strangle her with his one good hand. She was clearing away his untouched breakfast tray. "You didn't eat your breakfast again."

Ed looked at the petrified remains of a hospital breakfast of powdered eggs and Spam. "If you want me to eat, bring me some food."

"My, aren't we grumpy today." She acted to Ed as if she couldn't imagine what he might have to be grumpy about.

"I want a pain shot before I see anybody."

Ed knew that Emily was bringing the kids today for the first time. And she said that his best friend, Stormy, might come up, and maybe even Jack, his boss.

He pushed the control next to him and the bed raised his head up. He practiced his pleasant faces and waited for the pain shot. The shots made him groggy, but they made him kind of happy too.

Ed didn't realize until they were already in the room that he hadn't been prepared to see his children. They walked in first, with Emily running herd on them from behind. They all but had their little sneakers dug into the tile floor. They looked so scared, Ed wanted to jump to their rescue, then it dawned on him what they were afraid of.

"Come on, I won't bite." Ed sounded as merry as if he'd just come home from work.

The kids stayed an arm's reach away, so to speak, and Ed looked them over. Ed junior, the oldest, looked as out of sorts as a ten-year-old can. Red in the face, eyes on the floor, and hands on the move. Missy looked like she'd been crying. She held a rumpled crayon drawing in her hand. Little Corey, the four-year-old, just stood still and quiet like he did when he was being punished.

Ed looked up at Emily, and a moment of bewilderment passed between them. They realized at once that they should have talked about this ahead of time. There was a silence that hung in the room like anesthesia. Ed groped through his drugged head for something to say but could find nothing. He started to feel himself slipping deeper into the grip of the painkiller when little Missy broke the stupor.

"I drew you a picture, Daddy." She stepped forward just close enough to hand it to Ed, who pulled back out of his fog just in time.

He couldn't begin to make out what it was a drawing of, but he put his most admiring face on. "Well thank you, Missy."

"It's Peter Pan in Never-Never Land. Eddie says you're going to be like Captain Hook."

There was just one cold moment of surprise before Ed junior could react. "I did not!" he said, and started to lie further, but his dad cut him off.

"Wait a minute now, you two." Ed was running on parental auto pilot, and he put on his Dad voice. "I just might be Captain Hook. And I just might make you my Mister Smee."

Missy giggled. "I can't be Mr. Smee 'cause I'm a girl. I'll be Tinkerbell."

"Okay, you be Tinkerbell and this little pirate will be my Mr. Smee." Ed put his arm as far out to Ed junior as he could, and the boy couldn't resist the invitation. As he rolled up to his father's side, Missy was climbing onto the foot of the bed.

"And Corey can be Peter Pan," she said. " 'Cause he's so little."

"That's a great idea," Ed said, and even managed a wink for Emily before their little reverie was interrupted by a rowdy knock on the open door. Ed looked over to see his best friend, Stormy Storbock, waltz in with that great big twenty-dollar smile that could always get Ed to do anything for him. Including cheer up.

"Well, looks like we're all here," Stormy said.

"Speak for yourself." Ed actually pointed at his bandages to make his point. It was an irreverent and reckless thing to say. Even tasteless. The kind of thing he and Stormy always said to each other.

Stormy was taken a little by surprise at Ed's frankness, almost as much as Ed was, but saw he was in safe territory. "Ain't you bored with layin' in that bed yet? We gotta get you up and teach you how ta' shoot left-handed so I got somebody to go duck huntin' with."

"You just want to use my boat."

"No, actually I'm just butterin' ya up so you'll give me your bowlin' ball."

Emily watched with mock disgust as the two friends went at it. The wisecracks went right over the heads of the children, but they were giggling and grinning anyway, mostly at the atmosphere in the little room. Emily opened the window blinds and the light poured in like warm showers all around.

Stormy had pulled out a package of beef jerky and some Ding Dongs, and Ed was happily eating and jiving for the first time all week when his boss walked in the door.

Jack was a pretty serious character, and even though Ed had known him for ten years, he still would best describe him as *his boss*. Jack had some kind of flowered plant with a ribbon around it in his hand that he self-consciously set on the side table.

"My wife said this might cheer you up."

"What's it do—tell jokes?" Ed tried to stay with the frolic he was on, but Jack's grave manner brought him around. "Thanks for comin' by, Jack."

Jack fingered his hat and looked back and forth between it and Ed. "Ed, I just wanted to let you know that your job will be waiting for you whenever you're ready for it again."

The thought of his job sort of knocked the wind out of Ed. "Yeah sure, thanks," he said, like a person does when he's been given a promise that can't be kept.

Jack didn't like being called a liar, and he looked up solid at his senior employee. "Listen, buddy, you're better'n any two men I got. I want you in a rehabilitation program as soon as you heal, and back in your hard hat as soon as you're able." It was Jack's version of a tender gesture, and Ed appreciated it.

"Thanks, Jack." He meant it this time.

Jack left without a word like bosses are prone to do, and the feeling of reflection that remained in the room was everybody's cue to go.

Stormy shook Ed's left hand, and they both grinned foolishly at the awkwardness of it. The kids filed out in a lineup of kisses and hugs, and Emily gave him a long, long cuddle that took the fight out of every last muscle in Ed's exhausted body. Emily lowered his bed back down and Ed went with it. The painkiller washed through him into the farthest places and lit every fiber in such a way that for a moment he felt every part of him.

And the *better* part of Ed Flannigan floated off into a dream like Peter Pan and Tinkerbell looking down at his temperamental and sometimes cantankerous self. With a body as reliable and solid as they come. There were some hard miles on it, but lots left to go, and even if it was missing a few parts, he dreamed there was still hardly anything it wouldn't do.

THE BIG
BIRTHDAY BASH

MAYOR Richard Weekly wasn't entirely sure anymore why they'd decided to do it, but it was clear that blowing up the city's safe as part of the End of the Road Birthday Celebration was an ill-conceived idea. As his ears rang with the concussion from the blast, the good mayor tried to piece together the series of events that led up to this grand and explosive finale.

The twenty-fifth anniversary of the End of the Road sort of snuck up on everybody. It might not have been celebrated at all if the water main at Pioneer and Clearshot hadn't collapsed two weeks ago. What a broken water pipe has to do with illustrious occasions such as this might not be terribly evident to the casual observer, but few things around this town are, or have been for at least a quarter century.

What wasn't terribly evident this time around was, where exactly was the water main buried? It was this question that would set off the series of events leading up to the detonation of the city safe on the beach behind the Bluff Lodge last Saturday.

After a temporary water line had been laid on the surface to get people back in the wet, city manager Emmitt Frank began to research the damage in order to solicit some repair bids. The first thing he wanted to see was the original water system plans and specifications.

"That might be a little hard to find." Emmitt's assistant, Matty, was less than interested. "Those old pipes were buried over twenty-five years ago, before we were even incorporated as a city. I wouldn't know where to start looking."

There's no challenge that Emmitt Frank enjoyed more than a filing challenge, and he and Matty set themselves to the search. They fingered through all the current project files first and slowly worked their way down the cabinets and through the drawers. One cabinet downstairs, marked simply "1969," took them a day and a half to sort through.

"We didn't have a city manager that whole year." Matty sounded apologetic even though she didn't sign on until ten years later. "It looks like the mayor just kept stuffing everything in here and we're the first ones to find it."

Nineteen sixty-nine, though an interesting year by all appearances, did not hold the key to the water system. Neither did '68 or '67 for that matter, and the end of that first week found a frustrated Emmitt and Matty on their knees in the dim light of the city-hall basement going through the last of the cardboard boxes.

"I guess it just isn't here, Emmitt. We'll have to go ahead and repair it without the plans." Matty was brushing herself off, seeming relieved that they were done. Emmitt stood up brushing himself off too, but he looked anything but finished.

"I won't accept this. What kind of municipality would throw away its master water system plans?"

Matty answered his question by avoiding it. "I think you better go talk to the mayor," she said.

Mayor Richard Weekly sat at the big table in the back of Clara's Coffee Cup waiting for the lunch special. Ruby McClay and Argus Winslow were sipping coffee at the counter, and Clara was busying herself with the steamy business of Monday's pot-roast special.

Mayor Weekly groaned to himself when he saw Emmitt Frank come through the front door. Emmitt had his perturbed look on. The mayor hated it when his new city manager was perturbed. Emmitt was a good manager overall, but he tended to be a little persnickety when it came to details, and when the details weren't just what they could be, he got perturbed.

"The plans for the city water system are nowhere to be found, and we can't excavate without them," Emmitt said.

Details, thought the mayor, but he put on his most concerned face. "I'm sure they must be somewhere," he said, and might have gone on, but Clara interrupted from behind the lunch counter.

"They're in the time capsule." She lifted what looked to be the better part of a small pig from her big cook pot and let it settle onto her cutting board. "You guys put it in the time capsule twenty-five years ago." She commenced carving her roast and indicated with her back and elbows that it was all she had to say on the matter.

Argus Winslow turned on his stool. "Clara's right. We stuck those plans in the capsule, remember, Ruby? We kept looking for important historical documents to stuff in there, but all we could come up with was that fancy blueprint, a letter from the governor, the combination to the city safe, and Clara's pickled-herring recipe."

"Oh, that's right. It all seemed silly at the time—I guess when you think about it, it still does. But I guess we had to put something in there for posterity." Argus and Ruby both turned to face the plates of fresh pork Clara was doling out and lost all interest in the conversation at hand.

Mayor Weekly huddled up to his plate as Clara brought it around, leaving a somewhat puzzled Emmitt Frank standing alone listening to the satisfied smacking and snuffling of a mighty fine roast being eaten by most of the current city government.

"Would somebody mind telling me where this time capsule might be found?" Emmitt was addressing himself to the whole uninterested room.

Argus wiped his mouth and talked without turning. "It's in the safe, ain't it, Richard?"

"Yep." The mayor was addressing his mashed potatoes. "We put it in there twenty years ago. We were going to put it in the cornerstone of the new city hall, but then we forgot. It's just as well, though, we forgot the cornerstone too. 'Sixty-nine was a bad year for forgetting things around here."

Emmitt was trying to color in the picture forming in his head but wasn't getting far. "I don't know anything about a city safe. Why haven't I been told?"

Mayor Weekly finally looked up from his lunch. "No reason why you should know about it. It hasn't been used in twenty years. The only combination to the safe is in the time capsule and the time capsule's in the safe."

Emmitt could only respond with a look of pure disbelief, and the mayor added somewhat sheepishly, "I thought Argus had it wrote down."

"I thought you did." Argus finally turned on his stool and faced Emmitt, who was at least relieved to have somebody's attention.

"Now, let me get this straight. The plan to the municipal water system has been put in a time capsule for posterity and locked into a safe that nobody has the combination to? Surely you made a copy of the original plans."

"Didn't get the copy machine until 'seventy-two." The mayor sat back, waiting for Emmitt to get to his point.

"Where is the safe?" Emmitt revealed just about as much agitation as he dared.

"It's back in my storeroom taking up space like it has for twenty years." Clara never looked up from her work. "They said they'd move it when they built the city hall, but since nobody can get into it, they just left it here. Go see for yourself. It's under the lard cans."

Emmitt followed her finger around the corner into a dingy little room. In the back, looking important in spite of its uselessness, was a grease- and syrup-streaked old box safe.

Emmitt didn't know what his intentions had been. Just moments before, in his fit of frustration, he felt that he might just walk up to the thing and jerk it open with the pure power of impatience. But the sight of this three-foot-square hunk of solid steel added considerably to his tolerance of locked safes for the moment. "That thing must weigh a ton" was all he could manage to say.

"Twelve hundred pounds if I remember right." Argus Winslow was crowded in the doorframe behind him, alongside the mayor.

Emmitt took out a handkerchief and squatted in front of the safe. He tried the handle with the expected result, then gave a wistful turn of the dial while his mind worked over the situation.

When it came to bureaucratic procedure, Emmitt Frank was a warrior of no equal. He had a water main to repair, and in order to repair it he needed to solicit legal bids from licensed contractors, and in order to solicit these bids he needed to provide accurate job specifications. Specifications that could only be had from one document, which was only inches away from his hand. That was the situation of the world as Emmitt Frank saw it, and twelve hundred pounds of tempered steel was not going to stand in the way of procedure.

"Argus. I want this safe opened and I don't care how you do it."

Watching Argus drag the safe out to his junkyard behind the tow truck may have been what inspired Ruby McClay. Seeing the little vault bouncing along the shoulder pounding big holes in the road made it look playful, almost festive, and that must have been what moved her to the idea of a celebration. "Why, Mayor Weekly, we should have a birthday party!"

The mayor looked away from the pitiful sight going up the road. "What for?"

"Because we're twenty-five years old, and we're going to open the time capsule! It should be a great big to-do."

"Emmitt said he wanted that open by Saturday. How big a to-do you going to put together in four days?"

"You just watch." And Ruby strode off the porch with her best chamber of commerce booster gait raising a little dust behind her and leaving an anxious Mayor Weekly to look forward to the weekend.

Emmitt Frank heard every conceivable kind of commotion coming from Argus's junkyard all the rest of the week. There was scraping and grinding, banging, bashing, and dull thuds. There was screeching and flashing in the night and even a couple of small explosions.

When Emmitt went in Friday morning to see how the project was going, he was met by the sight of a badly gouged and scorched but wholly intact safe sitting in the middle of a clear spot in the junk piles. Lying around it in total disarray were torch tanks and hoses, levers, bars, pulleys, come alongs, chains, tree trunks, engine blocks . . . and one very tired old man.

Argus raised his head from his boots, but the bloodshot eyes couldn't hide his fierce determination. "Emmitt, I'm going to need a little more room if I'm going to open this thing properly."

Emmitt changed his focus and became aware that Argus was sitting on a pile of small wooden crates marked HIGH EXPLOSIVE and saw a potential public relations problem in the near future.

A good party can never be planned; it either happens or it doesn't. A good one comes of the accidental and magical blend of unrelated people and events that for a few precious hours in history come together in delicious perfection. The big celebration at the Bluff Lodge on Saturday was nothing like that.

Ruby McClay had rounded up Lars Luger and the Irish Polka Band, the perennial occasions group, as entertainment and they were noisily tuning up in the basement. Ruby was tapping a few beer kegs back behind the bar, while casseroles, desserts, and homemade breads came in escorted by various townspeople out for the potluck, the free beer, and any old excuse for a party.

Argus Winslow was down on the beach below the bluff studiously contriving the main event, and the folks wandered over one by one to watch him. It wasn't that they were so interested in the ceremonious opening of the time capsule. Word had already spread on what was in it, and nobody really cared about that. What they wanted to see was the explosion.

Argus was wiring together bundles of dynamite and strapping them to the safe with duct tape. Every few minutes he'd stand back to size up the situation, then grab another bundle, tape it up, or stick it into the sand underneath. The whole time, Emmitt Frank was wringing his hands over by the tow truck and advising against it.

"Isn't that an awful lot of dynamite?"

"Might be." Argus was twisting the rest of the detonator wires together in his hands. "I guess we'll find out soon enough."

Mayor Weekly stood with the small crowd on the edge of the bluff and watched as Argus drove down the beach in the tow truck while Emmitt stood on the rear bumper letting wire off a wooden spool.

The mayor smiled to himself at the sight of twenty-five years of city history sitting in the sand ringed with high explosives, while the devoted community sipped beer and waited for the fireworks.

When Argus waved his arms up in the air, Mayor Weekly stepped back from the edge of the high bluff. "Okay, everybody, he's gonna blow 'er, get back a little bit."

No sooner had he got the words out of his mouth when a deafening thud filled the air. It was the sort of concussion that pushes on your senses and sucks your breath all at the same time. The mayor blinked his eyes open after a pause to gather his wits and looked at several dozen of his fellow citizens wiggling fingers in their ears and working their jaws trying to get the ringing out of their heads.

The mayor pulled out of his own ringing symphony and turned back toward the beach. What he saw at first surprised him, then frightened him, then brought the smile back to his face. Out in the middle of a perfectly round crater in the sand where only moments before had stood the remnants of a quarter century of history was nothing but a little smoke and a bad smell.

The mayor's smile broke into a chuckle, and Ruby McClay started to laugh beside him, and then a few more started in, and pretty soon the whole tribe was laughing and wandering back toward the beer kegs, while a slightly stunned Lars Luger and the Irish Polka Band played a special dedication to this auspicious occasion that appears to have turned to vapor.

And out across town, a shadow formed on a patch of new sand and grew and grew and grew in a blink—and from out of the sun came a whoosh and a thud as dull as old news. And twenty-five years of municipal memory traveling in twelve hundred pounds of wholly intact tempered steel found its way down through a temporary city water line and came to rest on a much-sought-after antique pipe. A pipe that may not have been found in a more logical manner if they had another twenty-five years to work on it.

QUINTON'S CONFUSION

QUINTON Burrell couldn't figure out what was going on, and it worried him. He and Connie had lived here going on a year and it still seemed like they'd just arrived. They felt no more at home now than they had the day they rolled into town in their Volvo station wagon, fresh from their fast-track careers in St. Louis and nearly desperate to get at their "alternative lifestyles" at the End of the Road.

Quinton watched the bank customers coming and going beyond the glass partition of his office with uneasiness. The tellers were all smiles and small talk while the customers milled around pleased and sociable. But there was an undercurrent of tension in the air. Some sort of quiet acknowledgment that there was more here than met the eye. A stolen glance, a conversation bitten off in mid-sentence.

Quinton had been seeing and hearing these confounded signals for days and he was convinced it had something to do with him and Connie. And it wasn't anything good.

Quinton and Connie had finally completed the refinishing of their home and had been trying all week, quite unsuccessfully, to invite a few couples over for a quiet and belated house-warming. Everybody they'd asked had an excuse why they couldn't make it.

When he'd asked Stormy Storbock if he and Kirsten would like to come by for the occasion, the invitation was declined for the good reason that Stormy and Kirsten were finishing the Sheetrock in their own new place that night. Quinton would have accepted the excuse without question if it weren't for some twinge of feeling at the time. Again, something unspoken from Stormy. Almost a sadness or a pity all in a glance. Quinton thought immediately that he knew what it was.

One day months ago, when Quinton saw Stormy in the bank, he'd gone over to do some small-talking—find out how the

home and not eat rather than come visit with two people as spiritually misfit as he and Connie were.

It was proving to be a tough town to make friends in on every front. No matter what they did or who they did it around, they always managed to stick their foot in it somehow. Quinton even got on the wrong side of the fence from Ruby McClay, and that was hard to do.

Ruby is the president of the chamber of commerce, holds a seat on the city council, and is a community booster extraordinaire. There isn't a function within twenty miles or twenty years of here that Ruby hasn't organized or at least attended. So it was an especially painful blow to Quinton when she passed on their housewarming too. Quinton knew it must go back to that first chamber of commerce luncheon they attended when they'd just arrived.

Quinton and Connie wanted to make a good first impression on the business community and they were a little nervous. Being bank manager was an important job in a small town, and Quinton knew that the collective eye was on him.

They sat at the big table up front with Ruby and the mayor, making small talk and trying to find some common ground. Sliced turkey on toast was on the menu that day, and red wine was served in honor of the new manager and his wife.

Quinton was relieved to see the wine being distributed because that was one thing he knew something about. He rolled the wine around in the glass and held it up in front of his face to admire its viscosity.

Ruby watched with concern from across the table. "Is your glass dirty? We'll get you another one."

Quinton apologized with a look. "No, I was just appreciating the wine. Do you know what year this is?"

Ruby looked puzzled at first, then understood. "Oh, it should be pretty fresh. This year, I hope. You can go back in the kitchen and look at the box if you want, maybe it tells you."

Quinton started to explain, then tried to back out with a comment to his wife. "It has an arresting bouquet with a touch of fruitiness that I think you'll find amusing."

It was meant as a compliment, of course, but you'd have to know a little bit more about wine pretensions than Ruby McClay to appreciate it. "If you think the wine's so funny, maybe you should drink your water instead." Ruby wasn't so gruff as she was plainspoken. And Quinton sat through the rest of the luncheon without talking—making grand gestures of silent approval at everything he ate and drank. Right down to the carrot and celery sticks.

Quinton knew in his heart that Ruby did not want to come to the housewarming of pompous yuppie impresarios like them.

Quinton was sitting in his little glass office continuing to puzzle over the situation when the receptionist poked her head in the door. "Argus Winslow called and he wants you to meet him here at five o'clock."

Quinton managed to choke out a "Thank you" before his throat constricted with fear and realization. Argus Winslow had always scared the jeepers out of him. He was a grizzled and creased old man with the disposition of a badger. He was also Quinton's boss in a roundabout way.

Now this whole week made sickening sense to him. Argus was going to fire him. And everybody knew it. That's why nobody would come to their party, and that's what everybody was talking about him behind his back. Quinton's face ran hot with the realization that everybody knew but him. He was a laughingstock. He'd always been a laughingstock to these people. A Harvard MBA who couldn't even hold down a branch manager's position at a bank on the edge of the world because he was such a yuppie jerk. He'd learned everything at Harvard except how to get along with real people.

Quinton spent the rest of the afternoon straightening up his notes and files and avoiding contact with any of the faces beyond the window glass. The staff started trickling out around four-thirty, and by five o'clock Quinton was left alone sitting in an empty and lifeless bank like a condemned prisoner waiting for the footsteps of his executioner.

Quinton smelled his executioner before he saw him. The thick and rugged smell of metal and heavy oil preceded Argus into the office, and Quinton was already looking up at the door as it filled with the imposing form of his soiled director.

Quinton didn't even wait for the word. "Mr. Winslow, I'd like thirty days if you don't mind."

Argus looked at the serious young man behind the desk and tried to make sense of him. "Thirty days? That's a heck of a vacation, but I guess you've earned it if you want it." Argus plopped himself down in a chair and spit some tobacco juice in a potted plant.

"I just came in to tell ya that the directors up in Anchorage think you're doing a swell job, and I wanted to let you know that your probation is up. I know I'm a couple months late on this, but I been forgetting things lately and this one kept slipping by me."

Quinton could only gape. "You mean you're not firing me?"

"Firing you! Jeez Louise, we just got you broke in! Whatsa matter, don'tcha like it around here?"

Quinton straightened in his chair. "No, heck no, I like it fine. I just didn't think things were, well, I didn't think people were, I mean I think I was trying to . . . oh, I don't know—maybe I didn't think."

Argus looked at Quinton and shook his head. Not unkindly, but more like you do at a child who's said something goofy and terribly cute. "Maybe you think too much, Quint. And maybe you try too hard." Argus got up to leave. "I'd better get goin'. I don't want to keep you from your party."

Quinton hesitated. "What party?"

Argus stopped in the doorway and turned around with a wince. "Oops. I forgot and spilled the beans, didn't I? Oh well, I've spilled worse. I guess half the town's over at your house for a surprise housewarming. You better get over there before they tear up all that new wallpaper of yours and carry your wife off."

Argus walked out and left Quinton alone once again in the quiet and lifeless bank with a lot on his mind. For the second time that afternoon, everything made sense. They'd been planning a party all along. That's why nobody accepted their invitations. That explains what all the hush and fuss were about around the bank all week. It all came clear, and it all felt good.

Quinton sat for an extra few minutes and tried to figure these people out. Why they'd go to all this bother for someone like himself, who so far could only manage to amuse or offend them just by being the way he is?

And he could try all day and he could think all night, but only time was going to teach him that what people around here like most about Quinton Burell is that he has such a wonderful knack for just being the way he is.

ARGUS'S HEAVEN

ARGUS pretended to be irritated by the whole adventure, but Ruby could tell he was excited. How could he *not* be? It was his first time on a jet plane and the first time he'd been outside Alaska in over forty years.

He sat in the narrow airline seat huffing and making a big noisy deal out of banging his knees on the seat in front of him. "My God, Ruby, you couldn't stack firewood any tighter 'n this!" He stretched out his broad shoulders, compressing Ruby against the armrest. "Five hundred bucks a ticket, you think they'd let you breathe."

Ruby was born with the patience of a saint, but she'd developed even more than that thanks to her curmudgeonly old goat of a boyfriend Argus Winslow. Especially on this trip. Argus was going down to Seattle to have some more doctors examine him about his memory lapses. They weren't getting any better, and the Anchorage docs were throwing in the towel.

"I banged my head, that's all," Argus would say. "Maybe I oughta just go bang on it again to clear it up."

Argus fooled a lot of people with his reckless attitude but not Ruby. She could see he was scared speechless every time it happened. They never knew when they were coming. Sometimes months would go by without one, then they'd come again out of nowhere. Ruby'd been the one who finally convinced him to go see some specialists outside.

"I'll go if it'll make you feel better," Argus had told her. "Be nice to see what America's done with herself in forty years anyway. But I want you to go along in case I blank out again and forget to come home." Argus was kidding and he wasn't kidding.

When he had one of his lapses, he would suddenly stiffen, with utter confusion boiling in his eyes. He'd look around and

160

everything would be like the first time he saw it. If Ruby was around when it happened, she would gently touch his arm or rub his hand. And she would say, "Come back Argus." And the big, confused brute would come back.

She held on to the big arm of her quiet brute as the jet launched itself down the runway and leaped into the air. The process had gotten Argus's attention and no little bit of his respect. "Criminellie, this thing's got oomph, don't it?"

He was looking out the window, and she had to smile to herself at the boyish look of wonder on his face as he watched the ground disappear below them. All his discomforts were forgotten for the moment, and he could only beam.

Although he never forgave the small seats, Argus continued to be impressed by the airline in every other way. When he found out they served whiskey, he was beside himself with admiration. "Now, that's travelin'."

He teased the flight attendants, joked with Ruby, and when he got his choice for lunch of pepper steak or chicken cordon bleu, he went with the "blue chicken" just because he felt playful.

After about four of the little whiskeys, he put a fresh plug of tobacco in his lip and sat back philosophically. "Twenty-eight thousand feet in the air, the captain said. Can you believe that? Five miles high, eatin' chicken, gettin' drunk—by God, I think I've lived in Alaska too long, Miss Ruby."

Argus looked out the window at the clear, rich blue sky all around them with a thick white comforter of clouds below. "It looks just like heaven," he said, and quietly passed out with his face pressed against the window.

Argus was a little cowed by the crowds at the airport but delighted by the utter immensity of the terminal. "You could build our whole town inside this place." He was talking in his normal tone of voice, which was always about twice as loud as it needed to be and three times louder than people down in the real world were used to. They turned more than a few heads on the way to their bags, and it wasn't because they made such a handsome couple.

Ruby stood him by a post near the baggage carousel while she went for their suitcases. When she returned with their bags, Argus had one hand braced against the post and the other was covering his mouth in that oh-my way of wide-eyed astonishment that could only mean one thing.

"Argus, come back." Ruby held his arm until she saw the light come back to his look.

"Criminellie, that one scared the hell out of me." Argus slumped with relief. "I forgot where we was, and darned if I could make sense of these people chasing suitcases around that merry-go-round. I never seen anything like it before."

"You ain't been down here in forty years, ya daft ol' goat. I think you're gonna find a lot of things you ain't never seen before." Ruby led Argus out to the cab stand. "You stick with me, honey. We'll get that thick head of yours examined and then see what this town's got for a couple old war-horses like us."

Argus about rubbernecked himself to death on the way into the city. It seemed like everything in the world was in motion. The cars were spaced heel to toe and moving faster than Argus's tow truck has traveled in over a decade. He knocked the cab driver in the back of the head twice with his knuckles and told him to slow down. "Take it easy, cowboy. I've lived forty years without this place, I can wait a little while longer."

Ruby tried to explain to her old pioneer that you can't go around knocking strangers on the head like that, but Argus would have none of it. "If somebody's tryin' to get me kilt, I'll knock him any ol' place I want to." He gave his orneriest stink-eye to the young driver. "Ain't that right, cowboy." And there was a silent agreement to Argus's proposal as the cab eased into the right-hand lane and enjoyed a leisurely ride into the big city.

Argus kept waiting for something to become familiar but saw nothing. As the cab picked its way through the massive buildings of glass and brick, Argus grew quiet and still, but his eyes were on the move. First they'd follow the contour of a building up until it disappeared above the cab, then he'd fix on some woman on the street, who he'd follow until an unrecognizable brand of little sports car would break his field of view, and he'd look it over until it sped away or was replaced by some other curious matter or being.

It's important here to note that Argus Winslow was not unaware of the modern world. He was a voracious reader, an accomplished financier, and an admirer of modern gadgets from the space shuttle to frozen dinners. The problem was that, with the exception of frozen dinners, he'd been around very little of the modern world in person except for those parts of it that made their sorry way to the End of the Road and ended up in his junkyard. Seeing it all at once and all on the move unsettled and excited him in ways he hadn't felt in years. Maybe in forty years.

The war was over, and America was putting herself back together. The spirit of the wartime victories had given a momentum to a way of thought that filtered into everybody's attitude, including a young Argus Winslow. America was a land of limitless horizons. A land where young men could set their sights and go and get there—and get theirs. And the American dream was a giggling, playful thing full of bulging, bright-colored cars with good roads to drive them on and all the gas you wanted.

A person could look around and see what wasn't there and make it be there, and he would become rich. It was a time when ambition could run wild and free, with no barriers to hold it but a lack of imagination. All a man needed to know was what he wanted, and the young Argus Winslow knew exactly what he wanted.

He'd spent the war building roads and runways in Alaska, and as soon as he'd been discharged at Fort Lewis, he was down on First Avenue in Seattle spending all his GI pay on his outfit. He didn't know yet what he wanted with Alaska. All he knew was that everything he wanted out of life was in that great land, and he said that without even knowing what it could be. It was that magical time of a young man's life when nothing is spelled out but everything is clear. It was just a matter of picking the direction to go and setting out. They were invulnerable, young men like him. Picking their way up and down First Avenue, putting together their gear. Cocky, mischievous and, most of all, blessed. They were something, they were.

"The world was ours." Argus spoke out loud, not meaning to, and it woke him from his muse.

Ruby looked up from the bed to her tired old friend in the window. She hadn't heard exactly what he said, but it sounded wistful and weary and she took its meaning. "It's not the same world you left, sweetie, but there's parts of it out there. We'll go look around some after your tests tomorrow. So to bed, you old goat." Ruby turned the lamp off and watched the shadow in the windowpane until she fell asleep.

* * *

Argus was none too happy by the time he walked back out into the waiting room at the hospital. Ruby got up to greet him and was startled at his look. "Why, Argus Winchester Winslow, I believe you're blushing!"

Argus grumbled and reached into a pocket for his tobacco. "This place could make a dog blush. Hell, they could make a *politician* blush."

"What did the doctors say?" Ruby had to scramble to keep behind her man, who didn't even break his stride on the way through the reception area.

"First he said, 'Bend over,' and I says, 'The problem's on the other end, doc,' and he says, 'Bend over anyway,' and they got some kinda Roto-Rooter with a headlight on it, well— never mind. Then they strapped me in this thing looks like a nuclear reactor with a pillow in it and turn me around and upside down takin' pictures of my insides, and then I looked at lights and answered their fool questions about things that's none of their business, and then they sit me down and tell me I got a torn and sheared-off white-lateral sidewall hokus-pokus something or other, and they wanna drill a hole in my head with no promise they can fix it. My God, I need a whiskey."

Ruby knew her boyfriend well enough to see when he was scared, and she knew to leave this alone for now. "Well, let's go down to this First Avenue of yours and see if we can scare up some action."

Another mad cab ride with only one set of knuckles to the driver's head found our couple standing on First Avenue and Argus roaming around like a dog sniffing corner posts. "This is it, Ruby. I recognize some of these buildings, and *there*— look at that one!" Argus pointed down the hill toward the peaked roof of Smith Tower, the old Seattle landmark. "That was the highest building anywhere around when I was here last. You can hardly pick it out of the crowd now, but it was a handsome sight long before that Space Needler thing ever got put up."

They walked arm in arm, with Argus pointing out this or that thing he thought he remembered. They stopped for a drink at an old tavern. Argus could swear he'd been in before, and soon they were sitting on an iron bench on red-bricked Union Square and Argus knew he'd been there before.

The gas lamps, the bricked buildings and pigeons and the

throaty howl of a ship's horn leaving port. Ruby fed the pigeons popcorn and Argus looked down into the old red bricks. Bricks that had carried swifter feet than his were now, with a younger heart beating hard at the sound of the ship's horn. A horn full of promises for a young man. Promises for a lifetime. Or at least forty years. Promises that were kept. He'd done all he'd set out to do and more. Everything he ever wanted out of life was in that great land, and he'd found it all.

"Argus, come back." Ruby was touching his arm and rubbing his hand.

Argus looked at her and took hold of her fingers with a gentle squeeze. "Oh, I wasn't forgetting this time, Ruby. I was remembering." Argus stood up and lifted her with a gesture. "We've done all we can here. Let's go back where we belong."

Argus made no fuss on the airplane this time. He was strangely courteous, almost tame. Ruby had asked him only one time what he'd decided to do about his medical problem, and he'd said, "I decided to go home." The matter was closed for now. She saw that plainly, and she would never mention it again.

He made no remarks on takeoff, but when they broke through the overcast into the clear blue day of altitude, he touched her sleeve.

"I always loved going to Alaska." It was said almost sadly, and he let his chair back.

Argus stared out the window and Ruby read a magazine. She wondered what went through the old coot's head sometimes, and she worried a little, but not a whole lot.

She looked over at him and saw his attention fixed on the rich blue sky all around them with a thick comforter of clouds below, and his eyes were boiled with confusion. She started to reach for his arm to bring him back but pulled up short. The bewilderment in his eyes wasn't so much a panic as it was a surprise, and the look of it made Ruby glad for the moment. *It looks just like heaven*, he'd said.

And Ruby sat back and looked at the face of her friend, letting him believe everything he saw. Even if it wasn't real and even if it wasn't familiar, it was a place he deserved to be for at least a little while longer.

JOE'S CUP

JOE Miller waved to his buddies standing up on the cannery dock and took another hitch in his posture. He was standing alongside the pilothouse holding on to a mast stay of Lars Luger's big bottom trawler, the *Debi Jean*. Standing in his oilskins, with the light harbor breeze blowing at his hair and the weighty chug of a marine diesel urging them out to sea, Joe appeared just about as nautical as a person possibly could. He watched his friends looking after him to the stern and he felt arrogant, adventuresome, accomplished—and scared to death.

Joe Miller had never been on a vessel bigger than a rowboat in his life. And here he was a licensed commercial deckhand heading out into the perilous waters of Alaska with a German-Norwegian maniac for a skipper, and not the faintest idea what to expect.

He'd been after this job for months. Ever since he'd arrived in town after his miserable trip hitchhiking from Wisconsin. It was the trip that turned his head toward the sea for no good reason he knew of other than he was getting tired of the shore.

Joe had tried to get work on the oil-spill cleanup, to no avail, and had ended up working at the fish cannery and cold storage instead. Cannery work was okay. For a twenty-one-year-old college student on leave from Wisconsin, it even had its exotic moments. But skinning fish and jamming them into cans reached its romantic limitations soon enough even for Joe.

Joe first got the notion he wanted to try fishing by seeing the fishermen around the cannery. The boat skippers walked as gods among them. The deck crews, though not divinity, were at least royalty and they carried themselves as such among lowly dock and line workers like Joe. Joe studied their cocksureness and painfully noted the attention they commanded from the young women around the plant. It was rumored they

166

made thousands of dollars per trip, and standing on the dock watching them unload their holds placed an ache in Joe's heart and pocket that could not be quenched by cannery work.

Finding a position on a salmon seiner in this summer of the oil spill proved impossible. Every time the fleet was in town, Joe would walk the harbor docks asking after positions on the crews. There was nothing. The oil spill had fouled up most of the salmon openings in the area, and what boats were still fishing certainly had no lack of available crew and no apparent interest in a greenhorn from Wisconsin.

But Joe was diligent. He had nothing to lose but face, and being there was very little face to packing fish in the first place, he kept on his rounds of the docks, figuring sooner or later somebody would hire him just to get it over with.

And that's pretty much what happened. Lars Luger had offered him a job toward the end of summer, but not on his seine crew. He needed another guy for his flounder-dragging crew later in the year.

"Flounder?" Joe received the offer with mixed feelings. "What do you do with flounder?"

"I catch 'em an' sell 'em to people who eat 'em. Come time, I'll find you." Lars was a man of few words but true to every one of them, and one day months later, he walked up behind Joe in the Lame Moose Saloon. "Well, you goin' fishin' or ain't you?"

Heading out to sea on a flounder dragger didn't have near the maritime allure as, say, a yankee whaler, or even a halibut schooner might've had, but you wouldn't know it by Joe Miller. After the *Debi Jean* was out of the harbor and into the green tossing water around the point, Rudy, the other deckhand, went inside. Lars was up in the bridge at the wheel, and Joe stayed out on deck. He huddled against the back of the house, out of the chill wind, and studied the rigging.

He'd been helping Lars and Rudy rig the boat for dragging for two weeks, and he still didn't understand it. Lars was big on orders and short on explanation. The experienced Rudy had little to say either. Rudy was a professional, and although he was pleasant enough, it was clear that he considered crewing with a greenhorn a bruise to his integrity and he wouldn't be on this crummy trip at all if salmon season had panned out like it could have.

Nobody had revealed anything to Joe about the mysteries of dragging for flounder. They'd only told him what to lift, what to pull on, and which wrench to fetch.

It wasn't enough for Joe, but it would have to do. And it *would* do, because the vagaries and vulgarisms of life on a fishing boat would reveal themselves to Joe soon enough.

The first thing he was to discover was that Lars Luger, the quiet giant and lovable leader of a terrible and terribly popular local polka band, was in fact a seagoing megalomaniac with the sensitivity of an anchor winch.

Once they'd gotten around the point, the sea came up on them a little and the high, cold rolling green water made Joe a little nervous out on deck by himself. He came in from the chill and sat at the galley table leafing through magazines, not knowing if it would be proper to go up to the wheelhouse and join Lars and Rudy. He decided it would be if he took coffee up with him, and he did just that.

When he handed Lars the cup, the old sea dog took a look at it, opened the pilothouse window, and dumped it out.

"That's not my cup." He talked without taking his eyes off the sea and handed the mug back to Joe. Rudy was studying a chart, pretending to be oblivious to the scene, so Joe went back to the galley for another stab at it.

There were a half a dozen identical mugs swinging on hooks above the stove, and Joe picked one that for no good reason looked right to him. He took it up to Lars again, and again he dumped it out the window. "That ain't my cup either."

Joe was bewildered. "I don't know which cup is yours."

"I can tell," was all Lars said, and handed the empty mug back.

Joe returned to the galley, sat down at the table for a few minutes to think this over, and decided to be seasick instead. It wasn't a violent sort of seasickness. It was more of a hypnotic state. A head-swimmy sort of nauseous dream that would last several days and beg for sanity. But there was to be little sanity on Lars Luger's boat.

That night, after they'd anchored up in a protected cove, Joe was helping Rudy coil some cable out on deck. He was whistling a merry tune to cover up the fact that he was ill when Lars stormed onto the deck.

"Who's that whistling on my boat!" He stood glaring down at Joe, who didn't need to answer. "There's four things you never do on a boat. You never whistle, you never take a woman on board, you never make pea soup, and you never leave port on a Friday."

Joe faced his skipper, terrified and mystified, but he found his tongue. "But today is Friday."

"It is?" Lars face softened to puzzle for just an instant, then snapped back in place. "Sometimes you leave port on Friday, but never with a woman or pea soup, and you *never whistle*. It's bad luck!"

Lars went back in the house while Joe stood in the stupor that was to be his constant companion for the next four days.

The mysteries of dragging for flounder were cleared up for Joe in very short order the following morning. It consisted of being woken up by the insane scream of an 871 Detroit Diesel motor being fired off about three feet from his head. The resulting panic and dive for the ladder up out of the fo'c'sle is what set the pace for the rest of the day.

The actual fishing is a less than scientific process, which basically entails dragging a huge sock across the bottom of the ocean and scooping up whatever is not smart enough or fast enough to get away. Joe was delighted to see that flounder were apparently leaders among the dumber and slower sea life. Every bag that came to the surface and swung onto the deck was plugged full of flounder. It kept him and Rudy almost too busy to think as they got each set out of the net, put it back in the water, and went about weeding through the catch and shoveling it into the hold.

It was a giddy sort of labor. Seeing fish rising in nets from the ocean triggered something in Joe. When they'd pop the belly of the net open and the fish would fill the deck to their knees, still flipping, Joe would grin spontaneously. Sometimes he'd whoop or laugh in some vicious way and a new energy would take him over. He could see the cheer on Rudy's face, and even the berserk skipper at the winch showed signs of momentary goodwill toward earth.

It was something primal happening, and Joe found himself caught up with it. Little was said, because little needed to be said. An octopus came up with one load and Rudy told Joe to grab it before it got itself all wrapped around something. Joe had never had occasion to grab a large live octopus before, but he did anyway, and it was soon uncertain which one had a hold of the other.

Joe got progressively more worried as the slimy little suckers found their way onto his rain gear and attached themselves with impossibly hardy grips. He had two tentacles around his waist, one on each shoulder, one in each hand, and he didn't even want to think about where the other two were heading.

"Stop dancing with that thing and kill it." Rudy sounded impatient, but he might as well have ordered him to float in the air like a red balloon for all the notion Joe had about how to do it.

Finally Rudy stepped over, reached his hand up into the octopus, grabbed its beak, and yanked it inside out as smoothly as somebody'd do to a pants leg. He pinched some inside part of the critter between his fingers. It went immediately limp and pale and fell, dead, to the deck.

"They hate that," Rudy said, and went back to work.

The next few days were to be the most exciting of Joe's life. Although his head never did clear completely, he tuned himself to the rhythm of the rolling deck and worked effortlessly. His legs grew to the sea, and it freed his hands to do their job. He learned the knots by watching, and how to gaff a conger eel without getting bitten and how to hold a ratfish without getting poked or grab a crab without getting worried or pinched. He eventually learned the octopus trick and actually looked forward to seeing one mixed in with the catch. He could grab it by the beak, snap it open while he turned, and it would be dead in midair on its way to the hold pen Lars was filling with next year's halibut bait.

The whole while, the calm and efficient scuffling of a good crew permeated through the boat and occupied their minds and kept a watchful skipper with a critical eye quiet and satisfied.

Lars said very little. He'd come back to look at the fish after every haul and comment without explanation: "They're deeper"; "We're into a crab ground, we better move"; "The tide's turned them around." And Joe wouldn't know how he knew these things or why one spot on the ocean seemed better to Lars than another, but boy could that old lunatic catch fish.

It was the third day, or maybe the fourth, when they capped off the hold. It was dark and they brought the last set of the day in under the deck lights. It was one of the fullest bags yet. The rigging groaned, and the boat listed dangerously as the fish were hauled over the rail. As Rudy and Joe tossed and shoveled them into the hatch combing, Lars came back and looked it over.

"Well, boys, we better quit before we sink 'er." And it was as if a plug was pulled and all the strain on board drained into the sea from where it came. Like a cable gone slack, Joe looked up into the face of his captain, and his captain looked back. And it was a look that men pass between them at rare times in their lives. It is a look of sureness and gratitude, and of something so precious and scarce that it can have no value put on it. It was a look of shared respect for what they had and for what they'd done and for each other.

Late that night Joe sat his wheel watch alone in the darkness. The moon was clear and dead on their course as it laid a path of gold before them. Joe watched the compass and thought of their arrival at the cannery in the morning.

His buddies would be there to see them arrive with the deck on the waterline and the hold covers bulging with cargo. There was nothing more perfect in this world than a boat full of fish, and Joe was not just admiring it. This time he owned a piece of it. Whatever that bad dream was he'd been having, it was over. And strangely, he remembered very little of it.

Lars startled him when he came up behind Joe and nudged him with a mug of coffee. Joe took it and Lars held his and the old salt's craggy face shone amber in the compass light.

Joe thought a moment, then took a chance. "Is this my cup?"

Lars thought a moment too, and though his stony features didn't soften, his eyes seemed to as he checked their heading and answered. "Yeah," he said. "I think that's your cup."

YOUNG BUCKS

AS soon as Norman's feet hit the snowy beach, he didn't want to be there anymore. Deer hunting with his dad seemed like the stuff that dreams are made of when he'd been asked along weeks ago, but he was having a change of heart. There's something about the look of thin wet snow on a gray November beach that makes a young person wish he were back home curled into a warm spot on the sofa in front of a *Star Trek* rerun. Or better yet, on the phone making up to a disenchanted girlfriend.

"Grab the tent and the rifles, Norman. We'll camp just inside those trees." Norman's dad walked ahead with a pack slung across each shoulder. Uncle Stu was taking some other bags and bundles out of the skiff and laying them in a neat pile on the beach.

Norman looked out to their fishing boat, looking so familiar and warm, anchored peacefully in this protected little bay. "Uncle Stu, why can't we sleep on the boat?"

His uncle understood but challenged him with a smile. "The key to deer hunting is to go where the deer are, my good man. The deer are in the woods, not the water. Grab those rifles like your dad said. The sooner we get situated, the sooner we can get a fire goin'."

Norman followed his dad's footprints up the beach into the trees and tried to look forward to something.

It was a great honor to be along on this excursion. His dad and Uncle Stu had been coming over for this deer hunt on Stridelof Island every year since he could remember. They would always come back three days or a week later with whiskers on their faces and deer strung up the mast, hanging proud like scalps on a warrior's lance.

Norman had only a passive attraction to hunting. He'd done in his fair share of birds and squirrels around the neighborhood with his pellet gun, and two years ago he and Stanley Bindel had actually brought down a rabbit with Stanley's twenty-two. But there was no real passion to it, only that strange boyish fascination with killing things that Norman had never quite fathomed. Not that he'd spent a great deal of time thinking about it.

Norman's interest in hunting grew a hundredfold last spring, when his dad presented him with the thirty-thirty lever action Winchester he'd hunted with for years.

It was a bush-beaten old club of a rifle, but it was a real rifle, it worked, and it was his. He'd gone out to the gravel pit with his dad to target practice several weekends through the summer and had even become a passable shot.

Norman had pounded two big nails into his bedroom wall, where the rifle had hung importantly ever since. He liked the look of it. He liked what it could do. He didn't really know why he did. Again, it was just that baffling masculine fetish for the matters and means of destruction.

Norman ran the cleaning rod in and out of the barrel and watched as his dad stirred the stew pot over the fire. He took a sip from the spoon and cocked an eye as his tongue analyzed the result. "Normy, you're about to get your first taste of my world-famous camp stew."

"You'll soon discover why your mother does all the cooking around your house." Uncle Stu leaned back against his tree and winked at Norman through the smoke. Norman only grinned back and continued cleaning his rifle.

He was feeling better about things. The stew smelled fine, the tent was pitched, and the fire had already taken away most of his chill and all of his apprehension.

Campfires have a powerful narcotic effect on even the most reluctant campers. They're like nature's own Movie Channel. The flames stroke our eyes and spellbind our imaginations. Indiscriminate pops and wheezes hold us in suspense while the smoky heat rubs our hands and feet until we're called for dinner. And it always tastes good. There is nothing you can cook on a campfire that won't taste good if you're in the mood.

"This stew tastes worse than last year's." Uncle Stu was taking a big drink from his tin cup.

"Couldn't, it *is* last year's." Norman's dad sat on his haunches and talked to the fire.

Norman just ate his stew and listened. He loved the way grown men teased each other. They sounded so serious all the time, never laughing out loud or taking offense. Seeing the faces of his dad and uncle lit in the fire glow and listening to them jive each other gave him some sort of grand feeling he didn't want to interrupt. It was a sense of security. Maybe even intimacy.

With nothing but the wide world of autumn all around, the fire put them in the same small room together. He saw his gun glimmering at his side, and a sense of irrepressible . . . *manliness* came over him. Norman sat and heard the men and poked the fire, and he was glad he came.

Norman woke to the loud blue luminescence of a nylon tent in the bright sunshine. He was alone in his sleeping bag between two big empty bags, and he scrambled out into the morning. Uncle Stu was tending to a huge cast-iron pan sitting in the fire. In it, a solid inch of boiling oil floated an armada of eggs and bacon. A pot of coffee steamed away on a flat rock to the side, and the smell of it all on top of the fine morning was a glorious thing.

The gray despondency of the day before was lost to the blue sky and low-slung November sun that silhouetted their boat still at anchor off the beach and brought steam off the rocks and gravel, and warmed Norman more by its sheer look than anything he felt.

Uncle Stu looked up from his greasy work at the fire. "Good mornin', buckaroo. Soon's your ol' man gets back we'll have us some of this fine camp breakfast. It'll stick to your ribs all day—that is if it don't slip right through you."

Norman laced up his boots, tucked himself in, and wandered off into the trees for his morning business. When he returned to camp, his father was back, and dishing out the dripping eggs and bacon into three tin plates.

"These are what we call sliders." His dad handed over a plate to Norman. "You don't have to chew 'em, you can just suck 'em down."

Norman smiled at the thought and enjoyed his breakfast more than he had enjoyed one in a long time.

The men talked as they ate. Norman's dad had been scouting the trails and he had a plan. "There's nothing in the lower clearing, but they're around. Stu, I think you and I should head up on top from east and west and let Norman stand the clearing. They might head through there on their own, but if we jump some up top, they'll come in for sure."

Norman didn't know exactly what they were talking about, but he was pleased to be a part of the plan and anxious to get started.

"You might be sittin' a long time today, bub." Norman's dad stuffed a day pack with a thermos of coffee, some candy bars, and a wool blanket.

Norman followed Uncle Stu's lead and loaded his rifle, careful to leave the chamber empty like his dad had taught him. "Never leave a round in the chamber, and never pull the trigger until you're sure of your shot." He'd heard it a hundred times, and he was pretty sure he knew what it meant.

The weight of that responsibility felt good hanging on Norman's shoulder as he marched up the trail between the older men. All the talking stopped as soon as they left camp, and nobody needed to announce that they were hunting now.

He could see his dad's walk change. His feet landed differently, smoothly, and his hands reached out and guided branches and twigs quietly around him. Norman assumed the seriousness of the moment and he tried to ape his dad's movements.

Every so often the elder Tuttle would stop and look at some droppings or tracks on the path, and Norman would watch Uncle Stu searching through the brush and trees for signs of deer. It was very exciting, and Norman could feel the adrenaline pumping in his chest and his own attention riveting itself to the forest.

It was as if his natural senses were being colored brighter than they were. He was tuned to things. He could see a squirrel run up a tree trunk far, far away just because he was looking. He'd jump and wince at the scolding of other squirrels they passed by. He knew their position was being broadcast through the woods. As quiet as they were trying to be, he knew they must sound like a Mardi Gras parade to the deer who live in this peace all the time.

"This is where you'll roost, bub." Norman's dad talked in a low voice and pointed to a log lying in the tall brown weeds that made up the edge of a pocket meadow. They'd climbed a considerable ways and had reached a benchland. "This is where they like to come sometimes. You sit here and watch. If you see your buck, take the shot, but be patient, we'll work our way up each side of the ridge and see what's up there."

His dad gave him one long look that Norman couldn't read, but it felt fine, and he stood still in the gathering silence as the two men split and headed in different directions. The spare fall woods seemed to swallow them up as soon as they'd gone. He could mark their progress for a little while by the occasional chattering squirrel, but even that was soon lost to the drip-dropping of yesterday's light snow being chased off the trees by the sun.

It was as quiet as a day in the woods could be, and Norman searched through it with his eyes and ears for anything of note. There was the sporadic little clump of a spruce cone falling. The tick of little birds busying themselves with whatever it is little birds do. And most of all there was nothing. Some dripping snow and nothing at all.

Suddenly chilled from holding still, Norman unpacked his blanket and wrapped it around himself. He poured some steaming coffee, which he didn't particularly enjoy, but the company of it was good. He held his rifle between his knees and peered through the weeds. It became immediately apparent that deer hunting was a lonely business.

Norman didn't know how long he'd sat there. He hadn't been asleep. He knew that for sure. But he hadn't actually been awake either. Wherever Norman had been he hadn't been watching the meadow, because when next he noticed it, he wasn't the only thing in it anymore.

Right in front of him, not fifty feet away, stood a young buck indifferently rubbing its backside against an old tree trunk. Norman's heart leapt into his throat, and his rifle found its way up into both hands and lay across his legs. His first instinct was not the hunter's reflex, though, but the child's curiosity.

Norman smiled at the sight of a deer scratching its butt. It wasn't quite the picture he held of this noble beast. He'd envisioned a big-chested animal full of defiance, showing its proud antlers atop a grassy knoll in perfect outline against a scenic mountain backdrop. That's how they looked in *Outdoor Life*.

They weren't all leaned over into a fallen tree with a lip curled back in the exquisite pain of getting an itch scratched. And this one didn't have any antlers at all to speak of. Only a couple little forks. *This is just a boy deer*, Norman thought.

Suddenly the deer sprang to a position like it had been called. Norman watched, fascinated with this bird's-eye view of a wild animal's private moments. Without provocation the young buck leapt into the air, lowered its head, and charged the log he'd been scratching. His head hit with a hollow thud, and he staggered back a step or two before regaining his posture.

He was playing a silly game of battle with himself, and Norman's giggle slipped out before he could catch it. The deer sprang to attention again, and this time fixed its gaze square on Norman. Norman looked at the deer and the deer looked at Norman. A long look that Norman couldn't read, but somehow it felt fine. Two young bucks in the woods with nothing to do.

Everything was cut short by a sound like thunder, then another like it. They rolled down from the ridge and echoed through the woods. It froze the moment with a grim sense of purpose.

Dad and Uncle Stu, Norman thought. *They must have found something*. He stood up without thinking and the young deer bolted across the meadow away from him. Before Norman thought of anything for sure, he snapped the lever open and shut on his rifle, ramming a round into the chamber. The sound of it stopped the young buck in his tracks, and he looked back over his shoulder at Norman.

And Norman looked at him. Only this time it was through one eye down the barrel. It was a long look that Norman couldn't read, but it didn't feel so fine and it didn't feel so right. And he didn't know who was pulling on the trigger, but the gun jumped in his hand and left him and the deer standing in the inflated silence that a rifle shot leaves. A sound like a chord on a church organ. *Never pull the trigger unless you're sure of your shot*, his dad had said a hundred times.

And for a long and heavenly moment, Norman had missed. He looked at the deer and the deer looked at Norman. Then Norman saw the hole and his breath fell out of him.

The deer broke off his gaze without turning. He just stopped seeing. And he sat on his butt as his forelegs began to wobble with the two forked horns falling through the weeds. The blood drained from Norman's face as quickly as it did from the deer's heart, and their heads hit the ground together.

Two young bucks in the woods, with nothing to do.

FRITZ'S RETURN

MAYOR Richard Weekly drove the sign down into the heart of the greasy beach with the back of a shovel, and an old man four thousand miles away woke up and listened to the night.

The small gathering of volunteers on the Eden Cove beach cleanup effort applauded the quotation that had been painted on the plywood sign in spilled crude oil. The mayor collected his thoughts and breath to speak.

"We're here this evening as concerned citizens of the area to devote ourselves to the voluntary cleanup of Eden Cove. This beach has been special to many of us in our little town across the bay. Most especially for the man who made this quotation the motto of our city newspaper for over forty years, and pointed at a way to live for most of us here at the End of the Road. I hereby dedicate this effort to Fritz Ferguson's dearly departed wife, Meridith, whom he met and courted on this very beach and whose ashes rest here under this big mess, and to our simply departed friend Fritz, who couldn't bear to see this happen to our cove. Fritz and Meridith, this is for you." Mayor Weekly took one more thoughtful look at the sign, then grabbed his shovel. "Let's get to work on this mess."

An old man four thousand miles away rubbed his temples and saw the light come on in the hallway. The door space filled with a tent-size flannel nightgown with a woman's head in the middle.

"Uncle Fritz, we heard you stir. Are you all right? Would you like your sleep medicine?"

Fritz Ferguson sat in the shadow of his sister's oldest girl and held on to his knees. "No, I'm fine. A dream woke me, is all."

The big head moved back and forth in the doorway. "Fritz, you're going to have to just forget about that awful place. I swear, you worry me half to death sometimes."

Fritz lay back down and said nothing. The room brightened slightly as she stepped down the hall, then went agreeably dark with the click of a switch. He heard the floorboards of the old farmhouse groan back into a comfortable place after the woman found her way back to bed, and he listened to the still-unfamiliar sounds of an Illinois night.

A Great Plains wind moved through like static. A constant rush of noise with no peaks or valleys. Just the occasional interruption of a barn door banging or a train sternly commanding attention out across the endless fields.

Fritz sighed into his pillow like he had every night for the last six months and tried to clear his head of all thoughts of home. *Home.* He'd tried to stop calling it that. But it was no use. Even though he'd grown up on this farm and slept his first twenty years in this very room, his real home was still at the other end of four thousand miles of road.

He'd thought he could leave it. After Meridith had passed away, he thought he would live there until he died himself. But after the oil spill hit Eden Cove, he knew it would kill him to stay.

Coming back to the family farm was his only option, and it was clearly not working out. Most everybody he knew had died or moved away themselves, and those who were left he didn't know anymore. His only sister had died three years ago, and he hadn't seen his niece since she was a little girl. It was odd to live in this house with her and her husband.

Everyone was nice enough, but they treated him like some renegade old man who had finally come to his senses and returned home. As if his fifty-three years in Alaska were some kind of adolescent lark he'd been on. His dear gone wife was typically referred to in conversation as "that native girl of Fritz's" and every time he had a pain or a quirk, they tried to drag him off to a doctor or give him medicine.

They'd discouraged him from watching the evening news ever since the oil-company announcement that it was stopping the cleanup effort in September whether it was clean or not. It had enraged Fritz so much that they'd bought him sleep medicine. He'd even taken it on a few occasions, just to calm the storm of anger that had become so familiar in him.

Fritz lay in his bed and tried to talk to Meridith. The effort led to remembrances, and the memory of a motto lay before him in newsprint like it had for forty years. And before Fritz fell asleep again, it came clear what he had to do.

Mayor Weekly leaned on his shovel and tried to figure what two days' work had accomplished. It was unnervingly hard to see, but it was there. A line of volunteers with shovels and buckets huddled over their grimy work passing portions of rocks to the screen crew to be sorted for cleaning. All but the finest gravel was cleaned in the homemade rock washers with pressure sprayers then laid back down.

Basically, the top twelve inches of beach was being dug up, washed, and put back down. It was tedium to the point of lunacy, but there were no lunatics here. These were people intent on proving that the impossible could be done. And that the unspeakable be shouted from the treetops. *These beaches could be cleaned*. The mayor bent back to his work and thought of the meeting that had brought them all here.

It was at the Big Garage on Clear Shot the day the oil company announced its plan to cease all cleanup activity on September 15 and call it a job well done—at least done—even though state environmental agencies had not signed off a single mile of the nearly eight hundred miles of spoiled beaches. It was a heated meeting.

The oil-company representatives did little but quote chapter and verse from their own policies as to what constituted a "treated" beach.

"You guys float up to a beach and throw money at it and you say it's been cleaned." Ruby McClay was giving her twenty-nine cents' worth. "You're running a public-relations campaign, not a cleanup effort. Every time a TV crew shows up, you've got people in little rubber suits everywhere, and as soon as they go away, you lay 'em off. If the average American on the street knew half of what you're doing here, they'd tear you apart at the seams."

The oil rep sat at the front of the room with his arms folded and a look of counterfeit concern on his face. Like a person does when he's being bawled out by a drunk person or scolded by a child.

Tamara Dupree, who'd been sitting off to one side in a low simmer, suddenly boiled out of her chair.

"You fat, smug two-faced pipeline-sucking parasite!"

The whole room shrank back a foot or two. The oilman didn't budge. Only cocked one eye, like a gunfighter being called out. Tamara got a loose grip on herself and continued.

"Your company has measured the progress of this cleanup in dollars instead of results, and most of those dollars have gone right back into your own pockets. Isn't it true that successful cleanup techniques and solutions have been abandoned and kept quiet if they did not utilize products manufactured by your corporation?" Tamara didn't wait for a response.

"Isn't it true that workers who tried to do a good job on the beaches were fired? Isn't it true that you are doing everything you can to demonstrate the ineffectiveness of further cleanup so that the coast guard will let you go home? And isn't it true that some beaches do not even appear on your contaminated list? Isn't it true that you never had any intentions of cleaning up this oil?"

A vein appeared on the oilman's forehead, but his voice retained its professional cool. "These are serious allegations, young lady. I would like to see proof of any of it."

"What about the cleanup in Eden Cove?"

The oilman looked at some papers in front of him. "I show no Eden Cove as being contaminated by oil from this incident."

Tamara looked satisfied now. "There's your proof! Eden Cove is covered with crude. It's a dead beach!"

The oilman made a motion as if sorting through his papers. "I have no record of it." He looked up at Tamara with a cold corporate glare. A power so self-important it invents reality at its whim. The face of unchallenged authority.

Tamara's nostrils flared and her body had just begun its forward motion to challenge the face of authority, or at least rearrange it, when Bud Koenig shot up to the front.

"You know, I just had a thought." The sound of Bud's perpetually reasonable voice in this unreal situation caught the attention of all. Tamara of flared nostrils lost a beat in her charge, and Bud seized the moment further.

"I've been thinking that we've had nothing but trouble ever since these oil guys came to town to work on this cleanup. The town got split right in two. Some people made money, and others got nothing. We've got every state and federal agency in the phone book tripping all over each other's regulations so bad that nobody can hardly think straight. One group tells the oil guys to send in a hundred workers to some beach, and another group says, 'Yeah, but don't pee in the woods or lean on any trees or make too much noise,' and then we all yell and scream 'cause the oil company's not getting anything done just like it could if it wanted to."

Bud took a breath to make sure he still had the floor, and he did. "Tell me why we want this to go on. We should be driving 'em to the airport and giving out free tickets. Let 'em go home. They're tired of us and we're tired of them. And I'm tired of hearing all this complaining. If you want something done right, you gotta do it yourself. I say we pick a beach and clean it. Then the next time something like this comes around, we can show 'em how it's done."

The mayor continued his absent shoveling and became aware that his back was starting to hurt. He didn't know how much longer he could keep on it. He watched Tamara Dupree struggle with a wheelbarrow full of cleaned gravel across the beach and curse out loud when it dumped over onto the sticky rocks again.

Bud Koenig was underneath the homemade rock washer, adjusting a steam fitting with a wrench. Ruby McClay, with nothing to do while waiting for the repair, stood nearby looking blank and slightly overwhelmed in her gooey brown-streaked rubber rain gear, which had recently been yellow.

Argus Winslow was out in a skiff checking the moorings on the containment boom that caught any oil their operation might be flushing back into the water. He was pulling hard on something that wasn't cooperating, and a string of unrecognizable oaths and threats came across the water.

The mayor heaved a deep sigh, rubbed his back, and was about to sink into a weary posture of surrender when another boat on the water caught his eye.

It was a small skiff coming fast and straight from town. There was a lone figure in it wearing bright new safety-orange rain gear. *Probably another state inspector making sure we don't go to the bathroom in the wrong spot.*

Mayor Weekly turned his back to it. Everybody was used to frequent visits from officials, media, and well-wishers, and nobody paid any attention to the new arrival until they heard the harsh scrape of aluminum on gravel.

All eyes in Eden Cove were fixed in astonishment at the figure in the orange rain gear, but he wasn't looking back at them. A road-weary old man stepped from the skiff. While trying to find his feet underneath him, he kept his eyes glued with amazement on the plywood sign stuck in the middle of everything with crude and familiar letters streaked across the face.

The mayor scurried over the slippery rocks, worried that the old man was about to fall. "Fritz Ferguson! My Lord, what are you doing back here?" Mayor Weekly held one of Fritz's arms and could only stammer on. "Gosh, it's good to see you. You look great. No, actually, you look awful. Are you tired? Can I get you anything?"

Fritz regained his balance and his wind, and he smiled a warm old smile as he removed the assisting hand from his sleeve. "Yes, Richard, you can get me something. You can get me a shovel."

And Fritz Ferguson strode up the beach to enthusiastic greetings from his old friends and gave a passing nod to the smeared quotation that had served as his standard of journalistic integrity all his professional life. A two-hundred-year-old quote he'd dug up one day long ago in a dusty old book of writings from a British statesman and man of conscience.

It was just a small gathering of words that still rang true and clean and proper:

The only thing necessary for the triumph of evil is for good men to do nothing.

And they rang to the tune made by the busy shovels of a small gathering of people who'd just caught their second wind for a long and dirty job.

ED'S RIDE

IT all started late Thursday morning at the bank. Tamara Dupree was on her way in. Fanny Olmstead was on her way out. And Ed Flannigan was caught in the middle. It was one of those awkward doorway jam-ups that at their very worst leave somebody slightly off stride for a moment and are never given another thought. Seldom does having too many people in a bank doorway change the course of friendships or the way things are. But the gods must have been smiling on Ed that Thursday like they hadn't been in a while.

He had the door open and was about to walk in when he saw Fanny in front of him and became aware of someone on his heels. He turned, saw Tamara, and politely tried to stand aside and grab the door with his other hand. Unfortunately, he'd forgotten that he didn't have another hand anymore, and the door swung into the side of his head.

The bang in the noggin didn't hurt nearly as much as the strain on the stump of his right arm as it involuntarily wagged in the air as it would have if the rest of it were attached and trying to rub his head. The muscles were still pretty sore and he tried not to move it around too much, but he hadn't gotten control of these reflex actions yet. It still hadn't gotten all the way through Ed's thick head that he was one short in the arm department.

It was the first time Tamara or Fanny had seen Ed since the accident in September. Of course they both knew that Ed had lost his arm, but he hadn't been exactly parading it around town since he got out of the hospital. Neither one could help but gape at the empty coat sleeve that waved in front of them.

Fanny quickly looked away and brought a hand to her mouth to stifle whatever she might have been about to say. Her face burned with embarrassment, and maybe even shame, for Ed as she stood stock-still, completely crossed up as to what to do next.

Tamara, for her part, only looked away long enough to take control of the door, then she studied the curious hollow sleeve until Ed reached over to hold it still with his other hand. Tamara then looked at Ed's face just in time to catch the essence of the whole episode.

It passed in a flash, but before Ed could put the lid over it, Tamara got a glimpse of the pain. And not just pain from a knock upside the head or a healing ligament, but the deep pain of confusion and hopelessness. And there was a glimmer of rage and a measure of sorrow and a buried lonesome fear that almost poured out at their feet before Ed caught it all and stuffed it back inside.

If Tamara had looked away for an instant, she'd have missed it like Fanny did. When Fanny looked back to Ed, his face had reconstructed that sheepishly lovable Flannigan grin that said a shrug and a yuk and a how-do-you-do, like the world was a grand and funny business.

"Well thank you, kind ladies, for the dance. We better break it up before your husbands get jealous." And Ed moved out into the cool day with a masculine swagger that looked just the slightest bit impaired. The left arm swung long and low, and the right side just dangled without form or purpose or rhythm.

Fanny pulled her hand away from her mouth and found her voice. "The poor man." She looked to Tamara for company to her compassion but only got a look of preoccupation and a tight smile as Tamara handed the door over and went into the bank.

The whole affair had taken up less than ten heartbeats but would alter the direction of the day for all three of them, and maybe the life of one of them.

Ed slid behind the wheel of Emily's car and slammed the door harder than he had to. He saw his right arm reach up to turn the key, and a chill went right through him. Those ghost images were still happening. Not only did his absent arm try to grab for doors and turn keys, but he sometimes actually thought he saw it now and then. Just the mind playing tricks on him.

It wasn't as bad as the phantom feelings, though. He'd get

an itch or a stab of pain, and when he'd reach to comfort it, there'd be nothing. It really gave Ed the willies.

He shook it off and pointed the car toward home. Ed missed driving his truck, but there was no way he could handle the gear shift right now. The doc said he'd be able to use a stick again once he got fitted with his artificial limb, but it was backordered. Living in Alaska as long as he had, Ed was used to waiting for things, but he never thought he'd be waiting for his arm.

Ed chuckled to himself in the car. It was like him, lately, to do this. He maintained an iron curtain of good humor about him. He laughed and joked and kidded his friends with an impressive collection of one-armed-this-and-that jokes that kept everybody laughing, and eased everyone's tension but his own.

"I'd give my good right arm for that rig, whoops never mind. Guess I already spent it."

"I'd lend a hand with that, Stormy, but I'm down to my last one."

He could even get his kids to enjoy it. "C'mere, little girl, I gotta give you two hugs now 'cause they only come one half at a time."

He dazzled Emily with his proficiency at housework. She'd gone back to substitute teaching until Ed could work again, and while the kids were at school, Ed would do all the house cleaning and cooking chores. He called himself the one-armed bandit, and Emily would always come home with the kids to find her man cheerfully making a show of chasing a carrot around the cutting board with a knife or using his teeth to unscrew the ketchup bottle.

Emily was so proud of Ed and his good spirits. He seemed almost better now than when he was whole.

But that's because she never saw him practicing these stunts during the day. She also never saw him throw the pillows across the bedroom in a rage while trying for twenty minutes to put clean slipcovers on them. Or how he'd tried to shovel the snow from the walk but hired a passing teenager instead, and what it felt like to stand in the window with a dustcloth in his hand and watch the boy dispose of the chore with double-fisted ease.

Ed was being a good husband and good father and a good friend. He didn't want to worry anybody with his problems, and he had them all fooled. Most all of them.

*   *   *

Tamara couldn't stop thinking about Ed Flannigan. It had been over a year since she'd really talked to him. Oh, they'd talked since then, but they hadn't *talked*. Not like they used to last fall, when Ed was curious. Curious and adventuresome. Tamara knew back then, during those long and innocent evenings spent across the table from one another at her cabin, that it was the first time Ed Flannigan had taken a feeling and held it out in front of him to see. And he'd showed them to Tamara. And they'd talked about them and traded them and the whole thing had only lasted a little while.

Tamara had her Tony and Ed had his Emily, but Tamara and Ed had something. Something that Tamara hadn't thought of in a long time until she saw Ed split open for just that moment in the bank. She knew that macho pinhead too well for him to hide it from her. She could see he was riding this out alone just like the reckless cowboy he thought he was.

But this time Tamara could see he was riding a mean horse. A horse too mean and scary to tell anybody about. She knew he'd have to tell somebody or this horse would beat him. It would kick the heart out of him if he didn't talk. And as Tamara turned her van around in the middle of Far Road, she knew Ed would tell her about it.

Fanny Olmstead pulled into the Big New Store and wiped a tear from her cheek. *The poor man's life will never be the same.* She pitied the family. Those three sweet little children growing up with a crippled father. And Emily. She supposed Emily would have to work now until the kids were grown. Certainly, Ed wouldn't be able to support them. Not with his handicap. *Oh, what will the poor man do?*

Fanny felt compelled to do something for the Flannigans, so she went into the store to buy them a big tin of macaroons. Whenever she and the pastor were feeling low, they'd always get some macaroons and it would perk them right up.

As Fanny cut through the store, she chanced down the games aisle and she had another thought. *I'll bet the dear man is just bored to tears in that house all alone every day.* She looked around the shelves for something appropriate, but everything seemed to take either two people or require two hands. She thought maybe a good book would be better but was concerned he might have trouble with the pages. Then she spotted the jigsaw puzzles and knew she had her answer.

She picked out two puzzles that had happy pictures on them. One was a laughing clown and the other was of two ponies in a sunny field. As she was about to turn with her prizes and move on, she spotted something else. Something that lit her face with a knowing smile and a thanks to Providence for pointing her in the right direction. Marching straight up to a deluxe sixteen-color paint-by-number set, she thought, *Crafts: handicapped people love arts and crafts.*

She clearly remembered their summer-camp retreats, where they learned to work with those poor disabled children from Anchorage. *Boy, did those kids love to paint and do beads.*

Fanny tucked the paint set under her arm and strutted merrily toward the macaroons.

Ed Flannigan poured himself a whiskey and put the bottle back under the sink. It was a little bit earlier than yesterday's toddy, but well, his stump ached a little today. He took a drink, appraised his glass, dug the bottle back out to fill it again, then stuck it further back under the sink, where Emily wouldn't see it.

Ed lay back on the couch and closed his eyes. He heaved a deep sigh and waited for the scenes to roll. The scenes he played every day and drank to lately. He'd see the ghost arm coming and going and coming and staying. And he'd replay spectacles like what happened at the bank today. And he'd cringe with humiliation and take a drink and see the faces of Emily and the kids and put an *X* across them. They could never see him like this. He had to tough this out for their sake.

He'd see the faces of others when they looked at him. Pretending not to notice but not being able to keep their eyes off it. He saw Tamara looking at him and Fanny Olmstead staring in shock and pity. Everybody had pity in their face somehow, and he hated them for it. They thought he was finished. That his life was ruined.

And he hated them for it because he thought they were right. He knew he was crippled and could never do his job again. He couldn't even change a pillowcase. How could he ever drive a road grader? Cripples didn't work. They drew disability and watched game shows and learned how to weave baskets with their toes and paint duck decoys.

And Ed felt the tears come behind his eyelids, and he sat up and shook it off. He knew that none of it was true. That he would work and play and do all the things he did before

"It has to be true," he said to himself. But it didn't have to be true, did it? And Ed Flannigan rode his mean horse and held on with both hands—the good one and the ghost one—because he was going to slip and he didn't know which way he'd go.

He didn't hear the knock on the door right away, but when he did, he was jolted out of his muck mire and put on his feet. He got rid of the drink on the way through the kitchen and had his Flannigan face back on by the time he turned the knob.

Ed's mask briefly fell when he saw who it was, but he pulled it back up again. "Why, Tamara Dupree. What in the heck brings you around?"

Tamara smelled the liquor on Ed's breath. She was not going to be floated by his false buoyancy. "What are you doing, Ed?"

Ed tried his act again. "Oh you know me, busier than a one-armed . . ."

"Cut it out." Tamara couldn't stand friends lying to her. "Ed, *how* are you doing?"

Ed reacted to this dangerous question by folding a good arm and a ghost arm across his chest. "It's fine, Tamara. It's almost healed. Doesn't hurt hardly at all anymore."

Tamara closed the door behind her, seeing but ignoring the car pulling into the driveway. "I don't care about your arm. How are *you*?" She reached out and put a hand on each of Ed's shoulders. "I'm worried about you."

The boldness and strength of Tamara's touch welded Ed in place, and he looked into her unwavering eyes, searching for something to say. And he stammered and waited and breathed and started again, and everything he thought to say was lies, but Tamara's eyes wouldn't allow it.

Something moved inside Ed that shook him like a horse would kick his heart out. And Tamara saw it move and held him in her arms at the kitchen window while the sob boiled up out of her friend and lay him open in front of her, and the grief spilled out on her shoulder so mightily it made a sound. A sound like a great big tin of macaroon cookies hitting the sidewalk.

And they looked up in time to catch Fanny Olmstead, her hand over her mouth and her face burning in embarrassment, backing down the walk and fumbling the rest of her packages into the snow.

Fanny was clearly in the wrong place at the wrong time, but not for the reasons she thought, and she couldn't get away fast enough. She scurried back to her car, leaving behind spilled cookies and happy puzzles and deluxe paint-by-number sets and a kitchen window full of broad smiles.

And two good friends took ten heartbeats and stood apart. And they let a piece of quiet come around them like a deep breath, before a long talk . . . that was way overdue.

NORMAN'S GOOD INTENTIONS

NORMAN stood on the front porch of the Flannigan duplex holding a pepperoni-and-pineapple pizza with extra cheese. He took a deep breath—squared his shoulders, tucked his chin, and knocked on the door. He was the cavalry. The SWAT team. The knight in shining armor to his damsel in distress. And he knew he held the advantage.

Finally, the door opened and Laura Magruder, his distressed damsel, stood silhouetted in the frame like a portrait of a tortured saint.

The whole thing started four weeks ago, when Laura signed up for baby-sitting classes. She'd waited years for this, she told Norman. Baby-sitting was a chance to earn money. Her own money. And it was responsibility. Responsibility like she'd never been given in her whole thirteen years. And it would give her a chance to work with children.

Norman couldn't really understand. He didn't know why she wanted money. He had plenty of money. Norman fished on his dad's boat in the summers, and he had a savings account that would have been the envy of most working people, adolescent or otherwise. Surely Laura knew that he would buy her whatever she asked him for.

And working with children. *Yick, little kids.* Norman was the oldest of four. He placed little kids alongside gerbils and loose car parts in the social order of living things. He'd been left in charge of his riotous siblings too many times to ever comprehend a craving for the experience.

But Laura had been insistent, and eventually, they had let the subject drop between them. As close as our two young friends were becoming, there were still many things that they couldn't put to words with each other.

Laura couldn't explain to Norman the real reason she

191

wanted to baby-sit. The money would be fine, and being that she had only an older brother, small children did interest her mildly. But Laura's real motivation for the whole thing was respect. Thirteen-year-olds get precious little respect, and Laura's maturing personality hungered for it.

Laura knew from general observation that if there was anyone in this world that adults from all walks of life held in the highest regard, it was a reliable baby-sitter. They were talked about, even bragged about. They had their names posted next to telephones, along with best friends and 911. They were acknowledged enthusiastically in public. They were praised and taken care of. Good baby-sitters were so precious, they were hoarded. It was by far the most prestigious position a young person could aspire to hold.

But of course, she had no way of explaining all of this to her boyfriend. Even if she could, it was doubtful that Norman would grasp it. Sensitivity comes a little later in boys' development. Sometimes as late as their third or fourth marriage. Norman was far too busy worrying about himself to be able to appreciate Laura's desire for acceptance in the community of adults. Norman was content just to have a foot in the door of adolescence. Granted, being caught red-handed by Laura at child's play last summer didn't help his position any; he was holding his ground as best he could.

What Norman worried about mostly was that if Laura started baby-sitting, he wouldn't be able to see her on weekends. She'd be off all over the place every night, and he'd be stuck at home with his dumb family, or down playing pinball at the bowling alley with *Stanley*. He would sit home thinking about her, and she would sit someplace else *not* thinking about him.

But of course he had no way of explaining all this to Laura, and the two just skipped the subject and did what they had to do: Laura went to baby-sitting class. And Norman worried about it.

Norman's worst fears were realized Monday afternoon, when Laura rushed up to him at school to break their date for Friday. They'd had a big night planned of riding around aimlessly in a pickup truck with Laura's brother. Norman was appalled that Laura would interfere with the sanctity of their regular Friday night outing, but she seemed not to notice his aggravation.

"I'm the first one in our class to get a referral . . . and

it's the Flannigans!" Laura had gushed as if she'd just been appointed nanny to the royal family. All things being equal, she had been.

Ed and Emily Flannigan were a well-known and coveted client on the baby-sitting circuit. They went out often, but not too often, and they stayed out late. They paid well, and they paid cash. They were an excellent reference. And they had a VCR. Their three kids were a notorious nuisance, but the benefits far outweighed any disadvantages.

Much to Norman's chagrin, Laura would talk about nothing but baby-sitting all week long. She huddled up with her other girlfriends at every opportunity, to compare notes, and left Norman feeling very much like a forgotten detail. The more Laura tried to involve him, the less Norman felt a part of it and the more cynical he became.

Laura would often look off into space and speculate about her future. "I'm going to do such a good job with the Flannigans that *everybody* is going to want me to sit for them. The Storbocks. The Bindels. Maybe even your mom and dad."

"My parents will never hire a baby-sitter while I'm still alive." It was a long-standing complaint of Norman's that his parents wouldn't bring in any outside talent. He'd become reluctantly well experienced with the wiles and ways of small children.

Laura looked at Norman and raw enthusiasm gurgled out of her. "Oh, Norman. You're so lucky to have little brothers and sisters. It must be like baby-sitting every day! I'll play games with them and read them stories, like we learned in class. I know how to regulate their television, locate fire exits, and test smoke alarms. I know thirty-seven kinds of poisons that can be found in the home. Why, I even know how to save babies from choking! This is going to be awesome!"

Norman would not be swayed by any classroom propaganda. "You're going to wish you could choke them yourself by the time you're through. Ed junior's only three years younger than you, ya know."

"I know, and he'll be a big help to me with the other two." Laura left a doubting Norman standing in the hallway with a bright promise that she'd call him this evening just as soon as she got the kids to bed.

The series of events that led from Norman lying bored in his room sneaking mournful gazes at a photograph of Laura to his hand-delivering a pizza to the Flannigan duplex might not ever be fully disclosed. Norman himself didn't have the entire picture. He only knew what he heard over the phone.

The first time Laura called she sounded calm enough. She made a point of saying she was calm, Norman knew, because that's what it said in big black letters on the page of tips and regulations she'd gotten from her class—*Above All, Stay Calm*.

"It's not that I'm worried, really, but I am curious. Can four-year-olds scream themselves to death?"

"I don't think so. How long has he been screaming?"

"Over an hour. He's really turning colors."

"He'll get hoarse pretty soon and stop on his own." Norman sounded every bit the voice of experience, and it had its effect. Laura thanked him, kissed into the phone, and hung up.

The second call was a little more tense but still in control. "You're right. Corey can't scream anymore, but he still hasn't stopped trying. Norman, is it true that if kids don't have six Flintstone vitamins and a cup of hot cocoa before bed that they die of scurvy?"

"Who told you that?"

"Ed junior and Missy. They say that's what's wrong with Corey."

Norman set her straight on that point, and again Laura hung up with a grateful smooch. He lay back on his bed and bounced a Nerf ball off the ceiling with a wry smile. *She couldn't do it without me*, he thought. And even though Norman was none too thrilled about what she was doing in the first place, he felt a little better about it every time the phone rang.

"Norman?" By the third call, Laura was sounding positively rattled. "They won't go to sleep. Ed junior says it's because they all have hyperactive thyroids and they need something to eat, like pizza. Have you ever heard of that?"

Norman could tell that his partner was being seriously outclassed and it was time for drastic measures. He offered to have his mom talk to Ed junior for a minute, but Laura nearly jumped through the phone at him.

"No! You can't tell anybody about this trouble. My entire baby-sitting career depends on it!"

For a woman to put any kind of career in the hands of a neglected boyfriend is a mistake, but Laura can be forgiven her youth. Besides, not all men are as selfish and insecure as Norman. Well maybe they are, but sometimes they do the noble thing anyway.

Norman told Laura to put Ed junior on the phone. Having lived several years as a responsible older sibling, Norman had developed a comprehensive two-phased approach to child behavior manipulation. First, you threaten them, and if that doesn't work, then you bribe them.

Phase one backfired badly. Norman had tried to intimidate the younger Flannigan with hollow threats of physical violence, only to receive a much more potent counterthreat. Ed junior told him that he knew Norman slept with Laura's class picture under his pillow and Laura was going to find out about it if he didn't mind his own business.

"How'd you know?" Norman said going dry in the mouth.

"Your brother told me."

Norman made a mental note to murder his younger brother at his earliest possible convenience, then got on with phase two of the program.

It was phase two that had our hero at the Flannigans' kitchen table happily dishing out lukewarm pizza to three tightly wound children while Laura looked on nervously.

"They were supposed to be in bed hours ago," she said.

"Don't worry. This'll calm 'em right down. They've about had it anyway." Norman laid out the last piece and let the sound of his voice hang in midair. It sounded good to him. There was something authoritarian about it. Something . . . manly. He looked at Laura, and she'd heard it too.

"You really shouldn't be here," she said. "What if the Flannigans come home early?"

"They *never* come home early." Norman moved across the kitchen, and for the first time in four weeks he saw that there might be a silver lining to this baby-sitting business.

The kids grew unnaturally quiet around the pizza box, like a pack of wolves on a fresh kill. There was a little bit of horsing around from Ed junior, but with no spirit to it. Mostly, they sat pushing pizza into their faces, guzzling juice, and sitting in the satisfied manner of victorious children.

Laura and Norman stood off to the side like proud parents over a baby's cradle. They looked at each other and in an instant the fantasy passed between them. It showed red in their cheeks, and averted their eyes. It was a fantasy of marriage and children and happily ever after, and it warmed them and drew them close and their hands found each other and they stood like that—just watching.

For a good long moment, Norman stood at the edge of a thought that didn't revolve around him. It was a view laced with partnership and responsibility. A rugged terrain, but with a beauty suggesting devotion and overpowered self-indulgence. It was a respectable place, with good intentions.

It was the first taste Laura or Norman ever had of what could possible lie before them in the adult world. And although they knew it wasn't theirs yet, they felt it down into their hearts and marrow and they became impressed with themselves. So impressed that they never even heard the car pull up.

"What on earth is going on here!" Emily Flannigan stood poised in the doorway with a grim-faced husband peering over her shoulder. "What are the kids still doing up?"

Emily wasn't waiting for answers, she was already storming the place. "Ed junior, Missy, Corey. Up those stairs this minute. Look at this house, it's a mess. Where'd this pizza come from? Norman Tuttle, what are *you* doing here? You get yourself home this minute!" Then she turned on Laura and let the air out of everything. "Laura Magruder, I'm so disappointed in you."

Ed was showing Norman the way out with a look like thirty-seven kinds of household poisons, and Norman could only take the briefest looks back at his partner. His damsel in distress was stressed to breaking. She could only look at her shoes and fold around herself, and there was just Laura in there to face the music. No Norman, and nothing he could do.

Nothing but stand on the porch, alone and confused. He'd come in a hero and left everything a mess. Norman walked off toward home bathing in guilt and regrets and self-incrimination, and tried to find a place to hide from it all.

Thirteen-year-olds have precious few places to hide inside, and it took Norman some time to find his. It was hard to find, only because it was new to him and he was halfway home before he recognized it as a place to be.

A respectable place, with good intentions.

THAT LAMP

KIRSTEN stood in the kitchen doorway holding a fresh tray of cocktail weenies and took a moment to admire her circumstances.

It was only a year ago she'd stood not a hundred feet from here and watched her house of dreams collapse into flames and burned labors. *They lost everything*, people kept saying, but as Kirsten looked out over her new house loading up with old friends, she could see they hadn't lost a thing worth mentioning. In fact they were far richer now than they ever had been in more ways than could be figured.

They'd spent the past year living in the charitably empty half of the Flannigans' duplex, surrounded by other people's things. It seemed like everybody in town had given them something. Only days after the fire they'd been substantially endowed with clothes and bedding, pots and plates—soap, curtains, and places to sit. It was all secondhand stuff with little rhyme or reason and no sense of fashion, but it was something.

Even though for a whole year their home looked like a garage sale waiting to happen, it had gotten them through, and now here they were one year later in a fine new house filling up with fine new things, and none of it could have happened without the generosity of the people coming through the front door at that moment. They'd all helped build this house, and their faces kicked up a proud hitch as they passed through the door and looked around at what they'd done.

Kirsten watched Stormy greeting the odd stream of people making their way into the living room bearing more gifts and she went literally flush with wealth, health, and the love of good friends. She caught a new grip on her weenie platter and waltzed toward her guests with that lightness of foot that can only come from true and total delight.

197

* * *

There were only a handful of things on this earth that could have discouraged the prevailing spirit of goodness that settled on our little gathering up at the Storbocks'. And one of those was being lugged along Flat Back Ridge Road on the stooped shoulder of our dull-witted desperado Doug McDoogan.

Doug hadn't intended bringing anything at all to the party. It wasn't that he was selfish or insensitive, although he was. It was mostly that he rarely thought a foot ahead of his own boots, and he wouldn't have thought of this present either if he hadn't tripped over it while rummaging around the dump on the way up.

What it was, basically, was the ugliest lamp ever devised by the minds of man or demon. Innocent raw materials that could have been easily crafted into any number of tasteful accessories for the home had gone crazy. They'd taken the form of a creation so foul that not even Doug McDoogan entertained a moment's thought of keeping it for himself. It was a piece with less than no charm. It was a piece that took any charm in its presence and turned it into tack board and poster paint.

It was a nightmare with a plug on it. It called to mind leopard-skin vinyl barstools, Muammar Qaddafi, menthol cigarettes, long bus rides to Detroit, pimples, bad chicken dinners, and noisy little dogs in parked cars—all at a glance.

It was big but not in a grand way. It was big to excess, like vintage cars from the fifties with crummy paint jobs. The base was cast of some metal with the complexion of storm drains. Formed into it were glossy black figurines that seemed to climb up the stem like a biblical plague. They ascended into a pool of weak light emanating from a milk-glass globe. Crowning it all was a nearly opaque green crushed-velvet shade with royal-red brocade and powderpuff dangle balls.

It was a piece that begged to be given away. A quality that would prove to supply a valuable lesson in the fine art of giving to Kirsten Storbock and her gathering of generous good friends on the ridge.

"Oh, Emily, these are just darling!" Kirsten sat on the couch between Sissy Tuttle and Emily Flannigan holding up matching sunflower-print flannel bed linens. "These will go so well with Sissy's afghan." Sissy blushed and grinned while

Kirsten reached into the stack of housewarming gifts for another treasure.

Tamara Dupree and her man, Tony, were off to one side, enthusiastically explaining the workings of a solar-activated kitchen composter to a grateful but perplexed Stormy.

Argus Winslow and Bud Koenig had both brought a fire extinguisher to give and were arguing over the individual merits of each as the rest of the group mingled and grazed on weenies and bean dip, looking the place over and generally doing a pretty good job of warming a house.

The doorbell was a welcome sound to Stormy, who'd been groping for an excuse to tear himself away from Tamara and Tony's interesting but long-winded discussion of environmental responsibility. "Garbage could become the world's single biggest energy source in the next century. Garbage, Stormy, plain old everyday garbage . . ."

"Hold that thought," Stormy said, and went to let Doug in.

When the lamp appeared in the entryway, a chill swept through the front room of the house. Sentences were bit off. Bean dip oozed off Doritos frozen halfway from dish to lips. Even the dog stopped licking crumbs from the linoleum and raised its hair.

Doug was used to this kind of treatment and thought little of it as he thrust the lamp into a horrified Stormy's hands and closed the door behind him. Doug turned into the room, letting his body hang on his spine in that curious way of his, while Sissy Tuttle broke the silence with the two words that were about to leap from the throat of everyone in the room.

"That lamp!" She put a hand over her mouth as if to catch the color that drained from her cheeks, and Doug felt compelled to explain himself.

"I found it at the dump." He said it as if boasting of a bargain at JCPenney. And without another word he scuffled over to the food table, leaving *that lamp* to fend for itself and find its way into the lives of the assemblage.

Little did Doug know that his lucky find had already been through the lives of nearly everyone present. Passed from one to the other like a bad cold. His retarded sensitivities wouldn't allow him to notice the round-robin of shame and resentment that was commencing before he got the first deviled egg to his mouth.

Everyone's eyes were on Sissy Tuttle, who'd been the first one to make the mistake of recognizing this hideous excuse for a lighting implement.

"I threw it out yesterday." She looked around, ashen-faced, and stammered on like an accused murderer with a knife in her hand. "It wasn't mine, you know. It was left over from the charity bazaar. No one would buy it." She stopped talking and thought of the Organization of Fishermen's Wives Charity Bazaar and Flea Market last Saturday at the Big Garage on Clear Shot.

Not only would nobody buy the lamp, nobody would even come near it. Whatever piece of furniture or clothing it stood close to seemed immediately threadbare and overpriced, and it was bogging down the entire benefit. Many people would just stick their head in the door, get one glimpse of the lamp, and promptly leave with a false impression of the whole inventory.

Chapter president Donna Fitzwillie had asked her in front of the other women to put it back in her car, and she still hadn't completely unfolded from the cringe of embarrassment. She had risked her entire reputation as a conscientious home-maker by accepting the donation of that lamp in the first place. In a defensive reflex, she dodged. "Bud Koenig gave it to us."

Sissy eased into the cushions of the couch feeling spared, while Bud bristled across the room. It was true. He'd donated it to the charity bazaar because he couldn't stand having it around his store.

Somebody had left it on the front step of Bud's saw and chain shop one morning, and he brought it in. Most of Bud's furniture at home and in his shop had been carved out of big hunks of wood with a chainsaw, so he didn't have as keen an eye as some for interior decorating. Even so, it only took a few days for Bud to recognize that this lamp, and its dangly personality, was too unsightly even for a saw shop. Being of a generation raised not to waste, Bud couldn't make himself throw it away, so he called Sissy Tuttle under the pretense of philanthropy.

He felt bad about it when Sissy showed up to get it. Real bad. Like he'd given a dog a boot to eat because he didn't have any meat. Without saying anything in his own defense, Bud looked to the only person he knew who would wish such a dilemma on him.

"Now, wait just a minute." Argus raised a hand to hold back the judgment of the room. "I'm a junk dealer. I get all manner of things come through my junkyard. I could see that fruity lamp had no resale value, so I left it off, figurin' you could use it. It seemed a little dim in your shop last time I was in."

Nobody believed a word he said, and Argus himself knew full well he'd left it at Bud's store just to annoy him, so he did the only decent thing. He passed the buck. "Tamara Dupree brought it by and I gave her a dollar for it, figurin' she musta been desperate."

"I beg your pardon!" Tamara started to bluster a rationalization but realized before she started that she had none. She had been desperate. The Flannigans had given her the lamp one day, figuring it would be appreciated by two eclectic and creative minds such as hers and Tony's, and they'd allowed the flattery to blind them. Tamara figured the lamp would make a wonderful conversation piece, but it proved too ugly to talk about. It cast sort of a mildew-green light in their cabin. A lifeless light. A light like a dentist's lamp makes. It irritated the eyes. It foreshadowed pain. It had to go.

Seeing the lamp again filled her with such revulsion she felt insulted by its presence and the idea that anyone would possibly think she could like such an atrocity. She stared daggers at Ed, and he took it in the heart.

"Well, hell's bells, it was givin' my kids nightmares. What was I supposed to do? Kirsten and Stormy gave it to us, and I couldn't hand it over to just anybody." It was a flimsy justification and Ed knew it, but at least it put the heat back where it belonged. Which was firmly on the original and present owners of the awful unwanted item that had passed from one end of town to the other and back under the guise of generosity.

Kirsten was just finding her voice to explain her innocence in the whole thing and finger the real culprits when the doorbell rang again.

When Kirsten opened the door, a small sound escaped from her throat. She couldn't have been more unnerved if she'd looked out and saw the Messiah riding a buffalo across the yard. There in her doorway, beaming like picnic missionaries, were the culprits, Pastor Frank and Fanny Olmstead, holding something between them that sent Kirsten three steps back into the room.

It could only be described as a nightmare with a plug on it. A recurring nightmare at that. From the bottom of its seamy base to the top of its pallid green shade with dangling foolery and crippled posture. It was the dead ringer twin lamp of the one inside, and every bit as welcome.

"Yuck-oh!" Everybody in the room silently agreed with Doug's sentiment before they looked over and saw he'd been directing it toward a taste of avocado-nut roll Tamara and Tony had brought, and was oblivious to the pastor and Fanny's arrival.

Fanny bustled in and set their offering down next to its mate. Then she stepped back to the pastor and cocked her perky little head toward Kirsten and Stormy.

"We just knew you'd be surprised. When we gave you the first one last summer, we didn't want to tell you there were two. We wanted you to fall in love with it so you'd be just that much more thrilled when you found out there was another one. Don't you just *love* them?"

A fly could've made its way safely in and out of the mouths of everybody present. They all gaped in astonishment, not just at the dynamic duo of ugly before them but at the idea that somebody could actually stand them.

Kirsten looked into the pleased faces of her benefactors, and the truth of the whole matter came clear to her. Fanny and the pastor really did *like* these lamps. They liked them a lot. So much that Kirsten could see a glimmer of sadness in their eyes. A sadness of parting. They were giving something away that they wanted for themselves so badly that they could hardly contain it.

Kirsten suddenly realized that it was probably one of the sincerest acts of giving she'd experienced over this past difficult year. And certainly the sincerest one she'd heard about all evening. She looked around at the faces circling the room trying to conceal their distaste, and Kirsten felt ashamed. Ashamed for all of them.

And she looked over at Doug McDoogan, feeding his face at the table, and silently gave thanks he'd brought the lamp back to them. She also made a mental note to tell Doug at her earliest possible convenience that she'd kill him in his sleep if he ever mentioned where he found it.

Kirsten looked back to Pastor Frank and Fanny and resumed her air of true and total delight with the world. "They are special, Fanny. *Very* unique. They must be a family heirloom. I don't know how you can part with them." She took a long look at the lamps again. "Believe me, I have a hard time accepting them from you."

Pastor Frank, somewhat flushed and impressed with his own selfless deed, put a reassuring hand on Kirsten's shoulder.

"Now, now, my dear. There's no need for concern. These lamps mean the world to Fanny and I, and that's why we want your family to have them. As the Bible teaches us in the Book of Acts: 'It is certainly more blessed to give than to receive.' "

And as the sentiment draped itself across the room, everyone took a good long look at the two lamps, and there wasn't anybody who could disagree with that.

ARGUS PROPOSES

ARGUS stood in the sour blue smoke of eight spent .22 shells, and he smiled. Ringing out across his junkyard were the fading notes of the first few bars of the "Wedding March" as played on several stripped hot-water-heater tanks by a small handgun. This time it was perfect. His dog cautiously uncoiled his ears again, and Argus patted his head. "Barney ol' boy—this'll melt 'er heart for sure."

Argus had been working on his musical water heater tanks for three full days. He set eight old tanks on the snowbank across the lot and tuned them to pitch by adding different amounts of water to each one. It'd been a long and laborious endeavor involving an old harmonica, a ball peen hammer, and a lot of trips to the well house.

Argus's tin ear made just tuning up hard enough, but once he got to the business of sounding out the song, he wore himself out in a hurry. He'd set the tanks too far apart, and in order to play "Here Comes the Bride," as he called it, with any sense of cadence, he had to move from one to the other faster than his aging legs wanted to take him. He puzzled over this for some time, then remembered his eight-shot .22 revolver. It was just the thing.

He made the mistake of using the long loads at first and punched some leaks into a couple of tanks before he learned the trick of shooting high with short loads. He bought a case of proper shells and spent a long, cold afternoon on the front step of his house trailer trying to sound out his proposal of marriage to Ruby McClay.

Argus Winslow was not normally this musically inclined or romantic, but he was in love. It's hard to say what sparks such amorous behavior in the aging likes of Argus and Ruby. It may be that these two frontier swingers were finally facing the fears

of growing old alone—but not likely. Neither of them wanted
for friends or company, and the more logical cause for them
finally falling in with each other after all these years was that
they ran out of reasons not to.

Argus let Barney and himself in from the cold and poured
them each a whiskey. Barney lapped his up, then lay down
with a great grunt in front of the propane heater. He studied
his master with one worried eye, wondering just exactly what
had come over him lately. Argus sat at the table beating out
a steady rhythm with his meaty fingers and wondered the
same thing.

It was that blasted Bud Koenig who'd given him the water-
tank idea. Well, indirectly anyway. Bud happened to come
around the corner into Ruby's video store one day awhile
back and caught her and Argus in a smooch.

"Oh my, oh my," Bud had teased. "I think I hear weddin'
bells ringin'."

Argus blustered and Ruby blushed, but neither one of them
had done a very good job of denying the possibility. They
stood apart, sheepish and stymied like school kids, while Bud's
look turned from gentle harassment to curious appreciation.

"Yes indeed. I do hear those bells on the wind."

It was that sweet, awkward moment that gave Argus the
courage to pursue the idea of matrimony.

Argus had considered the proposition of marrying Ruby
before but had never really figured out how he would pop
the question. It wasn't the sort of thing that just rolled off
the tongues of seasoned junkyard tycoons from the End of the
Road. He was going to need a fancier and more subtle method
of proposal, and wedding bells seemed like the immediate
way to go.

Of course, seasoned junkyard tycoons are prone to make do
with what they have. Genuine regulation wedding bells are a
bit of a scarce commodity at End of the Road salvage facilities,
but scrap hot-water-heater tanks sure ain't, and it doesn't take
much research to figure out how all this came together.

Argus's first idea was to hang two or three of them from
the big spruce behind the trailer and let 'em bang around in
the breeze naturally like real wedding bells might. He hoisted
them up and let them dangle for almost a week before a wind
blew up that was strong enough to budge 'em. Argus stood out
in the gale watching the three tanks flop around and decided

the whole thing lacked a particular quality of romance he was looking for.

His next thought was to get these love chimes ringing the old-fashioned way—yanking on the rope and letting them pound together like a preacher does church bells. He might have gone with it too if Emmitt Frank, who was renting the old cabin behind the junkyard, hadn't come by during Argus's first test ring.

Argus was thrashing up and down on the rope trying to get a rhythm going when Emmitt pulled up along the driveway and rolled his window down.

"What are you doin', Argus?"

Argus continued his assault on the rope. "What does it *look* like I'm doing?"

Emmitt studied the situation for a few beats and offered the only logical conclusion. "It looks like you're trying to shake those old water tanks loose from that tree." He paused and looked some more. "But what I can't figure out is how they got caught up there in the first place. You need some help?"

Argus stopped his tugging and turned his annoyed face toward the car. But just as he was about to admonish Emmitt for his blatant disregard for matters of the heart, it occurred to him that flagging old iron appliances around in tall trees wouldn't necessarily translate into romance for everybody.

He decided the whole thing might be a little abstract even for his Ruby, and he reached out with his knife and cut the support rope, already working out another approach in his head. The cluster crashed down a few feet from the car, and Emmitt decided this meant Argus didn't need any help. He rolled up his window and eased down around the junkyard, as confounded as ever about his eccentric landlord.

Eccentricity is a wonderful thing. It allows ordinary mortals like ourselves to rise above worldly constraints and think, for a time, with the whimsey of angels. It's nonsense without remorse. Foolishness with function. It would be greatly admired if it weren't so darn idiotic most of the time.

And the nicest thing about eccentricity is that it's blind to its own shortcomings. Argus Winslow would certainly never think of himself as silly or dim-witted and would take grave exception with any individuals who might. Courting his intended with rusted cast-iron containers seemed no more ludicrous to Argus than if he'd straight out and ask her to marry him. And he never gave a moment's thought to why he didn't.

It wouldn't occur to Argus that he was being anything more or less than playful and poetic. The intention of the whole business seemed so clear to him that he never once stopped to question his motives. It never crossed his mind that burying a serious proposition in poetry and playfulness was just a way of shrinking from a serious reply. A straight question gets a straight answer. And then what?

Argus stood in the front door of his trailer, looking out at his melodic contraption across the yard. He finished his whiskey and let a chill run down him. He mistook it as the kick of cheap liquor when actually it was a rush of the sort one gets when touched by the incredible. Like Argus had been touched that very morning.

The final solution to his wedding-bell quandary had come to him in a rush of divine inspiration, if not actual intervention. He was kicking the water tanks from the tree fiasco off the bed of his truck onto a stack of others. One tank happened to land just right on the pile, and as it rolled down, it sounded out the opening notes of "The Beer Barrel Polka" just as clear as a winter sky.

The Lord works in mysterious ways, and it's a good thing for Argus Winslow, because so does he. The first thing that popped into Argus's head when he heard those coincidental notes was a couple walking side by side down the aisle into the waiting arms of holy matrimony.

The connection here between an old beer-drinking song and the institution of marriage might seem a little vague, but it wouldn't if you'd been to as many weddings in the last forty years as Argus Winslow has featuring Lars Luger and the Irish Polka Band and their modest repertoire of dancing music. "The Beer Barrel Polka" made up a good 25 percent of that song list, with the "Wedding March" filling out the first half.

Argus immediately saw what he would do, and the whole thing seemed so perfectly sensible and terribly touching that he laughed and thanked his Maker right out loud.

It was a different kind of mind at work here. Maybe one in a million. The quantum leaps of logic it takes to go from a comment about wedding bells to an accidental polka to the "Wedding March" played on junkyard flotsam with a small-caliber handgun as a marriage proposal could only occur once in this universe. Argus Winslow closed his door and went to bed, extremely pleased with himself.

Argus knew it had turned colder overnight as soon as he woke up and found Barney under the covers with him. He threw the blankets back and stepped into his pants.

"Get up, you sleepy old coyote. We got company comin'."

The dog ignored the command, but Argus was already too busy to notice. His beloved was on her way over for breakfast and there was lots to do. He went out to the food cache to get some side pork and shivered back through the trailer door with it.

"Barney, I bet it dropped twenty degrees out there last night."

Barney already knew how cold it was, and his only acknowledgment of the remark was to wiggle a little deeper into his snooze on the bed.

Argus went back about the work of putting together a romantic breakfast for two. There were all the standard accoutrements: sizzling side pork, sourdough pancake batter, strong coffee, fried potatoes—and topping it all off, the coup de grace, a fully loaded .22 pistol hanging on the peg by the door.

The two lovebirds chatted amiably through their meal. They talked about the cold snap, this year's snowfall, and some light gossip. This wasn't the first time they'd sat across a breakfast table from each other, and it was an easy place to be for both of them.

Barney got up just in time to clean off the plates, and Ruby and Argus left him licking under the table as they stepped out into the bright, clear morning for a breath and a stretch. Argus grabbed his pistol on the way out. "C'mere, Rube, I got somethin' to show ya. Somethin' important."

Ruby took note of Argus's serious tone and stood still to watch what he was doing. Argus blew air onto both his bare hands, gave Ruby one short, hopeful look that concerned her, then he leveled an aim at his masterpiece.

He peeled off eight even shots and listened to the high-pitched ringing from across the yard. What he heard turned his rugged old face white and set his jaw in confusion. Something was wrong. Terribly wrong.

Although Argus wouldn't figure it out until later, the water in his junkyard vibes had frozen solid and randomly changed the pitch of each one of them. His little outburst sounded no more like the "Wedding March" than it did "God Bless America," but it *was* familiar.

To Ruby it sounded a lot like a bunch of small bullets bouncing around a junkyard. She dug her hands into her pockets and shrugged. "Nice shootin', cowboy." She already knew that Argus was a crack pistol shot and couldn't begin to imagine what he was trying to prove with a display like that. "You just trying to wake me up this morning?"

Of course, Argus was shattered. He let the pistol hang by his side and shook his head in disbelief. It couldn't be. His ears must be playing tricks on him. He'd worked way too hard for this to have it fail. He looked at his girlfriend and made a defeated confession. "It was supposed to play a song for you."

Ruby puzzled for a moment, then broke out laughing with relief, figuring that her goofy ol' man was just playing a joke on her. She decided to play along with it just to humor him. "Yeah, yeah, I heard a song, it sounded like the, oh, what is it? . . . that 'Beer Barrel Polka,' " Ruby kept laughing and started to move as if to begin their walk when she heard her own words and stopped dead in her tracks.

There was a different kind of mind at work here—one, maybe two, in a million. Quantum leaps of logic went storming through Ruby's head so fast it wobbled her on her pegs a little, and a chill went through her like what happens when one brushes against the incredible. Those things in this universe that only occur once, but sometimes, when God is paying attention, they play twice.

Ruby turned back toward Argus, who was still standing there like a whipped dog, and she took a big breath. "Yes."

Argus pulled himself out of his own head to look at her. "Yes, what?"

"You senile old goat. You just asked me to marry you didn'tcha? You ask a straight question, you get a straight answer around Ruby McClay."

And as Ruby pulled up beside him and took his arm, Argus felt as confused as he ever has been, or is ever likely to be. Never had anyone been so inspired to work so hard, with so much dedication and so much love and so much purpose, to get something so screwed up that it couldn't possibly come out right—and then it does.

As the two walked out the junkyard drive hearing heavenly wedding bells between them, Providence smiled a mischievous smile, knowing better than anybody present that it was the perfect lesson to start a marriage with.

JOE AND DOUG

JOE Miller didn't know anything about Doug McDoogan when he moved into the apartment next door, but he got interested in that lukewarm way neighbors do with each other.

When the landlord showed Joe to his apartment the first day, he'd said, "The guy next door—he's a little . . ." And he'd made an odd expression with his face that Joe couldn't quite read. It could have meant the guy was mentally off balance. It could have meant he was simpleminded. Or he might have been telling him Doug was just plain ugly. Joe couldn't have known that it was a fairly even measure of all three, but it hadn't mattered to him at the time.

Joe had spent the last three months bouncing around on the stormy gulf waters with Lars Luger's fishing crew. Anything that wasn't a seagoing vessel looked like home sweet home to him, and he didn't care who lived next door. For now, a hot shower, a dry bed, and a new world's record for sleeping late was all Joe Miller was really concerned about. What the neighbors did was up to them, and it interested Joe not in the slightest. It was fine with him to be on solid ground and out of the miserable January weather.

Of course the relish of a warm dry home soon gave way to the realities of a bare and empty room. A man can stay fascinated with contentment for just so long, and then it's time to move on to the next appetite. At these times almost anything can bid for one's attention. Even strange neighbors.

It was Doug McDoogan's bathroom habits that first caught Joe's interest. Not that he was concentrating on them, really, but there was one he couldn't very well help but notice—the length of his showers. Doug seemed intent on showering at least twice a day. Each time until all the hot water was gone. This might not have bothered Joe at all outside of natural curiosity if the two apartments hadn't shared the same water heater.

Joe did the noble thing and complained to the landlord, who told him that the water heater was in Joe's closet so why didn't he just shut off the valve before Doug could run all the water out? He made that same peculiar gesture insinuating that Doug was too nuts, dumb, or ugly to ever notice the difference.

Joe tried it out that very afternoon, and true to predictions, nobody on the other side of the wall seemed to suspect anything. There was a muffled yelp through the wall, then silence. It was the first real communication the two men had.

The next morning Joe tried to ease the valve shut a little more gradually, but it took a few days of practice before the hoots and hollers quit altogether. Joe felt better about the whole situation, and that brightened him in a noticeable way against the backdrop of his bleak circumstances.

You see, Joe Miller wasn't quite sure what he was doing here. He'd left college for a long summer in the north country and never went home. It was as if his life decided to do the driving for itself. One day just sort of led on to the next. First it was work in the cannery. Then he'd got the job on Lars's boat and fished the grounds from Prince William Sound to Dutch Harbor.

Now he had a pile of money without so much as a wish to spend it on. The landscape of the past year had unraveled and dissipated from the wildness of new territory to the water stains on a rented ceiling. Joe seemed to be waiting for his life to come find him again, and in the meantime he was content to explore the nuances of one-handed cribbage and perfect the skills of hot-water deprivation on an unseen neighbor. There was a resemblance of companionship in the effort, although Joe wasn't aware of it.

Joe never really did become aware of how much his neighbor kept him company over the following weeks. But slowly Doug's activities through the wall wove themselves solidly into Joe Miller's lazy days. There definitely was a lot more activity going on in Doug's world than in his.

Doug seemed to have a lot of visitors. Even though Joe never saw anyone come or go, the door opened and closed constantly and there were voices other than Doug's. Joe never could make out what they were saying, but there was always a suspicious man's voice and a nervous woman's or a girl's.

It was hard to tell, even though it sometimes went on for an hour or more.

Other times it would be quiet for a long time, then Joe could pick out this dull and methodical thumping sound interrupted by an occasional distant "Aha!" or "Gotcha!" There would be more activity at the door. Another shower. Some voices at night.

Without realizing it, Joe grew resentful of all the socializing next door. He didn't know what kind of friends this fellow had, but they were more than Joe had and that was for sure. He figured out that these visitors account for all that extra showering and he began shutting the hot water down sooner and with less care. The barks and curses through the wall brought the occasional smile to Joe's face like nothing else had in a while.

The miserable weather outside encouraged Joe to continue to do nothing with himself. His days persisted, as Joe's days were prone to do, with countless hands of pointless cribbage, marking time with scoring pegs on a flat wooden board.

"Fifteen-two, Fifteen-four, and a pair is six." Joe worked the cards methodically on the table and kept one ear tuned to the revelry next door. "Aha—gotcha!"

The sound of it would be like a tiny knife in Joe's insides, bleeding loneliness and restlessness through his guts. He was developing quite a hair trigger on the water-heater valve, and there were days he hardly let it run at all. He openly enjoyed the chilled hoots from the next room, and sometimes even talked back to them. *Whoop!*—"Gotcha." They might be having all the fun next door, but Joe had all the hot water.

Of course what Joe Miller was dealing with here was a king-size case of cabin fever that if left unbridled might lead to any number of unpleasant encounters in the long haul, but this whole ordeal was not to be hauled that far.

The knock on the door startled Joe and momentarily confused him. He'd been counting points on his eighty-third consecutive winning hand against himself, and lost his train of thought. He expected no one and went to the door with that what-who frown that we greet strange knocks with.

The face on the other side of the knock took Joe by surprise at first, because even though he was sure he'd never seen it before, it looked familiar.

"Hi, I'm Doug McDoogan from next door." the face said. "I hear you over here sometimes. I was wonderin' if you wanted to watch a movie tonight."

Joe looked at the face, amazed. The odd expression the landlord had been using in reference to Doug was so accurate that Joe had recognized him from it. And even seeing it live, it was impossible to read. Touched, dumb, or ugly. It was a tough call, but one he had to make.

He thought cautiously for a moment, wondering if this mysterious guy from next door was simply luring him into a trap where he and his friends would rob and beat the ears off him for playing with the plumbing. But a long look at that face convinced him there was no masterminding at play here.

The prospect of seeing a movie and getting out of his room for the night was so tantalizing to Joe that touched, dumb, *and* ugly couldn't really steer him away. In fact, Doug probably could have been frothing at the mouth and Joe might have gone along just to see what kind of movies rabid neighbors watch.

"Well sure, I'd like a movie. Thanks," Joe said. "Oh—I'm Joe Miller."

Joe offered his hand through the doorway, but Doug had already turned and walked away. Joe let his arm hang limp and said after him. "What time you gonna start it?"

Doug looked back, and seemed thoughtful for a second, then said, "I don't know. I don't have a watch." And he disappeared through his door.

Joe could see there was going to be some guesswork involved with this Doug McDoogan fella, but that was just fine. He went back into his room and waited for some reasonable signal from next door.

Joe heard the door bang open once and slam a couple of times. Then a few minutes later he heard it being worked on some more, so he took that to mean the other guests were arriving. Joe was surprised to turn into Doug's door and find it wide open. Doug himself sat with his face about two feet from the image on a silent color TV and didn't notice Joe until he knocked.

"Oh, come on in. I suppose you can close that door now."

Joe stepped into the room, a mirror image of his own only fuller. Doug had supplied himself with an impressive number of amenities, including the TV, VCR, a toaster, lamps, a bullfight rug, and comic books. There were wood chips on the floor and half-carved pieces of driftwood set around everywhere. It was a pigsty, but the homeyness and activity of it made Joe immediately jealous.

"I thought everyone else was already here," he said, sitting on a chair just inside the door.

"Everyone is." Doug didn't understand his meaning, but Doug was used to not understanding about half of what anybody said to him, so he gave it no heed. "There's beers in the fridge if 'n you like beer." And his attention went immediately back to the small screen.

Joe declined to venture into this strange man's refrigerator unescorted and tried to be sociable instead. He looked around at all the carvings and picked up one within reach.

"This is a nice bear. You carve these?"

"Yep." Doug turned his head slightly but never pulled his eyes from the picture.

Joe could see that Doug was not going to be easily called away from his movie, so he turned his own attention to the screen, confused by the noiseless display and more and more mystified by his neighbor.

"Is this a silent movie?"

Doug turned his head again without moving his eyes. "Is now since I busted the sound knob off. It's called *Grease Pit Lizards*. It's about space monsters at a drag strip. I watch it all the time. I can do the parts for you if you want to hear it. I know 'em all by heart." And without further invitation Doug began lipsyncing with the images on the TV in eerily familiar voices.

A nervous woman's. "Oh, Speed, do you think they'll come back?"

A suspicious-sounding man. "I don't know, Clara Belle. I just don't know."

Then Doug looked at Joe with an expression like he'd just tossed a ringer. Joe could see he was seeking approval, and had no choice but to give it. "That's good, Doug. Real good."

"I know. I practice all the time." Now that Doug's eyes had moved from the television, his mind seemed to follow. He looked at the door. "It's hot in here again."

It was hot in there, and Joe watched as Doug pulled the door open, flagged it around in the room, and then left it slightly ajar. "It's always hot in here. I'm forever having to open this door."

"Why don't you turn the heat down?"

"Can't. Broke that knob off too." Doug moved over to the table and started absently straightening up a pile of playing cards turned all ways. He talked while he fumbled the cards. "I think I musta broke the shower too. There used to be all kinds of hot water in there, but there's hardly any now." Doug looked at Joe with an expression he couldn't name, but it made him squirm in his seat.

"I miss hot showers. Can't take enough hot showers if you ask me. I lived so long in shacks I got used to doin' without a lot of things, but I never got used to doin' without hot showers. I love hot showers so much sometimes I think I'm crazy over them. I miss them that much." A loose card fell to the table, and Doug slapped it suddenly with his hand. "Gotcha!"

Joe came completely up off his chair and was about to stammer his confession when Doug held the card out to show him. It was a jack of hearts.

"Slap jack," Doug said, grinnin' his mudshark grin. "I always play it. It's more fun with two, though. You play cards?"

"Uh, sometimes." Joe backed himself through the open door, fixed on Doug's expression. *Touched? Dumb?* or— *Foxy?* "I'll see you around." And soon Joe Miller felt better about being alone in his room than he had in a long time.

He lay on his bed that night and listened to his neighbor with new ears. Spirited card games were replaced with a childish diversion. All the comings and goings stopped and in their place was just an empty door in the wind. Overheard conversations turned to bewildering play-acting. Just filling in the blanks of a picture with no sound.

"Oh, Speed, do you think they'll come back?"

"I don't know, Clara Belle. I just don't know."

Joe Miller closed his eyes as the water next door ran long and hot and tried to fill in the blanks of a curious new acquaintance. Just a sound, with no picture.

ARGUS AND EMMITT

A ball of fire flared up out of Argus Winslow's junkyard and retreated as quickly as it had come. A dull explosion like thunder and glass rushed through the night and was gone.

A quarter mile away, inside a squat log cabin a piece of wood shifted and popped in the wood stove. Our city manager, Emmitt Frank, looked up from the letter he was writing. It didn't startle him really, but it got his attention. Almost any little noise would have.

It was generally quiet in the stout old cabin even on the rowdiest of winter nights, but tonight was particularly quiet. It was one of those cold midwinter evenings that seemed motionless. Like it had frozen to a halt. The clear December sky lit itself with the playful curtains of the northern lights while the stars stood silent guard over a world topped and tucked in with a comforter of new snow. A snow so soft it grabs any clatter or voice in the night and puts a finger to its lips.

Emmitt sat still in the glow of the oil lamps and let himself slip into the mood of the room. The rusty, rugged complexion of the cabin walls. The white glaze of frost on the windowpanes. And the reliable old wood stove in the corner. He heaved a great peaceful sigh and returned to his letter with a new zeal satisfied that all was well with the world, and having no way of knowing otherwise.

Emmitt had grown to enjoy these quiet evenings alone in the cabin more than he'd ever thought possible when he moved in last summer. He'd become captivated by the power of the landscape of Alaska and he was drawn to it at the same time he was terrified of it. He wanted so much to feel its natural touch, but was so afraid to lay himself bare to it that he might never have found the guts to do it without the prodding, wheedling, and conniving of Bud Koenig.

Bud Koenig thought of the frontier as a place to live. Something to savor, and to admire. To Bud, it had almost religious significance and he was keen on teaching Emmitt how to appreciate it, which he was. Argus Winslow thought of a frontier as a temporary inconvenience to be developed into something better. He'd lived the life of a pioneer only as long as he had to, then went immediately to the luxuries of electricity and propane. Argus'd been mystified nearly to the point of disgust as he watched Emmitt, over the past several months, adapting to his rugged life-style with such enthusiasm.

The luxuries of electricity and propane have a lot to recommend themselves but only if kept in the proper proportions and at appropriate distances from each other. A failure to do so might lead to consequences much like the scorched pair of refugees who broke into Emmitt's rustic reverie with a sound thrashing on the front door to the cabin.

Emmitt wasn't accustomed to visitors at this time of the night and the commotion on the porch startled him. He laid his letter aside and went to the door, slightly annoyed. But when he threw the big bolt back and pulled the door open, his irritation turned to shock.

Before him stood a sooty-faced old junkman with conspicuously absent eyebrows, and at his side was a singed and somewhat stunned black Labrador retriever.

"Argus, what in the world happened to you?" Emmitt stepped back from the door, half in welcome and half to get away from the aggressive odor of a scorched dog.

Argus walked through the doorway, and Barney limped in behind him. "Criminellie, didn'tcha hear it? My trailer blowed up right in my face." He turned and squatted next to his dog. "Poor Barney took the worst of it. I was at the front door; he was all the way in. Light switch must've set off a gas leak in the heater. Nothing' left of the trailer but a black mark— wonder we weren't kilt."

Emmitt looked at the old man comforting his pet and tried to come up with something appropriate to say. It was an awkward moment that Emmitt knew would require careful handling.

"Argus, would you like some water?" Emmitt reluctantly closed the door behind them. "I believe your dog is still smoldering."

* * *

The unexpected entry of Argus and Barney into the quietly ordered existence of Emmitt Frank represented two very clear likelihoods: trial and tribulation.

There were no two men in existence less likely to get along. Argus thought Emmitt was an idiot to live out in the rough like this. Chopping wood, hauling water, tending gardens, curing meat, digging outhouses, and everything else it took to live had lost some, if not all, of its luster for Argus over the years. He viewed those activities as burdensome chores that only served to keep a man away from more important matters.

Argus's more important matter was the procurement, assemblage, and resale of junk. He'd devoted most of his life to placing a value on the things that other people threw away. Anything that Argus himself would throw away was less than worthless, and he let few things go.

"You got a mirror anywhere around this shack?" Argus stood up from the burdensome chore of shaving the burnt spots off his dog. "I think I got all the singe off Barney, now I gotta get the rest of these eyebrows off. The stink is makin' me sick."

Emmitt sat at the table, horrified and speechless, and could only point to his little shaving mirror above the washbasin. He looked back to the dog lying behind the wood stove, and a shiver went through him.

Barney lent a whole new meaning to the expression *hang-dog*. Argus had been fairly arbitrary about his pruning and left Barney looking much like a road kill. He had a bald spot on top, like he'd hung up his hat somewhere. He had one leg shaved, and a piece of one hindquarter and a few spots here and there about the size of a man's hand.

Dogs have their vanity too, especially black Labs, and poor Barney was low-slung, trying to be as inconspicuous as a damp, shaved dog in a one-room cabin can be.

Emmitt looked over to Argus, who was scraping at his eyebrows with the same dull razor he'd used on the dog, and another shiver went through him. He wondered what had happened to his idyllic country evening.

It seemed like only minutes ago he'd been peacefully listening to the wood stove pop and waxing poetic in a letter to his ex-wife about the good life on the last frontier: the occasional flicker of the lamps; the cheerful silence of the new snow; and the reassuring aroma of freshly split spruce.

Now he sat in a dank room that smelled like a crematorium, with a desecrated dog and his cantankerous master, who was at that moment cursing and shaving his forehead into the bowl Emmitt brushed his teeth in.

Argus seemed a little peevish, and it made Emmitt nervous. Despite the fact that the man's house and home had just blown up on short notice, and maybe that had left him slightly annoyed, Emmitt still felt like it might be something he said. He tried to warm up to the situation.

"I hope Barney wasn't burnt too badly."

Argus wiped his face on his shirtsleeve and raised what would have been his eyebrows at Emmitt's sympathy. Argus really was peeved, and he was obviously just spoiling for a place to vent it.

"I don't think it burnt his skin. He don't act like it did, but who can tell in this dark hole of a hut you live in?"

Emmitt sank down into his chair without an answer, and Argus took his silence as encouragement. "I mean, criminellie, Emmitt, they pay you well enough at the city. Why'ntcha get some electricity out here? This light'll wreck your eyes!"

Emmitt looked at the oil lamp on the table casting a long light across the table. Two more were lit across the room, and what had been a feeling of intimacy and warmth did seem a little close and dim now that it was mentioned. "I can light some more lamps if you'd like to see better."

Argus shook his head at the offer and walked toward Emmitt into the lamplight. The rugged old bald face shone in the weak light and sent yet another shiver down Emmitt's spine, like he was being spoken to from beyond the grave.

"You just don't get the point, do ya? These are modern times. You're livin' back here like a . . . like a *hippie* or somethin'. Look, you don't even have a phone so I can call to tell somebody I got blowed up!" Argus waved his hand around the room as if to persuade Emmitt that, yes indeed, there was no telephone.

"I could drive you to town if you'd like." Emmitt was growing more and more uneasy with Argus's disposition.

"What, ya ain't gonna take me on your horse?" Argus started to pace the room, finding his rhythm. "You're carryin' your water in here by hand. Ya gotcher food stored in a box outside. You got your little wood pile parked out front and the outhouse seat warmin' by the stove. Who do you think you are, Daniel

Boone? You act like nobody's had a good idea in a hunnert years."

Emmitt sat dumbly fingering the pages of his letter pad. His nervousness was settling down into his stomach and lower. He just wanted to leave the whole thing alone, but he could see that Argus was waiting for some kind of reaction.

"Argus, I thought you and Bud Koenig set me up in this place together."

Argus got riled again. "I was just humorin' Koenig. He's crazier'n you are. He never got over bein' a homesteader. He thinks it's some kind of honor to live like a caveman, and I see he's convinced you it is too. Well I'll tell you, Emmitt, it's no honor, it's a darn insult. It's an insult to me and everybody like me, who worked hard all our lives to civilize this place and turn this land into somethin' useful. I just don't see what you're tryin' to prove."

Emmitt might have been able to work up an answer, but the anxiety of the evening had sunk as low inside of him as he dared let it go. "Excuse me, Argus," was all he had time to say before he grabbed the toilet seat from its peg on the wall and headed out the back way.

Argus needed no explanation of Emmitt's departure, and he bent low to pat Barney, who was now sound asleep by the stove, oblivious to the commotion.

"Ugliest dog I ever saw," Argus muttered to himself as he took a seat at the table to wait for Emmitt's return. He picked up the pencil off the letter pad just for something to fiddle with in the meantime.

Now, Argus Winslow, for all his flaws, was not a man to read another person's private letters, but this would be an exception. It wouldn't have occurred to him to read this one either, but his eyes were drawn beyond his will when they noticed a very familiar couple of words spelled out in Emmitt's even hand: *Argus Winslow.*

Seeing one's own name in print is one of life's intoxicating little joys. It sends a ripple of delight through us that sparks an irresistible urge to see what circumstances it was used in. A person had to know if it was bitter or sweet, and what Argus read was a good measure of both.

Argus Winslow and Bud Koenig, it said, are the most incredible people I've met here. They built this cabin I described to you almost fifty years ago. On nights like tonight I can sit here in the lamplight and almost feel like it might be then. When this land was a raw frontier and people like Argus and Bud were clinging to small pieces of it for their dear lives and futures. They were pioneers. Real pioneers. And I am so excited to know them. I can live like they lived, but I don't think I can ever be like they were. It's too late for that, I know. These are modern times. I don't have to live this way, but I'm so glad that I can. On these quiet evenings when I'm alone with it all here in Argus's cabin, I feel like I can finally see what's really worthwhile, and I wish I could show it to you. There's someone on the path outside. I'll finish this after . . .

Emmitt came back in the door and saw the guilt on Argus's face. He immediately realized what Argus had done, and it made him hot with embarrassment. Argus could see it, and he worked up a mighty blush for himself.

They cleared their throats as men do in their perpetual loss for words, and Emmitt hung the seat back on the peg. Argus got up from the chair quickly, as if ordered out. "Here, Emmitt, you take your place back. I was just thinkin' I might lie down over there with Barney if you got an extra blanket for the night. We'll stay out of your way and let you get back to what you were doin'."

Emmitt felt something give in the room and his insides calmed. He sat back down at the table and tried not to look at the letter pad. "It was nothing important."

"Seems to me it might be." Argus sat down next to his sleeping dog and let his back rest against the wall. The heat from the stove covered him, and he took a long look far into the dim cabin light. A light to see new things by. And a clearer head than he'd had in a while prevailed.

Both men let a silence fall between them that became a part of the bigger quiet that lay across the night, and it rested on the landscape like a patient hand that'd been there for a hundred years.

NORMAN'S DILEMMA

NORMAN sat in the backseat looking at the rear side view of his father's head and waited. He was going to do it again. Norman just knew he was going to. For as long as he could remember, every time the family went someplace together, his father drove. And for as long as he could remember, every time they hit a pothole or other rough spot on the road, his father would cheerfully say, "Bumpity-bump-bump-bump!"

His mother's head would bob pleasantly like she'd never heard it before, and all the children would giggle with dutiful delight at their father's playfulness. All the children except Norman, that is.

Norman had grown to hate this foolish little habit of his father's. On this eve of the fourteenth year of what he had figured as a tortured and dreadful life, he'd grown to hate it with such passion that he was obsessed with the mere thought of it.

He looked at the cheek on his father's rough face for any sign of movement. They were coming to the Y where the snowplows always tore up the intersection. He saw his dad take in a breath and hold it for a moment. Norman gritted his teeth as he first heard the pop and thud of radials on potholes, then the inevitable "Bumpity-bump-bump-bump!" from the front seat.

Norman saw his mother's head in front of him bob along in pleasant agreement. The three creepies, his beloved little brothers and sisters, giggled absently and dutifully beside him while they busied themselves with the dismemberment of a Barbie doll.

"Big deal," Norman said snidely, and leaned his head against the window, gazing out at the roadside. He was thinking of the long day of "family fun" that lay ahead at the Winter Carnival, and wishing he were going anywhere in the world but there.

The dumb parade. The dumb ice skating party. And the dreaded Winter Carnival Dance that night. Norman groaned out loud at the whole tiresome agenda.

His father frowned into the rearview mirror at Norman's bad attitude, and while he wasn't watching the road, they hit another large pothole. One that pounced them hard enough that Norman whacked his head against the doorframe. He grabbed his cheekbone and looked sharply at his dad in the mirror.

With no cheer in his voice, and looking Norman square in the eye, his dad said, "Bumpity-bump-bump-bump."

It had been a bad year for Norman so far. Ever since he'd been caught after hours at Laura's baby-sitting job and put on restriction, Norman's life had taken on all the luster of a prison work-release program.

All he was really allowed to do was go to school and do chores around the house. He could talk to Laura on the phone for ten minutes a night, but only if he could prove he'd finished his homework. He was only allowed to see her at school.

Under these strict confinements, Norman was becoming overexposed to his own family. His brothers and sisters were certifiable lunatics born and bred solely for the purpose of tormenting their oldest brother into nervous conniptions. Conniptions that were becoming more and more frequent, driving Norman more often to his room and for longer periods of time each trip. He'd scream frustrated obscenities into his pillow, then lie back on the bed making lists in his head of everything he hated about his life.

It wasn't just the three creepies he had to share his immediate space with that was making Norman crazy. It was everybody in his life right now. His parents, his teachers, his best friend, Stanley. Even Laura had changed lately, become someone else. Norman couldn't figure out what this world was coming to.

Norman never even got out of the car for the parade. He didn't see much sense to standing out in the cold just to watch a fire truck and a police car go by. The Outhouse Races used to make him giggle out of control. But that was long ago in another life. Almost a year now.

Now it was embarrassing to be a witness to. To see his mom and dad laughing and pointing. Calling out to the contestants, who rode their contraptions in silly costumes, grinning and waving like they were really somebody doing something. It was all so dumb, Norman thought, and he sank lower into the backseat and slid further inside the collar of his parka and climbed deeper inside himself.

For two years Norman had suffered through the growing pains of adolescence. His physical growth had been awesome. "You can stand him still and watch him grow out of his clothes," his dad would tease him to his mother. "This isn't a kid, this is a science project."

On top of the actual pain of rapid growth, Norman had the equal discomfort of not knowing exactly how big he was at any given moment. His battered head and knees, ill-conceived posture, and perpetually misfit clothing did little for his peace of mind at this age, when vanity takes its first icy grip on our pride.

His voice had changed, his face had broken out, and the main motivating factor in his life had shifted from his bicycle to his pituitary gland.

With all this in mind, it isn't surprising then that Norman would begin to see the world as a changing and increasingly hostile place to live.

"Norman, hey! Stormin' Norman!" Stanley Bindel speed-skated toward him on the lake and Norman could see he was raising his hand up for a fly-by high five. Norman hated slapping five. It was stupid. It looked good when athletes on television did it, but they really *did* it. Their fives were crisp and vital. Fives had to be robust or they were less than worthless. They became some glancing effeminate gesture that meant nothing and only added tension to what are usually totally irrational moments to begin with.

Norman held his hand up reluctantly and Stanley glanced it awkwardly with his own as he slipped and gyrated, and skidded behind him on his backside. Stanley was really starting to get on Norman's nerves.

"Coordination, Grace." Norman said it out of habit, but he couldn't even pretend the meanness. He just didn't care anymore. There are many things that separate the men from the boys, so to speak. But none so literally or so effectively as biology.

Norman and Stanley were only a few months apart in age, but nature's way with boys has, for the time being, put Norman light-years ahead of his friend. There is nothing in this world more destructive to friendship and loyalty than a badly placed hormone or two.

Stanley pulled himself up and staggered to get back on top of his skates. Norman couldn't conceal his aversion to his nerdy old friend for very long, and luckily he didn't have to. Over Stanley's shoulder he spotted Laura Magruder by the warm shack, and the sight of her took him over.

"What is it, Norm?" Stanley clowned at Norman's look. "A death in the family? Indigestion?" He turned with mock surprise. "No it's Laura, queen of Norman."

"Oh stuff it, Stanley." Norman pushed past his friend without a look back.

As Norman was skating across to the warm shack, Laura looked up and spotted him coming. He sent her a meaningful smile, glad to see her for the first time out of school in weeks. But what Laura did in return unsettled Norman in ways he'd never felt before. She looked at him but pretended not to see him. She quickly turned to her girlfriends, and they shimmied out into the rotating mass of townspeople gallivanting about the lake. Norman coasted to a stop at no point in particular and looked bewildered. A look as if he didn't know what this meant when every fiber in his body knew exactly what it meant.

"Whadja do, lose your sweetie, Norman?" Laura's older brother, Burt, sat on the hood of his high-rider pickup with three of his friends. They all sent Norman the peculiar sadistic sneers that only seniors in high school can deliver. The force of it drove Norman into the throng of skaters.

He'd gone in to hide, but when he looked up he found he'd skated right up beside Laura, who was just about as surprised as he was.

"Norman, oh hi!" she said, and pretended to have to concentrate precisely on her feet.

The chill from Laura was colder than what was coming from the lake, but Norman found the words. "Are you going to the dance tonight?"

Laura continued her precision skating. "Everybody's going to *be there*," she said, and Norman knew then for sure that she wasn't going to be there for him.

The strength seemed to go from his legs. "Maybe I'll see you," Norman mumbled, and let himself drift to a stop outside the skaters. He leaned up against a stack of old tires from the ice derby and surveyed his miserable world.

Norman saw Laura, skating easily now, talking earnestly with her girlfriends, who stole curious glances in his direction. His heart felt like it had exploded in his chest. Stanley Bindel darted by, and Norman had to look away. One of Stanley's goofy looks or stupid remarks right now might lead to serious felony charges if Norman caught up with him.

He saw Burt and his buddies over on their pickups listening to loud, obnoxious music and sipping from brown bags in their jackets. Burt looked over again and narrowed his eyes with some unintelligible threat. To avoid it, Norman turned his attention back to the warm shack.

The three creepies were spilling hot chocolate all over themselves and giggling at their mom and dad hamming it up out on the ice. They were both graceful skaters, and they seemed to float across the ice backward and forward, arm in arm, and beaming good cheer. His dad would pretend to lose his balance, flail his arms, and wobble his knees for the benefit of his small audience.

It would have been very funny, Norman thought, if it wasn't so stupid. If everything wasn't so stupid. And he went to wait in the car until the whole silly business was over with.

Norman was even quieter on the way home than he was coming in, if that was possible. His dad eyed him from time to time in the rearview mirror but said nothing. He could tell Norman was steamed, but didn't really feel like dealing with it right then. Norman was being a bit of a pain in the pants lately, all around. It was a day of family and fun, and there didn't seem to be very much of either in his oldest boy today.

Norman had his head leaned against the window again, and all he could do was swirl his misery around in his head like the skaters on the lake. Laura and Stanley and mean seniors and demented siblings and . . . BAM! The window frame came up and cracked him right in the chin.

"Bumpity-bump-bump-bump" came cheerfully from the front seat. His mom bobbed her head appreciatively, the three creepies giggled, and Norman lost his good judgment.

"Would you please stop saying that stupid thing every time we hit a bump! You say it *every time*, and it drives me crazy! So would you please just stop it!"

A silence hung in the car like frozen batteries. His mother's head stood stock-still in front of him. The three little kids sensed danger and shrank together in a wad of snow pants.

Norman heard this tone of voice still fresh in his ears, and his blood ran cold. There were going to be consequences for this, and he felt a moment of white terror, not knowing what form they might take.

His dad continued to drive, but spent most of his time looking in the mirror at Norman. He was taking those long, deep breaths like he did before he was going to pull on something really hard. And then he spoke in a tone so cool and even, it made Norman tremble.

"There's only two people in this world I'll let talk to me like that—and you ain't one of 'em. What in blazes has come over you lately?"

Norman looked at his dad's face, and the emotion of falling from grace with a father overcame him. It gushed out of his eyes and out of his mouth in one smooth ebb.

"Laura broke up with me, Stanley Bindel's a total nerd, and everybody hates me! Including you!"

And another silence filled the car. A little warmer one than the last. The man in the front seat studied the road for a long mile, then studied the boy all alone in the mirror, sunk down in his parka like he'd just as soon disappear.

The soreness and sorrow of fourteen flashed at him as plain as skate blisters. It wasn't a time for speeches and reprimand. It was time for something else, and he searched deep inside for the words.

He wasn't watching the road very well, and the car hammered in and out of a series of potholes like gunfire. Words sprang to his lips and he met the eye of his son in the mirror. A sad young man who didn't need any needling right now.

"It's a rough road, isn't it, Norman? Don't you wish somebody could fix it for us?"

His mother's head bobbed appreciatively in front of him. The three creepies giggled with relief. And Norman agreed with his father for the first time in several weeks.

TAMARA AND TONY GET TRAPPED

TAMARA and her man, Tony, were in high spirits as they kneeled over their work on the cabin floor, making up slogans and painting them on poster board: ONLY THINGS ON ALL FOURS SHOULD WEAR FURS. FURS ARE FOR FOOLS. TRAPPING IS MURDER.

"This is fun!" Tamara said as she globbed some red paint on her sign and let it drip down like gore. She smiled as if she'd just arranged a flower in a window box.

Tamara and Tony were heading up to Anchorage to do a little recreational protesting at the Fur Rendezvous. The Fur Rondy was the one time of year when trappers, fur buyers, sellers, and fans of the genre all got together to celebrate a mostly extinct life-style and times. Every natural enemy Tamara ever dreamed of all gathered at one convenient place to be goaded, teased, riled and insulted.

Our conscientious couple were accomplished protesters and usually wouldn't bend to such accessible harassment. They would have felt much more challenged by, say, chasing nuclear submarines in rubber boats, but it had been a slow winter and any protest in a pinch would do.

It gave them a good reason to get out of town for a few days, and they'd have a chance to spend some time with their friends Brandon and Willow, who were wintering in a tepee a little further up the peninsula. Brandon and Willow shared Tamara and Tony's love of controversy, and they'd chewed the bone of contention together many times. Tamara and Tony would pick their friends up along the way and they would become a fearsome force of four.

Tony situated the signs in the back of Tamara's VW bus while she loaded up the packs and went through a mental checklist. "Cheese, veggies, water, tea—I'll bring some poetry to read. Did you gas up the bus? That gauge still doesn't work."

"Um-hm." Tony, not really listening, agreed to her tone of voice more than anything else and slammed the door shut. "Yep, I think we got everything we need." He said it with such calm satisfaction that Tamara relaxed and thought of nothing further.

The ride up the peninsula was quiet. Tamara looked wistfully out the window at the frozen forest picketing past them along the highway. She read some poetry to Tony and they both ate a little cheese and basically just cruised.

"We'd better start looking for the turnoff to Brandon and Willow's place." Tamara hated to break out of their road reverie, but they were entering the foothills below the pass and she knew they were getting close. "It's to the south just after a big spruce with a split trunk."

"What's the name of the road?"

"I don't know. It doesn't matter—I can find it. I have a good memory for places."

Tony looked around them to the thousands of acres of big spruce and became privately infuriated at Tamara's methods. She believed she had a great natural sense of direction and a keen memory for wilderness trademarks, but she'd proven herself to be mostly misguided most of the time. But then again, he thought, how many side roads with big split spruce by them could there be along this desolate stretch of road?

As it turned out, there could be at least two.

"There it is." Tamara pointed with great satisfaction to a tall, deformed tree marking the entrance to a narrow lane that twisted off into the woods.

Tony pulled the bus off the highway and turned into the forest.

"The tepee is just up around those turns." Tamara sat forward on her seat, visibly excited to be there.

Tony drove confidently up the narrow road, relieved that the snow was soft and shallow, thanks to the thick canopy of treetops. Tamara's look of anticipation grew wide as they pulled around the second turn and then her face collapsed into consternation.

"Well, I *thought* it was right here." The tip of Tamara's tongue appeared as she deliberated, and Tony moaned to himself. Tamara only thought with her tongue out when she didn't have a clue to what she was doing. "I remember now, it's further up in a big clearing. There's no clearing here. Keep going."

And Tony kept going. And going. And going. Past one forgotten landmark after another, until every last shard of faith in his navigator had evaporated. But just as he was about to call an end to the chase, Tamara sat another hitch higher in her seat and pointed down the road one last grand time. "*There*, that clearing ahead. I feel it in my bones."

When they broke through the trees into the open, they were greeted by a conspicuously tepeeless clearing. Tamara's spirits sank, Tony's mood sank, and the rear end of their 1968 VW bus sank, with a sound like lost hope, into the thick heavy snow of an exposed clearing in a remote wood.

"Well, we're one with nature now," Tony said, and got out to diagnose the situation.

"Terminally stuck," was the prognosis, and our duo stood still in the gray afternoon looking into the woods as if to find solutions.

The particular clearing that had Tamara and Tony in its grip was not made by nature. Someone unknown, a long time ago, had carved this nick into the endless forest to make a place for himself. This wasn't evident until Tony spied a collapsed old cabin poking an ear out of the snow back against the trees.

Tony pointed. "Maybe we can get some old boards or something to put under the wheels."

The pair waded through the snow and speculated on the origins of the shack.

Tony thought it might be an old homestead, but Tamara thought better of it. There was no farming around here. It must be a mining claim, she thought, but Tony didn't—there wasn't a creek or river nearby and it didn't make sense.

It wasn't until they reached the ruin and starting kicking around looking for loose planks that the answer to their speculation glared up at them. Dangling from a nail across one caved-over wall was a small cluster of rusted old leg-hold traps.

"It was a trapper's cabin." Tamara said it as if she'd just uncovered a den of snakes. Long since driven off by elements, age, or economics, some far-gone trapper had left nature to dispose of his modest attempts at civilizing the wilderness.

Tony kicked at the wall with a force that looked like fury, but he was just trying to break the planks loose. The useless traps disappeared into the snow and vanished from their minds as the boards showed signs of surrender.

Tamara grabbed hold of the loose ones, and with a few squeaky whimpers they came free in her hands. A quick glance of accomplishment passed between our heroes, and they marched back toward the foundered bus with their spoils.

Tony used one plank as a shovel to move some snow away from the wheels, then jammed both boards behind the tires. "You drive," he said. "And I'll get around front to push."

Tamara watched her man's face through the windshield as she dropped the bus into reverse. As Tony bit his lip and strained against the front, the valiant rattle of a Volkswagen engine gave way to the sound of rubber on wood as the bus climbed on top of the planks and lurched back the way it had come.

Tony staggered triumphantly alongside until Tamara stopped again on top of the tamer snow inside the woods. She switched off the motor and there between them hung an air of victory. The feel of transportation snatched from stagnation. Human will wrestled once again from nature's firm grip.

And there was something else. A sound, a presence. Something almost otherworldly. It was a sound immediately familiar, and Tamara and Tony's high spirits began deflating about as quickly as the right rear tire on the bus was. A tire neatly gouged open with a rusty old trapper's nail left in a decrepit old trapper's shack.

The protest signs looked small and impotent stuck in the snow around the bus. They'd had to unload everything to get at the jack and spare tire. As Tamara and Tony stood looking at their daring slogans aimed at a blind wilderness, an idea started to gnaw at them.

When the lug wrench jumped off the nut and Tony clipped the tops from three knuckles, it was taking form in his head. Tamara stood quietly off to the side, feeling the heat begin to rise in her body, out of her feet. She stomped them around in the snow and that was all it took to shake it out of her.

"If it wasn't for trapping, we wouldn't be in this trouble."

Tony sucked a knuckle and was quick to grab her meaning. "If it wasn't for the fur industry, we might not be within a hundred miles of here. The Fur Rondy is what got us away from home, and that trapper's shack is what blew our tire."

Tamara's cold feet reached all the way to her head now. "We could be home in front of the fire drinking hot tea."

Tony talked in bursts as he tightened the nuts on the spare. "We could . . . at least . . . be at . . . the tepee . . ." and the wrench slipped again, skinning three cold knuckles on his other hand. It sent Tony into a fit of snow-kicking rage, and Tamara into the driver's seat for escape and warmth.

She started the engine and tightened her whole body into a knot of icy bitterness. She stared through the windshield at the bleak clearing and conjured up images of the monstrous people who were responsible for all this trouble. The kind of people who killed things for money.

She saw large, dangerous desperadoes. Slopeheads with rough manners and reckless habits—angry sneers and noisy opinions. There were greasy jackets, bad teeth, poor skin, and smelly breath. They were trappers, she thought. That's all. Macho moral mutants who only brought pain and harm to the world, even when they weren't around.

Tamara was just getting herself good and whipped up about the matter when the engine sputtered and quit. She reached up and turned it over, it sputtered for a few beats, and quit again. Her shoulders drooped with recognition. She'd driven this bus long enough to know every symptom of every ailment, and she'd played nurse to this one a thousand times.

She climbed out and went around to Tony, who was just gathering up the tools. "I thought I asked you if you'd filled the gas tank."

Tony thought for a moment. "I thought you were telling me that you did." There was no blame in either of their voices. Tamara and Tony held each other in far too high a regard to condemn each other over minor foibles. Whether it be Tamara's poor directions and stubborn confidence or Tony's poor listening habits, it only took simple human kindness to forgive these.

The two looked at each other and they both felt colder surrounded by the silence that blares from dead machinery. Tamara looked at their protest signs stuck around in the snow. A new anger rose in her, and as she looked out at the clearing in the fading light, she knew exactly who was to blame for all this. She opened her mouth to start in on it but stopped short when another sound came out of the woods. A muffled sort of scream.

It was an eerie sound at first, but then when she saw the lone light bouncing across the clearing, she realized it was a snowmobile. The person riding it must have spotted the bus, because he suddenly stood up and turned directly toward them.

Tamara and Tony could see now that it was one man and that he was pulling a small sled behind him. They stood blinking into the light as it came around beside the bus and stopped.

"You folks need some help?" The voice from behind the light was curious but friendly. Confident and resourceful. The kind of voice you like to hear when you're out of gas in the woods about twenty miles from anywhere in particular.

"We're out of gas, is the only problem we've got left." Tony talked over the idling machine.

"Well, you're in luck," the voice said, stepping back to the sled. "I always carry an extra gas jug, and I won't be needin' it today." He handled some elastic straps on the dark load, and before Tamara or Tony had said another word, he was walking up to them with a metal can in his hand. The man was full of energy, and rather than offer the can to Tony, he walked right up to the bus and unscrewed the gas cap.

Only after jamming the can in the opening did he pause to look around. He was an older man, and Tamara and Tony could see he had a face that was used to facing people with a dependable smile that rarely left—like it did the moment he laid eyes on the signs leaning over here and there around the bus. FUR IS FOR FOOLS. KILLERS. CRUELTY HAS NO EXCUSES.

"What brings you folks out here?" The warmth was gone from the man, but there was no menace.

Tony sensed the change in mood and felt suddenly self-conscious. "We were looking for some friends. They live in a tepee around here."

"Oh yeah, I know 'em." It was clear the man took no great comfort with the fact. "Two more roads up and to your right."

He finished pouring the gas and went directly back to his sled with the can. "This here was my dad's place. I was born in a little cabin right over there." He gestured a hand toward the clearing that was sinking quickly into dusk. "Please take your litter out with you."

The warm smile came back across the man's face. It was obvious it never stayed away for long. He climbed back on his machine and revved the motor while Tony and Tamara stammered their appreciation.

It wasn't until the man was already by them that they finally saw the sled and what was on it. A pile of steel traps, a loose stack of fresh pelts, and a gas can. It was a flash in front of them, and then it was gone in the dark with the friendly man and the eerie wail of a snow machine.

"A trapper." Tamara went white. Even felt a little dizzy.

"A real one." Tony and Tamara looked after the sled, and their heads went into tailspins.

Tailspins like when everything you think you know for sure—every suspicion and judgment, every rough manner, reckless habit, angry sneer, and noisy opinion—turns out to be wrong.

And all you're left with are a few ideals, a good heart, three people in the wilderness, and a simple act of human kindness between them.

Why, it is enough to make you dizzy.

THE TRUTH ABOUT DOUG

DOUG McDoogan had a big problem, and as usual, he'd caused it himself. As with most of Doug's self-inflicted misery, his current dilemma stemmed from his absolute inability to tell the truth about anything. His gift for deception was so constant and uncalculated that one might think it was a genetic difficulty. Something as positively beyond his control as the cut of his nose or the texture of his voice. Because whatever Doug McDoogan said or whatever he did, it was for all the reasons but the sincere ones.

Sending two thousand dollars to his family in Idaho might at first glance seem like an admirable gesture no matter which way you turned it, but Doug knew better. He knew he only sent it so they would see he had two thousand dollars to give away. He told them that his Alaska gold mine had paid off.

Through the patronage of the mysterious blue-haired lady from Anchorage, Doug's driftwood carvings were continuing in their meteoric rise to commercial success and Doug was continuing in his grand ascent to commercial excess. Including, it seems, giving away large amounts of money for the wrong reasons.

It never entered his mind that it might make them feel good. In fact, he'd sorta hoped it would make them feel kind of bad somehow, like didn't they wish they had that kind of dough to send around to people they didn't like? It certainly never entered his mind that they would use the money to come visit for a week.

Doug wrestled with a carving of a fox and worried. Having Mom, Dad, and his sister, Doreen, around the place would be his worst nightmare come true, and Doug has dreamt some doozies. There is nothing in this world that a habitual liar fears more than a visit from his past.

It would take a genius of enormous talent to track the perpetual fabrications of a fraud such as Doug, but unfortunately, Doug's mental abilities did not even register on the dipstick of brilliance.

The trick to lying all the time is to keep moving. And Doug had been doing precisely that for the last ten years (fifteen, to hear him tell it). Ever since his dad threw him out of the house when he was sixteen. (Actually, he was eighteen and he was begged to stay by the whole family, including his dad.)

He had gravely informed them that he was going off to join the army and fight the war in Vietnam. The McDoogan savvy being somewhat of a shared family trait, no one took notice that the war had ended four years earlier. They dutifully and patriotically worried, until they got a call from Doug saying he was alive and well, traveling with a circus through Europe when, in fact, he was washing cars in Boise at the time. Or is that when he was working the deep frier on the night shift at a Spokane truck stop telling them he was logging on the Oregon coast? He'd never be able to keep it straight.

Doug had never before considered that he'd have to account for any of his tales. He'd never stayed anyplace long enough to have it happen. Apparently, he'd hung around the End of the Road a little too long.

Suddenly, Doug's mind did a dangerous shift of perspective, and he realized that the flip side of this counterfeit coin was every bit as troublesome. Not only would he have to account to his family for everything he'd said to them about his travels and conquests over the years, but he'd have to justify to the people around here everything he'd said about his parents.

Doug's jaw slid forward like it does when he's trying to bring something to mind or add something to it, and he thought of all the things he'd told people about his family. How they'd forced him out of the house and chased off him off when he was sixteen, claiming he ate too much. How his father had taught him to swim by throwing him off a railroad trestle when he was four. He'd repeated that story so often he wasn't sure himself anymore that it didn't happen. It was the reason he always gave for not being able to read.

"Bumped my head on the bottom of the river and never read another word," he'd say sadly, adding that he began to read when he was three and would probably be a world-famous reader by now if it wasn't for his father's cruel ways. In reality, Doug couldn't read because he was dumb and lazy and his father had been far too big of a jellyfish of a disciplinarian to make him do anything about it.

Doug let the chips fall from his carving and fretted over what would happen if people found out the truth of the matter. The thought that people might see him as he actually was gave him a sense of nakedness that unsettled Doug considerably, but he needn't have been worried. Everybody around here had Doug's number a long time ago. The saying goes that the way you can tell if Doug is lying is that his lips are moving. Everybody has a special quality. And Doug's particular quality was his knack for distortion.

He sat in his kitchen and worked with his knife. A piece of raw wood was turning into the beginnings of an arctic fox. Half in, and half out. It suggested a fox more than it said it, and Doug laid it aside. He never knew why he finished with these things, he just knew when he was done.

Doug's hands sweated heavily when he saw the three familiar figures come through the door into the airport building.

"They call this an airport?"

It was amazing to hear his older sister's voice again. Doug stepped forward, ramrod straight, and said the first thing that came to his mind: "Boy, you really got fat, Doreen."

Doreen squinted through her winged eyeglasses and raised a Kleenex to her nose. "I caught a cold as soon as we touched the ground. I told Mommy and Daddy I was going to get a cold if we come to Alaska, and I did. Didn't I say I was going to get a cold, Daddy? I wanted to buy a big-screen TV with your money, but Mommy said, 'No, we should go surprise little Doug,' and so here we are and I got a cold and ain't you surprised." Doreen rolled closer, bounced a large arm off Doug's shoulder, and made a kiss face all in one motion. "Well I see you ain't got any smarter. Go say hello to your mommy and daddy, for goodness sake!"

Doug had forgotten all about his mom and dad. Something that had been fairly easy for him to do all his life. They stood inside the doorway side by side as if they were joined at the hip, just the way they'd been standing the last time Doug saw them, ten years ago. His dad was introducing himself to a stranger while his mom smiled on and patted his arm, bobbing her head up and down proudly at everything her husband had to say.

"Hi, I'm Phil McDoogan. Just in from Idaho to see my boy. He's a gold miner. I'm in sewage." The stranger looked down at Mr. McDoogan's feet, puzzled at his meaning.

Doug's dad has been a pond skimmer at the sewage-treatment plant back home for the last twenty-three years. He took his work very seriously and was eager to talk about it. "It's not for everybody. You couldn't have told me there was a future in sewage twenty years ago, but here I am."

The stranger walked away absolutely at a loss as to why he should care about all of this, and Doug stepped into his place.

"Hi, Dad, Hi, Mom."

The Idaho McDoogans stood still for a moment and dressed their faces with interpretations of looks of parental approval they'd seen on television.

"You've grown into a fine young man, son." Doug's dad paused, then he looked over to Doreen. "You got a Burger King in this town? Doreen's got hypoglycemia or some darn thing, and she's gonna pass out like a hog if we don't get a Whopper in her quick."

Doug was worn out by the time he got his family settled around his kitchen table in the apartment. They'd hitched a ride down to Clara's Coffee Cup in the back of Bud Koenig's pickup and had to leave Doreen in the truck because she was too weak to haul herself over the tailgate. They got burgers to go, and Bud was kind enough to wait and haul them home.

Doug had been frantic, trying to keep conversation between his family and Bud to a minimum lest one of them discover a fabrication of his from the other. It wasn't as hard as it might have been, though, because his dad talked mostly about sewage treatment and Doreen kept interrupting about her cold and how sick she was going to be if she didn't get a double cheeseburger and how pickles make her throw up.

Doug sat silent and watched his dad's eyes roam the room. He'd call them three times over the last year since the blue-haired lady started giving him money. He'd told them how he'd struck it rich in the gold field. How he'd bought the best of everything for himself and was living like a king.

His dad looked from the bullfighter wall rug over his bed to the Farrah Fawcett poster. He watched Doug's garage-sale lava lamp ooze a bit, and then fixed on the jumbled entertainment center, which appeared to be a pile of appliances roped together with extension cords. There was the TV and the blinking VCR, a stereo and a Mr. Coffee, and a hopeless wad of wires all crisscrossing around a crooked stack of bricks and boards.

Doug's dad looked him in the eye from across the table.

"Son, it's even nicer than I pictured it. That gold mine is treating you good, ain't it?" Doug's mom nodded and patted her husband's arm agreeably while Doreen flipped the last french fry by her big lips. It was plain she was getting her strength back.

"What in heck is that supposed to be?" Doreen pointed her head, the only moving part of her body, toward the driftwood fox Doug had crafted.

Doug looked at his carving and looked at his family and opened his mouth to speak, but stopped. He groped around in the dim light between his ears, opened his mouth again, and stopped again. Doug was stunned. For the first time in his life he'd been asked a question that he couldn't find a decent lie to.

As hard as he tried to find some fantastic or deceptive reason for that piece of art to be on his kitchen table, he couldn't. Nothing was more fantastic than the truth. "It's a fox," Doug said, to his own surprise. "I whittled it last week."

Doreen squinted her eyes at her brother. "You did not."

Doug's mouth was caught half open again. Now he was stunned *and* stumped. After spending his entire lifetime trying to keep one step ahead of his fraudulent past, he was in the very uncomfortable position of having to defend the truth. No immediate method presented itself, so he let his sister ramble on.

"You didn't make that, and it ain't no fox anyways. Foxes have big tails, and there ain't no tail. That looks like a dog, don't it, Daddy? It looks just like that yappy little dog the Criders over in the trailer park got." Doreen started to reach for the carving, but Doug snatched it.

"This is no yappy trailer dog. This is an arctic fox. I saw one once, and it don't have a tail 'cause the tail's still in the wood. I don't whittle 'em all the way out. I let 'em out as far as they want to come and then I give 'em to the blue-haired lady, who pays me money, lots of money. She sells them to rich people all over the place."

A painful silence draped across the table. Doug looked down at his fox, hearing his own words in his head, but was unable to comprehend how ludicrous and unbelievable it sounded. It was Doug's first brush with integrity, and he didn't know where to take it from here.

Doreen swiveled her head back and forth and turned her attention to her parents. "Daddy? Mommy? Did you hear that? I told you Doug was all lies. He's always been all lies. I told you he never went in the army and I told you he never joined no circus and I told you he never owned no gold mine, and God only knows where he got that money. And you always defended him. You always said it was true, and you sit right here and tell him how much you like this dump of his just to make him feel good, and here he is lying right to our faces! I told you we should have just bought that big-screen TV and stayed home."

Doug's dad let his eyes drop to the table in resignation while his mom patted her husband's arm reassuringly.

Doug's head was twirling with the complexity of what was happening here: These three odd people whom he'd lied out of existence years ago had come into his home, and one of them was using every major perjury he had ever committed as proof that the only true quality in his life to date was in fact a lie.

Had it been a lie, Doug would have known what to do about it. He would have just continued to repeat the lie until it was believed or resigned to or somebody smacked him. That's the business of lying. But somehow he realized that with the truth, a person only needs to say it one time. And he'd already done that. Doug looked at his parents' downcast faces and his sister's squinty little eyes sunk in her head and he didn't have another thing he wanted to say.

He put on his coat and wondered if he could hitchhike all the way to the blue-haired lady's house before dark.

"You folks go ahead and stay here the week. I gotta go check my gold mine."

And it might have been the second time that day Doug McDoogan told the truth and wasn't believed. But he wasn't thinking about that. He was looking at the face of an arctic fox starting to come out of a piece of wood tucked under his coat. He never knew why he finished with these things. He just knew when he was done.

Epilogue

by
Ruby McClay

WHEN Ed Flannigan's new arm got here, he was back in his road grader within a week. I knew a natural sporting man like him would master that gizmo just like he did. He's got a clamp on the end of it that he can use to grab things. He likes it fine. He told me, "You can't skin the knuckles on it, and it cracks crab like nobody's business."

I see Norman and Laura together every once in a while now. I think she just wanted to cool the boy off a little. I see Norman just as often with Stanley Bindel, so they've either worked out their differences or decided to live with them. There's nothing wrong with Norman that a few years won't heal.

I heard from Doug one time since he left. He wrote me a letter. Can you believe it? I'm so proud of him! He's staying with his lady friend and learning how to read and write. He said he'd be back but he didn't know when, and he asked if Joe Miller would look after his stuff.

Argus and me are getting married as soon as my dress gets here (darn thing's been back-ordered twice). Argus asked Emmitt Frank to be best man. He wanted Bud Koenig to be my maid of honor, and I'm afraid Bud's going to do it just to be contrary. (Those two will be the end of me.)

Argus hasn't had a memory lapse since he blew up his trailer. The doctors think he might have cured himself, and now Argus is claiming to have done it on purpose. It doesn't matter. The new trailer is a real beauty, and I'll be moving in right after the wedding.

Tamara and Tony are getting married the same day as we

are, only in a tepee up on the ridge. (I never will understand it.) Argus says we ought to have the receptions together so nobody misses one of them. It's a good idea, I suppose. We do share so many friends around here.

I'll have to talk to Mayor Weekly about using the Big Garage on Clear Shot. When we do things together like this, it's still the only place in town big enough to hold us.

The Best in Biographies from Avon Books

IT'S ALWAYS SOMETHING
by Gilda Radner   71072-2/$5.95 US/$6.95 Can

**JACK NICHOLSON: THE UNAUTHORIZED
BIOGRAPHY** *by Barbara and Scott Siegel*
                                     76341-9/$4.50 US/$5.50 Can

ICE BY ICE
by Vanilla Ice   76594-2/$3.95 US/$4.95 Can

CARY GRANT: THE LONELY HEART
by Charles Higham and Roy Moseley
                                     71099-9/$5.99 US/$6.99 Can

I, TINA
by Tina Turner with Kurt Loder
                                     70097-2/$4.95 US/$5.95 Can

ONE MORE TIME
by Carol Burnett   70449-8/$4.95 US/$5.95 Can

PATTY HEARST: HER OWN STORY
by Patricia Campbell Hearst with Alvin Moscow
                                     70651-2/$4.50 US/$5.95 Can

PICASSO: CREATOR AND DESTROYER
by Arianna Stassinopoulos Huffington
                                     70755-1/$4.95 US/$5.95 Can